THE CAUSE

THE CAUSE

*The American Revolution
and Its Discontents,
1773–1783*

JOSEPH J. ELLIS

LIVERIGHT PUBLISHING CORPORATION

A Division of W. W. Norton & Company
Independent Publishers Since 1923

Frontispiece: This Benjamin West portrait of the men who negotiated the Treaty of Paris remains unfinished because the British diplomatic team refused to pose. Left to right, they are John Jay, John Adams, Benjamin Franklin, Henry Laurens, and William Temple Franklin, Ben's grandson.

Copyright © 2021 by Joseph J. Ellis

Printed in the United States of America
First Edition

Maps by Jeffrey L. Ward

For information about permission to reproduce selections from this book, write to Permissions, Liveright Publishing Corporation, a division of W. W. Norton & Company, Inc., 500 Fifth Avenue, New York, NY 10110

For information about special discounts for bulk purchases, please contact W. W. Norton Special Sales at specialsales@wwnorton.com or 800-233-4830

Manufacturing by Lakeside Book Company
Book design by Ellen Cipriano
Production manager: Lauren Abbate

Library of Congress Cataloging-in-Publication Data
Names: Ellis, Joseph J., author.
Title: The cause : the American Revolution and its discontents, 1773–1783 / Joseph J. Ellis.
Other titles: American Revolution and its discontents, 1773–1783
Description: First edition. | New York : Liveright Publishing Corporation, [2021] | Includes bibliographical references and index.
Identifiers: LCCN 2021028335 | ISBN 9781631498985 (hardcover) | ISBN 9781631498992 (epub)
Subjects: LCSH: United States—History—Revolution, 1775–1783. | United States—History—Revolution, 1775–1783—Causes. | Great Britain—Colonies—America—History—18th century. | United States—Politics and government—To 1775. | United States—Politics and government—1775–1783.
Classification: LCC E210 .E45 2021 | DDC 973.3—dc23
LC record available at https://lccn.loc.gov/2021028335

Liveright Publishing Corporation, 500 Fifth Avenue, New York, N.Y. 10110
www.wwnorton.com

W. W. Norton & Company Ltd., 15 Carlisle Street, London W1D 3BS

1 2 3 4 5 6 7 8 9 0

In memory of William S. McFeely, who lived a full life, sharing with readers and students his contagious enthusiasm for the promises and pitfalls of American history.

CONTENTS

PART III: TRIUMPHS AND TRAGEDIES, 1780–1783

PREFACE

Lest We Forget

I do not mean to say, that the scenes of the revolution are now or ever will be entirely forgotten; but that like every thing else, they must fade upon the memory of the world, and grow more and more dim by the lapse of time.
—Abraham Lincoln, Lyceum Address, January 27, 1838

Real historical understanding is not achieved by the subordination of the past to the present, but rather by . . . attempting to see life with the eyes of another century than our own.
—Herbert Butterfield, *The Whig Interpretation of History* (1931)

The pages that follow represent my attempt to tell the story of a highly compressed historical moment that subsequent generations called the American Revolution. No one called it that at the time. The British called it the American rebellion, an accurate description of the eight-year war fought by former British colonists who sought to secede from the British Empire. These former colonists did not regard themselves as Americans, but rather as New Englanders, Virginians, or Pennsylvanians. No such thing as an American national identity yet existed. The term they used to describe their war for independence was The Cause, a conveniently ambiguous label that provided a verbal canopy under which a diverse variety of political and regional persuasions could coexist, then change shape or coloration when history threw choices at them for which they were unprepared. Thus my title.

Whether The Cause was truly a revolution remains, over two hundred years later, a controversial question. My former mentor, Edmund S. Morgan, liked to resolve the debate with a wink, defining a revolution as a sudden change in human affairs so traumatic that no one understood it, either at the time of its happening or thereafter. No less an authority than George Washington observed at the end that any historian who managed to write an accurate account of the war for independence would be accused of writing fiction.

The earliest and most articulate advocates of The Cause insisted that they were *not* proposing a revolution. Quite the contrary, it was the British government that was attempting to impose a revolutionary change in the structure of the British Empire by insisting that Parliament was empowered to tax and legislate for the colonies without their consent. They opposed that change because it violated their historic rights as Englishmen, hardly a revolutionary agenda. Moreover, when some of the most ardent champions of The Cause embraced the radical implications of its meaning—the end of the property qualification to vote, the expansion of women's rights, a gradual emancipation program to end slavery—a chorus of voices, led by John Adams, insisted that such drastic changes must be deferred.

We can, and should, argue about the wisdom of that deferral strategy. There will be those who embrace the conviction that justice delayed is justice denied. But they must contend with the inconvenient truth that any attempt to implement the full meaning of The Cause would have undermined the unity necessary to win the war and thereby rendered American independence impossible. In her *On Revolution,* Hannah Arendt has called attention to the irony of it all. The French Revolution is admired for attempting to implement its radical agenda all at once and failing. The war for American independence is criticized for deferring its full promise and succeeding.

Wherever one chooses to take a stand, there can be no question that we must come to terms with an unusual kind of political animal, the prudent revolutionary. In several senses, their prudence proved wise, in fact brilliant. But, as we shall see, when it came to slavery, the outcome was tragic, and we are still living with the residue of that failure.

Chronology, so they say, is the last refuge of the feeble minded, but the only reliable refuge for the historian. The story told here fits into the decade from 1773 to 1783, though the neatness of that fit obscures the messy origins that precede and outcomes that follow, which cannot be ignored. Keep in mind that the past is not history, but a much vaster region of the dead, gone, unknowable, or forgotten. History is what we choose to remember.

My choices have been guided by the simple question: what is the story? Lots of note cards have been consigned to oblivion because they led the narrative down intriguing byways that transformed the story into a series of interesting asides. Once I realized where the story wanted to go, it often led to events that have been forgotten or that were never remembered in the first place. It turns out that telling the story of a revolution, much like making one happen, is an inherently improvisational act.

The British side of the story requires several trips across the Atlantic in order to understand the reasons why the government made the biggest blunder in the history of British statecraft. While writing those pages, it occurred to me that American readers are now, perhaps for the first time, equipped to grasp the British side of the story. For it is the story of a newly arrived world power moving onto the global stage with overwhelming confidence, brimming over with a bottomless sense of its omniscience and invincibility, stepping into a military quagmire in a war that was both unnecessary and unwinnable. That should have a familiar ring.

The American side of the story requires a different kind of movement from the top to the bottom of the social scale in order to grasp the reasons the American resistance proved so intractable. For it fused together the political arguments of a colonial elite with the passionate intensity of ordinary citizens throughout the vast American countryside. Over the years historians have tended to divide between those emphasizing the top tier of elite spokesmen and those emphasizing the bottom tier of local activists. In the following story both are necessary and interdependent players, the words and music of the revolutionary song.

Similarly, the distinctive character of the nearly eight-year war requires several trips back and forth between the military and political sides of the story, which interact and become comprehensible only when recovered together. It was simultaneously a conflict between armies and a war for hearts and minds; a conventional war and a civil war. Many military historians argue that the American victory was a virtual miracle, an interpretation that Washington endorsed. If it were only a conventional war, they would have been correct, but it was not. In truth, Great Britain never had a realistic chance to win the war, despite its military and economic superiority. American victory was not a miracle; it was foreordained. How that end happened, however, was a function of chance, accident, and what Washington called providence.

There are some ugly moments in this story that will require a revision of our prim and proper picture of eighteenth-century warfare as a polite exchange of muskets between two perfectly aligned rows of statuesque soldiers. The savage character of battle that Rick Atkinson has unmasked so splendidly in *The British Are Coming* is also exposed here. After the first exchange, most battles were fought at close, face-to-face quarters with bayonets and rifle butts. Men were expected to remain calm as the adjoining soldier was decapitated or disemboweled by cannonballs or grapeshot. Casualty rates in major battles were high, often approaching 30 percent killed or wounded.

In fact, more Americans died per capita in the war for independence than in any war in American history save the Civil War. If hit in the torso, your chances of surviving were less than 50 percent. If captured and made a prisoner of war by the British, less than 40 percent. British foraging patrols, especially Hessian and loyalist troops, often gave no quarter, and presumed that plunder and rape were privileges of the profession.

My cast of characters has been assembled according to a modified version of the Casablanca Principle. Which is to say that I have "rounded up the usual suspects," many old friends from previous books. But I have also given greater prominence to characters customarily cast in supporting roles. In my judgment, John Dickinson, Nathanael Greene, John Jay, and Robert Morris were more highly regarded as major players by their contemporaries, and rightly so, than they have been by posterity.

Nor could my story be fully told without a British cast that gets short shrift in most American histories. British historians have tended to make George Germain, the American Secretary throughout most of the war, the chief offender and most conspicuous culprit for the unprecedented British defeat. In my judgment, Germain became the scapegoat for His Majesty himself. John Adams was not just joking when he refused to take credit for making American independence happen, insisting that the lion's share of credit belonged to George III.

Finally, there are profiles of certain players—women and men, Blacks and whites—with distinctive perspectives on the relevant issues at stake in the unfolding story. Most of them fit into the "never remembered at all" category. As you will see, I believe they belong in the story, and are often stories unto themselves, which I try to tell in profiles at the end of each chapter.

Be forewarned that there is an ambush lying back there in the eighteenth century for all those incapable of learning to think in a foreign language. We will be traveling to a premodern world, which means it was pre-democratic, pre-capitalistic, pre-internet. Distance still made an enormous difference. Composing a letter was a more deliberative process than typing an email. Death by disease and a high rate of infant mortality were taken for granted. The average American was born, lived out his or her life, and died within a three-hour horse ride of his or her home.

We must strive to inhabit their world, not just pass through like tourists—especially the kind of American tourists who criticize Londoners for speaking with a foreign accent, or, even worse, who condemn the indigenous people of Samoa for failing to follow the child-rearing practices of Dr. Spock.

We must avoid at all costs the "presentistic fallacy," presuming that the revolutionary generation is a fixed object against which we do our politically correct isometric exercises. All moral and political judgments can come only *after* comprehending their lost world. Looking back, we should expect to encounter imperfect human beings struggling to control events during the most consequential crisis in American history. We have much to learn from their failures as well as their considerable achievements. Indeed, if they were demigods, what could we possibly learn from them? It is time to put away childish things.

Finally, we must also be capable of thinking paradoxically. The American Revolution succeeded because it was not really a revolution. Which means it succeeded because it failed. Moreover, the tragedies, both the failure to end slavery and avoid Indian removal, were rendered inevitable by the terms of the triumph, which demonized any national government empowered to shape domestic policy as a second coming of British tyranny. The two abiding legacies of The Cause, American independence and slavery, established the central contradiction of American history at the very start. Thus my subtitle.

PART I

Origins
and Arguments,
1773–1776

CHAPTER ONE

The Rubicon

The die was now cast; I had passed the Rubicon;
swim or sink, live or die, survive or perish with my
country, was my unalterable determination.

—John Adams, June 1774

There was surely a mischievous twinkle in his eye when Benjamin
Franklin made his outrageous prediction. It came at the end of his
Observations on the Increase of Mankind (1751), which provided demographic evidence showing that the population of the British colonies
in North America was doubling every twenty to twenty-five years, a
rate over twice as fast as the population of England. This led Franklin to imagine a future Anglo-American empire, about a century later,
in which the capital had moved from London to somewhere on the
Susquehanna River in western Pennsylvania. Intriguingly, although
Franklin's reading of the long-term demographic and economic trends
allowed him to foresee the looming power of a large continent over
a small island, he could not imagine a wholly independent American
nation. He presumed that America's expanding significance would
occur within the protective shield of the British Empire.[1]

Franklin was describing the eventual emergence of what came to
be called the British Commonwealth, with the United States cast in

the role subsequently played by Canada and Australia. Given his vantage point in 1751, and his presumption that long-term change would occur gradually in response to America's sheer geographic and demographic size, that is how American history could, perhaps should, have happened. Even now, references to the "special relationship" between the United States and the United Kingdom suggest a filial bond of mutual affection as English-speaking peoples with shared political values, almost as if the American Revolution was a mere bump on the historical road, now beyond memory, and in that sense, never occurred.

Of course, it did. Unlike Franklin, who was predicting the future, historians have the much easier task of predicting the past, indeed are virtually omniscient in that regard. They know beyond any doubt that American independence occurred in the late eighteenth rather than the mid-nineteenth century, on a revolutionary rather than evolutionary schedule, in the crucible of a highly compressed political crisis that generated ideas and institutions which continue to define what has become the world's oldest and most enduring nation-sized republic.

There is also a nearly unanimous consensus among historians that the imperial crisis that culminated in American independence had its origins in the Treaty of Paris (1763). The historical templates shifted at that moment because of the enormous British triumph in the Seven Years' War with France (in America called the French and Indian War). In addition to acquiring several French possessions in Africa and the Caribbean, the great prize was the former French empire in North America. This included all the land from the Appalachian Mountains to the Mississippi River, between Canada and the Floridas. The Treaty of Paris effectively laid the global foundation for the first British Empire, with its base in North America.[2]

There was a palpable and broadly shared sense that Great Britain was entering a new chapter in its history that was simultaneously glorious and ominous. The most experienced and informed British student of American colonial policy, Thomas Pownall, sensed a dramatic shift in the atmosphere, "a general idea of some revolution of events, of something new arising in the world." Pownall did not fall back upon the fable of the gnat that swallowed an elephant, but his previous experience as a royal governor in several colonies made him more fully aware of the unprecedented size and scale of the American theater and the management problems it posed. "There is a universal apprehension," Pownall warned rather vaguely, "of some new crisis forming."[3]

A similar sort of ill-defined apprehension came from an anonymous writer who styled himself "Cato" and who sought to speak for ordinary inhabitants of England and their somewhat baffled sense of inheriting a strange new world. The question posed in his "Thoughts on a Question of Importance," succinctly put, was "What have we done?" As far as he could tell, "we now have from the Gulf of Florida to the North Pole, and how far West I really do not know." Meanwhile most of his friends could not tell the Mississippi from the Danube or the Alleghenies from the Alps. Were these acquisitions new jewels in the British crown to be admired? Or new burdens to bear in the shape of taxes and military obligations? "Cato" claimed he did not know enough to answer his question, but at least for the present was stalled in some zone of apprehension with a blinking sign saying "PROBLEMATICAL."[4]

A less speculative, more managerial perspective came from Francis Bernard, then serving as the royal governor of Massachusetts. Like Pownall, Bernard sensed a dramatic shift in the global templates. As Bernard saw it, Britain's policy toward the American colonies for the preceding century was not to have a policy, what Edmund Burke subsequently called "salutory neglect." There was no foreign secretary in the British government with exclusive responsibility for the American colonies. The foreign policy expertise on America consisted of six officials in the Board of Trade and their respective secretaries. As far as most British subjects were concerned, events in North America could be occurring on the moon. In his *Principles of Law and Polity, Applied to the Government of the British Colonies in America* (1764), Bernard, ever the earnest administrator, argued that the era of complacent negligence needed to end, and he proposed no less than ninety-seven specific reforms to launch the new chapter in British imperial policy.

His major themes were consolidation and control. The various colonial governments had assumed many different shapes, each a product of shifting political imperatives over the past century and a half of English history. Bernard proposed a uniform model for all colonies modeled on the structure of the British government: a royal governor appointed by the king; an upper house or council akin to the House of Lords, which over time might serve as a nursery for the establishment of an indigenous American aristocracy; a lower house or assembly that functioned as a colonial version of the House of Commons and retained control over taxation while acknowledging Parliament's authority over trade; finally, despite the obvious logistical problems, some kind of American representation in Parliament, a political gesture toward accommodation and inclusion designed to keep the colonial planets, at least symbolically, within the gravitational field of Westminster and Whitehall.

This last concern weighed heavily on Bernard's calculations, since he, unlike Franklin, viewed the long-range forces contained within the expanding population of the North American continent as a relentless pressure leading inevitably toward American independence. Imperial reforms that would avoid, or at least delay, that outcome were therefore an obvious and urgent priority: "This is therefore the proper and critical time to reform the American governments upon a general constitutional, firm, and durable plan," he insisted. "And if it is not done now, it will probably every day grow more difficult, till at last it becomes impracticable."[5]

THE FIRST MANIFESTATION of a new imperial policy came not from Parliament, but from George III. As the first Hanoverian monarch to be born in England and to speak English fluently, George III recognized the Treaty of Paris as an opportunity to rescue the British monarchy from what had become a murky, almost symbolic significance. The result was the Proclamation of 1763, which announced the creation of an invisible border running down the western rim of the Appalachian range from the Great Lakes to the Gulf of Mexico. No American settlements would be permitted beyond the new border, purportedly to protect the resident Native American tribes from white encroachment, not so incidentally to restrict the expanding American population to the confined region between the Atlantic coast and the Appalachians.

It was unclear what legal authority a royal proclamation enjoyed at this point in British history, but no sustained opposition to the Proclamation of 1763 emerged on either side of the Atlantic. The primary reason for the silence was simple: everyone knew there was no way that the designated deployment of ten thousand troops could police the imaginary line. Over a thousand settlers every year were already streaming across the mountains, most of them traveling in ox-drawn wagons as early-day pioneers. None of them needed to crawl between the far-flung British garrisons to reach the promised land. Within a few years the surge of Irish and Scotch-Irish immigrants transformed the westward flow into a flood, all oblivious to the fact that some monarch an ocean away, with a scratch of his pen, had proclaimed their destination off-limits. In the crucible of the moment, the most important fact about the Proclamation of 1763 was that it was a wholly arbitrary and presumptive attempt to impose an unprecedented level of British control over the colonies. In retrospect, the most significant fact was that the proclamation could be completely ignored. Projecting power across an ocean onto a vast continent was not going to be easy. Governing the American colonies was not going to be like governing Scotland and Ireland.[6]

The next installment of the new imperial policy came in the form of three acts of Parliament: the Sugar Act (1764), Stamp Act (1765), and Townshend Acts (1767). The ministries of George Grenville and Charles Townshend justified the legislation in financial terms, as responses to the economic problems generated by the Seven Years' War.

That war, like most wars, had proven longer and more expensive than anticipated. It had doubled the national debt to £140 million, a worrisome figure when measured against the £8 million annual budget. The ten thousand troops needed to police the trans-Appalachian region were estimated to cost £200,000 annually, a sum that quickly began to balloon, as all such estimates do. Since the revenue raised by the new taxes and duties was specifically designed to reduce a postwar debt incurred in the American colonies in a war fought on their behalf, it seemed only fair that the colonists should assume their share of the financial burden. Grenville made a gesture toward requesting the colonial legislatures to impose the new taxes on themselves, but the gesture soon became nothing more than that.

Beneath all the economic rationales and entries in balance sheets by faceless accountants in Whitehall, a major shift was occurring in Great Britain's new imperial direction. Control over colonial policy was moving from the Crown to Parliament. (George III even justified his Proclamation of 1763 as a royal effort to facilitate Parliament's expanding agenda.) From a British perspective this made perfect sense. The constitutional settlement of 1689, also called the Glorious Revolution, had achieved its glory by brilliantly blurring the distinction between the two major branches of British government, locating sovereignty in an awkward designation called King-in-Parliament.

The royal side of this partnership was always designed to be secondary, though somewhat more than merely symbolic. By 1760, with the accession of George III, Parliament had become the unspoken but unquestioned dominant player in the political partnership, the center of power within the British government. The fact that Parliament was now assuming control over policy for the American colonies was therefore completely understandable, for if the projections of power abroad were a mandate for the recently arrived British Empire, Parliament was now the place where that wellspring of power resided.[7]

⁂

AT THAT VERY MOMENT, the leading British legal scholar of the day did what skilled lawyers have always done and always will do. He discovered what his client, in this case the parliamentary side of the British government, required. In his *Commentaries on the Laws of England* (1765), William Blackstone found a principle that had always been lurking in the unwritten British constitution, or so he claimed, indeed a principle as old as Aristotle. In every state worthy of that designation, Blackstone intoned, "there must be one singular source of sovereignty beyond which there can be no appeal." And within the British constitution, despite rhetorical dalliances with the King-in-Parliament formulation, the seminal source of governing was Parliament. Its power was inherently unlimited and, as Blackstone declared, "it can do everything that is not naturally impossible."[8]

Blackstone's *Commentaries* appeared just as Parliament was launching an unprecedented campaign to impose its authority over the American colonies. Its publication, in fact, coincided with passage of the Stamp Act. The doctrine of parliamentary sovereignty therefore made perfect sense as a legal rationale for doing what the Grenville ministry—indeed, the entire governing class of Great Britain—wanted and needed to do in order to implement its new imperial agenda. But within the grand sweep of English history, the unlimited supremacy of Parliament, as Blackstone now framed the constitutional argument, was strange. The inherently absolute doctrine of sovereignty that Blackstone proposed for Parliament was the very same claim to unrestricted, nonnegotiable authority that medieval monarchs has been claiming for several centuries and that the entire Whig tradition in English history, itself embodied in Parliament's ascendance during and after the English Civil War, had rejected as a tyrannical vestige of feudalism.

In that sense the sovereignty principle as Blackstone defined it effectively provided Parliament with a secular version of unquestioned power previously reserved for kings claiming divine right and popes claiming infallibility. In fact, both as a word and an idea, "sovereignty" implied the rightful exercise of supernatural powers previously possessed by the gods in the ancient world, and by privileged princes in the medieval era with unique access to God's will. Blackstone's argument that a legislative body of otherwise ordinary human beings owned the same mantle of presumed omnipotence and omniscience was, at best, more than slightly bizarre.

No one in the vicinity of Westminster noticed the ironic implications of Blackstone's sovereignty agreement. (Given its obvious utility, dissenting thoughts were ruled treasonable before they could even be uttered.) But outside of Boston, in the town of Braintree, treasonable thoughts were occurring to an aspiring young lawyer named John Adams. At the same time that Blackstone's *Commentaries* appeared in London, Adams published four essays in the *Boston Gazette* with the off-putting title *A Dissertation on the Canon and Feudal Law* (1765).

Looking back years later, Adams pronounced *Dissertation* "a Sermon upon Plymouth Rock." This accurately described his eulogy to the political legacy of his Puritan ancestors in New England, which Adams contrasted with the prevailing vestiges of what he called "the canon and feudal law in England, the two greatest systems of tyranny ever conceived by the mind of man."[9]

For well over a century his Puritan forebears had planted, cultivated, and institutionalized values that, as Adams described them, "stimulated the common people to aspire at independency, and to endeavor at confining the power of the great within the limits of *equity* and *reason*." As a result, in New England there was no titled aristocracy, mandatory support for public education had created nearly universal literacy, ministers were selected by their congregations, local leaders were elected by their neighbors, and knowledge was "diffused thro' the whole body of the people." All this contrasted dramatically with England's class divisions, enforced ignorance, and illiteracy, and what Adams described as "those phantastical ideas, derived from the common law, which had thrown such a glare of mystery, sanctity, reverence and right reverence . . . as no mortal could deserve." As Adams saw it, and Blackstone seemed almost eager to confirm, most Englishmen still lived within a contrived set of political and religious assumptions designed to suppress personal freedom, assumptions that validated domination by the privileged few over the muffled many.[10]

The Adams analysis had major implications for the ongoing constitutional argument about Parliament's imperial agenda. That argument had become a legalistic exchange between two different views of representation, with the colonists claiming that the members of Parliament could never understand, and therefore never represent, their interests. The main problem according to the American argument was distance. Westminster was an ocean away. Adams now added a new variable. While he claimed to be speaking only for New England, the deeper difference, which rendered Parliament's legislative initiative wholly unacceptable, was that America and Britain had become two fundamentally different societies. Although the colonists were basing their constitutional argument on their historic rights as Englishmen, those rights had assumed a newer and more expansive meaning on American soil over the preceding century.

In addition, the Adams diagnosis of England's lingering liaison with the vestigial remnants of feudalism predisposed him to regard any projection of parliamentary power claiming to be absolute as the imminent arrival of despotism. The very word "sovereignty" was symptomatic, suggesting consolidated political power that defied compromise or negotiation. Just such an ominous phalanx of parliamentary initiatives was hovering over the American colonies, all unprecedented, all couched in the presumptively omniscient language of an arbitrary ruler. "The prospect, now before us, in America," Adams warned, "ought . . . to engage the attention of every man of learning to matters of power and

of right, that we may be neither led nor driven blindfolded to irretriev-
able destruction. Nothing less than this seems to have been meditated
for us, by somebody or other in Great-Britain. There seems to be a
direct and formal design on foot, to enslave all America."[11]

If this sounded hyperbolic, perhaps even paranoid—and over the
years historians have used such terms—mutual misunderstanding was
built into the imperial crisis of the 1760s. British apprehension that
all the American colonists were leaning toward independence, and
therefore required a potent push back into a more submissive posture,
was just as irrational as the colonists' fear that the British program to
consolidate its American empire was really a plot to enslave them. The
American fear, in truth, was rendered more credible by the unlimited
version of the sovereignty argument that Blackstone had provided the
British ministry, as well as by the emphatic way members of Parliament
embraced the intoxicating idea that their will was law.

Indeed, the conventional interpretation of the imperial crisis
needs not just revision but reversal. Great Britain did not launch a
parliamentary initiative to tax the colonies for economic reasons (i.e.,
to reduce the debt caused by the Seven Years' War). Instead, the British ministry imposed new taxes on its American colonies in order to
establish the new principle of parliamentary sovereignty. The defining
issue was power, not money.

From a purely financial perspective, in fact, the taxes and duties
enacted by Parliament in the decade after the Treaty of Paris actually
cost more money to collect than they raised. During the debates over
the Stamp Act, for example, reports from the Board of Trade revealed
that the tax would cover less than half the revenue required to enforce it.
Similarly, the small army of customs officials needed to collect the duties
imposed by the Townshend Acts was more expensive than the projected
revenues. All such calculations did not take into account the impact on
British merchants if the colonists responded, as they predictably did, by

boycotting the enumerated commodities, thereby placing a huge dent in the annual revenue flowing into British coffers, by 1770 estimated at £5 million.

Finally, if economic considerations were the highest priority, any imperial policy that put the lucrative trade with the American colonies at risk was problematic at best. The long-standing Navigation Acts, which the colonists accepted as a justifiable expense for membership in the British Empire, had become a silent and reliable money machine that by the 1760s was transferring over £2 million annually to the British treasury. And that did not include profits accruing to British merchants because of their monopoly of the American market. Enforcement of the Navigation Acts was haphazard at best: smuggling had become a wholly legitimate occupation within the colonies; corruption within the customs offices was rampant; but the leaky pipes continued to deliver a constant flow of revenue that overwhelmed any plan to fix the leaks. Indeed, the system worked so well because of, rather than in spite of, its inefficiency. Any change in direction by the British ministry that endangered this steady stream of income was economically indefensible, the imperial equivalent of killing the goose that laid the golden egg.[12]

It would therefore be misguided to imagine the British ministry reaching a decision to adopt a new policy toward its American colonies after assiduously scanning the ledger books like dutiful accountants focused on the bottom line. A generation of British statesmen named Grenville, Townshend, and North was scanning the horizons. What they saw was a newly acquired empire in North America that needed to be placed under more stringent control. They embraced the sovereignty doctrine with such zeal because it provided the essential rationale for them to perform their obligatory roles as custodians of an emerging empire. And within that empire, the American colonists needed to adjust their new role, not as slaves, but as second-class British subjects, in other words as colonists.

THE AMERICAN SIDE of this story has not gone unnoticed in the nation that eventually came into existence as a consequence of Great Britain's imperial crisis. A veritable mountain of scholarly writing— books, articles, collected letters, edited documents—has built up over the years that now defies mastery by a single mind. The wicked remark by Lytton Strachey at the start of *Eminent Victorians* (1918) seems eerily relevant: "The history of the Victorian Age will never be written; we know too much about it."[13]

After a full century of predictably patriotic treatment, four distinctive schools of thought have come and gone like waves onto the beach, each inevitably reflecting the currents of opinion of their own historical waters. (They have been called Progressive, Imperial, Neo-Whig, and Neo-Beardian schools, but such labels need not deter us.) It would be misleading to claim that the accumulated wisdom has generated what constitutional scholars call "settled law," for unlike the law, history is an argument without end. Instead, consensus has emerged along two overlapping lines of argument, each with ardent advocates. Rather than affix labels to these two interpretive options, better to describe them as top-down or bottom-up perspectives on the coming of the American Revolution.[14]

At the top-down level, the most conspicuous feature is the remarkably consistent constitutional argument that emerged in all the American colonies in response to Parliament's imperial initiative. Edmund S. Morgan and Bernard Bailyn were the first historians to call attention to the gallery of American writers, most of them lawyers, all of them previously obscure, who seemed to pop up out of nowhere up and down the Atlantic coast between 1765 and 1770. The major players were: John Adams and James Otis in Massachusetts, Stephen Hopkins in Rhode Island, Daniel Dulany in Maryland, Richard Bland in Virginia, and John Dickinson in Pennsylvania.[15]

Dickinson's *Letters from a Farmer in Pennsylvania* (1768) became the most comprehensive and influential version of the American argument.* Dickinson drafted a succinct version of the argument as the official statement of the Stamp Act Congress, a gathering of nine colonies at New York in October 1765: "That it is inseparably essential to the Freedom of the people, and the undoubted right of Englishmen, that no Taxes be imposed on them, but with their own Consent, given personally by their own representatives as assembled in the respective colonial legislatures."[16]

Instead of a cacophony of voices, there was a colonial chorus. All critics of the new imperial agenda agreed that the amount they were being taxed was not the issue, but rather the principle itself; Parliament lacked the authority to tax its American colonists or to impose duties for the explicit purpose of raising a revenue. The argument that the colonists were "virtually" represented by members of Parliament was so effectively ridiculed that spokesmen for the British ministry stopped making the claim. At this early stage of the debate, American writers focused their primary attack on taxation, leaving conveniently obscure what other forms of parliamentary legislation they found unacceptable, though there was a clear consensus that the Navigation Acts were not within their sights.

The great strength of the American argument was its conservative character. The colonists could legitimately claim that Great Britain was proposing a fundamental change in the Anglo-American arrangement. The Americans were insisting on their historical rights as defined in the British constitution and presumed as inviolate prior to 1763. It was an argumentative framework that placed the British ministry on the permanent defensive.

---

* Hardly an American farmer, Dickinson was born into a prominent Quaker family, married into an even more prominent Quaker family, was educated in the law at the Middle Temple in London, and carried himself like a natural aristocrat strolling to his appointment with destiny.

❧

MEANWHILE, at the ground level, what has impressed several generations of historians is the stunning speed with which the well-framed resistance to British authority seeped down to the county, town, and local level, effectively rendering enforcement of the new taxes and duties impossible. Almost instantaneously, American colonists created a communications network that generated the first truly national dialogue in American history.

If only in retrospect, there were several preexistent conditions that provided a foundation for the emerging revolutionary dialogue. The American colonies happened to enjoy the highest literacy rate in the world, approaching 90 percent in New England. By 1770 there were also nearly 150 newspapers in circulation, which routinely reprinted stories from other publications in distant precincts. The emergence of the pamphlet as a cheap, readily accessible vehicle for authors, often styling themselves "Cato" or "Publius," offered the perfect instrument for what we might regard as early-day blogs. In effect, despite the primitive conditions, to include the sheer nonexistence of roads, especially south of the Potomac, ideas could travel on a virtual highway for the printed word that defied distance.

New England led the way in what came to be called "circular letters" and "committees of correspondence." Massachusetts, under the leadership of Samuel Adams, created a routinized communications network connecting all the roughly two hundred towns and villages of the colony to headquarters back in Boston. If John Dickinson was the preeminent figure in shaping the American argument in the 1760s, Samuel Adams was the dominant figure in orchestrating the spread of that message to the countryside and beyond.[17] The groundswell of opposition to Parliament's imperial initiative had rendered the entire tax program just as ludicrously inoperable as the ill-fated Proclamation of 1763.

Several shifts in British ministries—from George Grenville, to the

Marquis of Rockingham, to Lord North—created what was effectively a bimodal policy: Parliament would repeal the specific enactments of the imperial principle but retain its commitment to the principle itself. Thus, the Board of Trade simply stopped trying to collect the duties mandated by the Sugar and Townshend Acts, then, after a highly contested vote in the House of Commons, it repealed the Stamp Act. But by an overwhelming vote Parliament also passed the Declaratory Act (1766), which asserted its right to bind the American colonists by legislation "in all cases whatsoever." In order to underline the principle at stake, albeit symbolically, Parliament retained the tax on tea while dropping it on the other enumerated commodities.

The Tea Act (1773) represented a perhaps overly clever scheme by the British ministry to score a symbolic victory against the American boycott of tea. The act retained the three-pence duty on tea owned by the East India Company, but allowed the company to bypass the middlemen in England and sell it at a discount rate in the American colonies. The point was to lure the tea-addicted colonists into paying the duty and thereby succumb to the dictates of Parliament.

The transparent scheme was exposed and ridiculed in all the major American newspapers. Committees of correspondence in all the port cities agreed on their strategy: all the British ships carrying tea would not be permitted to unload, and would instead be forced to return to England with all the tea aboard. This arrangement worked in New York and Philadelphia, but in Boston the governor, Thomas Hutchinson, would not allow the tea-laden ships to leave port. By early December 1773 matters had reached a standoff as three ships laden with 342 chests of the finest Bohea tea rested in sight of two British frigates charged with blocking their departure.

On December 16 more than seven thousand Bostonians gathered in Old South Church to debate their options. After listening for several hours, Samuel Adams, looking for all the world like a Boston dockworker but sounding like a Puritan minister channeling God's word, rose from the chair and pronounced the discussion at an end. "This meeting," he said, "can do nothing more to save the country." It soon became clear that these words were a coded message to implement a plan decided on weeks earlier if all else failed.

A group of forty men unconvincingly disguised as Mohawk Indians gathered at the doorway. As they marched toward Griffin's Wharf, they were joined by forty more men with painted faces and hatchets, moving in a column of twos like the trained militia they mostly were. In less than three hours all the chests of tea on the *Dartmouth,* the *Beaver,* and the *Eleanor* had been split open and unceremoniously tossed into Boston Harbor. According to strict orders, no other property on board the ships was harmed or stolen. Even the broken locks on the cabin doors were all replaced. The next day Samuel Adams let it be known that what had just transpired was not a mob action. "These people," he observed, as if reading from a decidedly American version of scripture, "have acted upon a pure and upright principle." From the British perspective, of course, that principle was pure treason.[18]

GIVEN THE WINTER WAVES and ocean currents, it took five weeks for the news of the Tea Party to cross the Atlantic. The response of the British ministry also came in waves: first shock, then outrage, then catharsis. Writing from London as a colonial agent for Massachusetts, Benjamin Franklin warned that the third wave had the look of a tsunami: "The violent destruction of the tea seems to have united all parties." It was as if a parent, confronted with a delinquent teenager, suddenly realized that earlier efforts at leniency (i.e., repeal of the Stamp Act) were misguided. The time had now come to end all pretenses of parental patience and show the imperial face of the British Empire.[19]

George III set the new tone in his message to Parliament. What he described as "the violent and outrageous proceedings of the Town and Port of Boston" had crossed a line and done so defiantly. It was now incumbent on both houses of Parliament "to put an immediate stop to the present disorders [by imposing] permanent provisions for securing the execution of the Laws, and just dependence of the Colonies upon the Crown and Parliament of Great Britain." The American colonists had created this crisis by their brazen display of disrespect for Parliament's authority, which now must be reasserted in no uncertain terms. "The die is now cast," the king wrote to Lord North, "and the colonies must either submit or triumph."[20]

Submission meant subordination and, if it proved necessary, subjugation by military force. If it should come to that, the king's military aide, General Thomas Clarke, assured him that the outcome was preordained. With a mere regiment of grenadiers, Clarke boasted, he could "march the length of the American continent and, along the way, geld all the Males, partly by force and partly by a little coaxing." If you were deciding to cross the Rubicon, it was comforting to know that the victorious outcome of all battles on the other side was already assured.[21]

During the spring of 1774, Parliament set the course that would define Great Britain's imperial agenda for the next seven years, culminating with the surrender of General Cornwallis's army at Yorktown in 1781. Knowing as we do that a catastrophe was in the making, perhaps the most salient feature on the political landscape—what leaps out, if only in retrospect—is the utter certainty of Great Britain's governing class in the direction they were taking the empire. Nothing less than the ultimate and absolute sovereignty of Parliament as the epicenter of power within that empire was at stake. And it was equally clear that the epicenter of resistance to that sovereignty resided in New England, more narrowly in Massachusetts, most visibly in Boston. The name given to the legislation passed by overwhelming majorities in both houses of Parliament in spring of 1774 was utterly accurate. Called the Coercive Acts in England, somewhat later the Intolerable Acts in America, the legislation was explicitly designed to coerce the residents of Boston in ways that felt intolerable, and thereby send a signal to all their co-conspirators in New England and beyond that the same fate awaited them if they proved equally defiant.

The Boston Port Act closed the harbor to all exports as of June 1, effectively ending all commerce on which the economy of Massachusetts depended. Only provisions for the occupying British army and a few essentials like firewood could be imported. Enforcement of the boycott rested in the capable hands of the British navy. All these devastating restrictions would be lifted only when the king was satisfied that the perpetrators of the so-called Tea Party were properly punished and full restitution provided to the East India Company for the destroyed tea.

The Massachusetts Government Act significantly revised the Massachusetts Charter of 1691 in ways former governor Francis Bernard had recommended a decade earlier, chiefly by enlarging the authority of the royally appointed governor at the expense of the popularly elected branches of government. The Council or upper house would be appointed by the governor rather than chosen by the legislature. All judges and sheriffs also became royal appointees. Finally, all town meetings, which were generally regarded as the engines of discontent in the colony, were confined to one meeting a year and prohibited from discussing issues beyond their local orbits. In order to implement the new political structure, General Thomas Gage was chosen to serve as governor-general, thereby imposing martial law for the foreseeable future.* In the commission appointing Gage, the colonial secretary, the Earl of Dartmouth, saw fit to mention that his new assignment would quite likely demand the display of military power, since "the sovereignty of Parliament over the Colonies requires a full and absolute submission."[22]

The Administration of Justice Act revised the court system so as to remove control from local juries in all cases involving customs officials or British soldiers accused of a crime. Trials of such offenders were

---

* Gage was the senior British officer in America, married to a prominent American woman who was rumored to harbor sympathy for The Cause, and who himself carried doubts about the Coercive Acts and the aggressive direction of British policy.

transferred beyond the borders of Massachusetts to Halifax, Nova Scotia, or, if necessary, all the way to London.

There is a strange discrepancy between the huge majorities that supported passage of the Coercive Acts and the record of the debates in Parliament, which make it appear that a robust opposition was present to contest the eventual outcome. Most likely, the majority of members realized from the start that their voices were unnecessary because the conclusion was foreordained. Prime Minister Lord North, whom Horace Walpole described as having a face that "gave him the air of a blind trumpeter," felt disposed to permit opponents the full range of their eloquence, since such generosity won him the respect of his peers while costing him nothing. As a result, anyone reading the historical record must guard against concluding that there was a sizable faction in Parliament that recognized the ominous path down which their colleagues were taking the British Empire.

Here is a sample of the dissenting voices: Alexander Dowdeswell: "You are not contending for a point of honor, gentlemen, you are struggling to maintain a ridiculous superiority." Colonel Isaac Barre: "Parliament may fancy that they have rights in theory, but these rights can never be put into practice short of war." General Henry Conway: "These acts, respecting America, will involve this country and its Ministers in misfortunes, and I wish I need not add, in ruin." Most eloquently, and certainly at greatest length, there was Edmund Burke, a one-man Irish army on his feet, who, despite his youth, had already earned a reputation as the most impressive speaker in the House of Commons. Burke compared the Boston Port Act to "an order—delivered to the British navy to bombard and destroy the town and people of Boston. This is the day, then, when you decide to go to war with all America."[23]

Finally, most poignantly, there was William Pitt, still regarded as the most distinguished statesman in Britain for the brilliance of his leadership as prime minister during the Seven Years' War. Recently elevated to the peerage as Earl of Chatham, Pitt was beloved in the American

colonies as the Great Commoner for his impassioned opposition to the
Stamp Act and his famous pronouncement, "I rejoice that America has
resisted." (His pro-American legacy is enshrined forever in the major
American city that bears his name.) If Pitt had been slightly younger,
less ill—several of his biographers think he was bipolar—or perhaps a
less singularly independent figure, there is no question that he could
have commanded the field of British politics in 1774. It is therefore, in
retrospect, almost impossible not to imagine Pitt as prime minister in
lieu of the wholly managerial, willfully vague, comfortably inadequate
Lord North. And once imagined, the entire history of Anglo-American
relations flows forward in the more enlightened direction that Franklin
had forecast more than two decades earlier.

BUT IT WAS NOT meant to be. Pitt himself let it be known that he
was no longer up to the challenge. He appeared in the House of Lords
only once during the debates over the Coercive Acts. "My Lords, I am
an old man," he explained to those accustomed to looking toward him
for leadership. He did muster the energy to urge his colleagues "to
adopt a more gentle mode of governing the Americans." His reasoning
echoed Franklin's vision: "For the day is not far distant," he predicted,
"when America will vie with these Kingdoms not only in arms, but in
arts also." Instead of worrying about America's growing strength, he
encouraged all liberty-loving Britons to welcome it. As for the sovereignty question, he described the current obsession with enforcing that
principle at the expense of the Bostonians as a sign of weakness rather
than strength. (One British historian has called Pitt's recommended
policy the doctrine of "sleeping sovereignty.") Based on the votes on the
Coercive Acts, fewer than one in ten of his fellow Lords were prepared
either to listen or comprehend what he was saying.[24]

There was another prominent presence in Parliament during the debates over the Coercive Acts who also invites a retrospective fling of the imagination, though he does not appear in the records as uttering a word. Edward Gibbon had just been elected to the House of Commons and assumed his position on the backbench in the spring of 1774. In his correspondence with Lord Sheffield, a longtime friend in the House of Lords, Gibbon registered the same sense of shock as the other members upon learning of the recent Tea Party in Boston. "We are now arrived at the decisive moment of preserving or of losing forever both our trade and our Empire," he observed. Then the record goes silent.[25]

What was Gibbon thinking? The question becomes mandatory since we know that he had been working on his history of the Roman Empire for eleven years; and the first volume of his magisterial *The Decline and Fall of the Roman Empire* would appear two years later. Even those dates suggest a striking historical coincidence: Gibbon began his magnum opus in the same year that Great Britain acquired its American empire, in 1763, and he completed the first installment the year she lost it, in 1776. Along the way, the man who was thinking more deeply than anyone in the world before or since about the historical forces that cause empires to rise and fall was witnessing that same imperial narrative play out from his seat in the House of Commons. And he said nothing.

There is this cryptic remark in a letter to Lord Sheffield a year later, when news of the outbreak of war at Lexington and Concord reached Westminster: "In this season and on America the Archangel Gabriel would not be heard," Gibbon wrote, "and for myself, having supported the British, I must destroy the Roman Empire." These words suggest, albeit elliptically, that Gibbon did not bring his knowledge of Rome's history to bear on British history in the making, but the other way around. Which is to say that he brought his experience as a bystander witnessing his British colleagues blunder into an imperial debacle to bear on his analysis of Rome's imperial history.[26]

Although the connection has long since been lost to us, the first three chapters of *Decline and Fall,* which describe the enlightened approach to Rome's far-flung colonies between the reigns of Augustus and Hadrian, were a prescription for the path not taken by the British ministry in 1774. The Roman Senate was confident that it possessed sovereign authority, and therefore felt no need to exhaust its energies over distant provinces, which were allowed to conduct their own internal affairs without Rome's intrusion. Augustus was the wise emperor that George III could never be, "for it was reserved for Augustus to relinquish the ambitious design of subduing the whole earth, and to introduce a spirit of moderation in the public councils." Augustus understood that "Rome had much less to hope than to fear from the chance of arms; and that, in the prosecution of remote wars, the undertaking became every day more difficult, the event more doubtful, the possession more precarious, and less beneficial." It seems plausible to conclude that Gibbon was too reserved a man to share his insights in the public arena of Parliament, but as the greatest historian of the age, he instead filtered his knowledge through Rome and thereby shared it with posterity. Such ironies were surely not lost on the most masterful stylist of irony in the English language.[27]

Another accomplished stylist had in fact recently published an essay containing a satirical version of Gibbonesque wisdom aimed squarely at the audience that Gibbon could not bring himself to address. The essay was mischievously entitled *Rules by Which a Great Empire May Be Reduced to a Small One* (1773). The author was the most prominent American in England, Benjamin Franklin.

Franklin's clear intention in *Rules* was to force the British government to view the current imperial crisis through the eyes of the colonists, and to frame his argument in a satirical format that rendered it impossible to rebut without appearing ridiculous. "I have held up a Looking-Glass in which some Ministers may see their ugly Faces," he explained, "and the Nation its injustice."[28]

Here are three of his mock recommendations to the members of Parliament:

If the colonists happen to be zealous Whigs, Friends of Liberty, nurtur'd in Revolutionary Principles, remember to treat their Principles with Prejudice, and contrive to punish it. Suppose them always inclined to revolt, and treat them accordingly. Take care that they are not incorporated with the Mother Country, that they are governed by severer Laws, all of your own enacting, not allowing them any share in the choice.[29]

Franklin's satirical essay appeared in several British publications to mixed reviews before it traveled across the Atlantic, where it met with nearly universal acclaim. In terms of Franklin's political career, the publication of *Rules* marked the moment when he stopped serving as an evenhanded arbiter between the two sides of the Anglo-American argument. A few months later, in January 1774, he was forced to stand in silence before an assemblage of Britain's most prominent officials while being demonized as the embodiment of American insolence and ingratitude. By then the gap between the British and American camps had widened into a chasm that could no longer be straddled. It was now clear for all to see that Franklin stood squarely on the American side. The British had just lost the American Prometheus.[30]

The passage of the Coercive Acts in the spring of 1774 represented Parliament's willful decision to transform Franklin's clever satire into a bad joke. It was almost as if Lord North's followers in Parliament took their cues from Franklin's essay. His catalog of British blunders became the political framework for their nonnegotiable imperial agenda. Looking back to this moment a year later, Edmund Burke delivered the epitaph for the Anglo-American vision that he, Pitt, and Franklin had tried so hard to defend, in words that Franklin could easily have spoken: "A great empire and little minds go ill together."[31]

⚜

THE AMERICAN RESPONSE to the Coercive Acts was instantaneous
and predictable. "For flagrant injustice and barbarity," Samuel Adams
proclaimed, "one might search in vain among the archives of Constan-
tinople to find a match for it." Down in Philadelphia, John Dickinson
observed that "the insanity of Parliament has operated like inspiration
in America. The Colonists now know what is designed against them."
The new rallying cry, which began to appear in pamphlets and newspaper editorials up and down the Atlantic coast, was "Common Cause,"
which described a shared sense of solidarity uniting all the colonies in
support of their besieged Boston brethren. The transparent strategy of
the British ministry to isolate Massachusetts had backfired, producing
exactly the opposite outcome. The Americans, it turned out, were also
prepared to cross the Rubicon, but in the opposite direction.[32]

Once again, American resistance to Parliament's authority mobi-
lized at two levels. At the higher altitude, the old argument against
the Stamp and Townshend Acts required revision because the political
threat posed by the Coercive Acts went beyond taxation by raising the
larger constitutional question of whether or where a line could be drawn
between Parliament's purported sovereignty and American rights as
Englishmen. Within a matter of months, three pamphlets appeared,
authored by James Wilson of Pennsylvania, William Henry Drayton
of South Carolina, and Thomas Jefferson of Virginia. All agreed that,
given Parliament's version of sovereignty, there was no middle ground
where colonial rights and parliamentary authority could coexist. The
new consensus was the mirror image of the Declaratory Act, which
had proclaimed Parliament's unlimited sovereignty. Parliament had no
authority whatsoever to legislate for the colonies.[33]

Meanwhile, even as the revised constitutional argument was forming in the atmosphere, more urgent concerns were circulating on the
ground through the same communications network that had mobi-

lized against previous parliamentary efforts to impose taxes. Samuel Adams saw to it that circular letters went out to prospective allies in Maryland, Virginia, and South Carolina as early as May 1774, urging them to join the Common Cause. Virginia needed no prodding, having already declared June 1 "a day of Fasting and Prayer" to recognize the date when the Boston Port Act went into effect. In the Virginia House of Burgesses, Richard Henry Lee read out loud from letters sent by his brother, Arthur Lee, currently serving as colonial agent in London, warning that failure to declare solidarity with their Boston brethren would validate the British strategy of isolating New England. "The shallow Ministerial device was seen thro instantly," Richard Henry assured his brother, "and everyone declared it the commencement of a most wicked system for destroying the Liberty of America."[34]

Virginia proved symptomatic of a resistance movement that flowed like a giant wave up and down the Atlantic coast in the summer of 1774, simultaneously soaking into the counties, towns, and farming communities where ordinary Americans lived their lives. In July almost every county in the Old Dominion drafted resolutions pledging support for a boycott of British imports and endorsing a recommendation that "Deputies from the several Colonies of British America meet in general Congress at such a place and time as be thought most convenient." By August ten colonies had endorsed the same resolutions, often in language so similar that the authors appeared to be copying from a prearranged script.[35]

Somehow, ideas and a shared vocabulary of resistance were traveling at electronic speed long before electricity made modern modes of communication possible. It seemed that the British ministry had designed the perfect instrument to galvanize the vast majority of American colonists. Previously, the only identity the colonists shared in common was membership in the British Empire. During the summer of 1774 a major shift was occurring. They now shared a common conviction that their equal status within the empire was being downgraded.

What was happening to their brothers and sisters in Boston was a preview of what soon could be happening to them.

MEANWHILE, up in New England, it was gradually dawning on Governor-General Gage that the orders he had received in London from the Earl of Dartmouth did not translate into the conditions he faced in Boston. His mission, as Dartmouth put it, was to enforce the Coercive Acts, by persuasion if possible, by military means if necessary. The sovereign power of Parliament required nothing less than "a full and absolute subjugation." The military means at his disposal should prove more than adequate to that task, Dartmouth observed, since it included three thousand troops, once reinforced by an additional two regiments from Ireland. And of course, he also enjoyed the matchless firepower of the British fleet in Boston Harbor and off the New England coast. He therefore possessed military supremacy more than sufficient to crush any imaginable American resistance. During the summer of 1774, however, Gage began to realize that his superiors in London needed to make a major adjustment in their calculations.[36]

The core of the problem was sheer numbers. As Gage discovered, beyond Boston's borders it was impossible to enforce any form of British authority. For example, all persons named as prospective royal appointees to the Massachusetts Council were immediately targeted for intimidation. "My house at Cambridge, being surrounded by about four thousand people," reported Thomas Oliver, "I hereby sign my name and resign my seat in Council." The same fate befell Joshua Loring of Jamaica Plain, where the mob outside his house was estimated at five thousand and a noose was hung in his front yard.* In Worcester, Timothy Paine read his resignation speech to a crowd of fifteen hundred onlookers, several cocking and aiming their muskets when he hesitated.[37]

---

* See the profile of Loring at the end of this chapter.

The same level of mass resistance forced the closing down of all courts outside Boston. No jurors would agree to serve, lest their names be listed in the local papers as traitors. Sheriffs who hesitated to enforce the closing of the courts had their houses surrounded by mobs. When one sheriff persisted, his house was demolished. In Springfield, three thousand protesters gathered outside the courthouse as four judges took a solemn vow to cancel all trials for the foreseeable future. One recalcitrant judge in Hatfield suffered the indignity of being "smoked" overnight in a smokehouse until he emerged appropriately penitent.[38]

It was now obvious to Gage that the military force under his command was inadequate for the task at hand. Gage urged his superiors across the ocean to recognize that the scale of the strategic problem Great Britain confronted in New England defied all earlier estimates or expectations. Nothing less than twenty thousand additional troops would be required to subjugate the population, and even those numbers might prove inadequate. Gage described a long and extremely costly campaign that, even if successful, would require a large occupation force for the foreseeable future, plus the permanent deployment of a major portion of the British fleet. The pressure such a commitment would put on manpower demands throughout the empire would probably require the costly but necessary hiring of mercenaries from the Germanic principalities or Russia. Nothing less than this level of commitment would suffice.[39]

Whether he knew it or not—and there is reason to believe he did—by sending such a realistic assessment of the strategic dilemmas posed by the wholly hostile theater in New England, Gage was committing professional suicide. For once the full scope and cost of implementing Britain's imperial agenda in America was fully exposed, the rationale for that agenda became highly problematic. And since such a conclusion was inadmissible within the corridors of Westminster, Lord North chose to blame the message on the messenger.

North's cabinet voted unanimously to relieve Gage after receiving

his latest report to Dartmouth. Upon hearing the news, one retired
British officer counted it a sad day for Gage, who had clearly aged overnight and lost his courage. After all, it was well known among British
veterans of the American theater that "any two regiments of soldiers
would be able to defeat the whole force of the Massachusetts Province." A much more accurate requiem for Gage would have been that he
demonstrated the courage to tell his arrogant superiors the truth. But
no one in the British ministry was prepared to hear it.[40]

ON THE AMERICAN SIDE of the same story, it was impossible not to
hear the steady chorus of voices floating up from every town, county,
and colony beyond the Massachusetts borders, from Connecticut to
Georgia. The resolutions were too diverse in their origins and accents
to be orchestrated from above, but ended up sounding the same notes:
Massachusetts must not be permitted to stand alone; the Coercive Acts
must be repealed; Parliament's claim of sovereignty must be repudiated; a boycott of all imports from Britain, Ireland, and the West Indies
must be enacted; whatever differences existed among the colonies must
be subordinated to the larger purposes of a unified resistance; colonial
unity should find political expression through a gathering of delegates
in Philadelphia sometime in early September.

And so, on September 5, 1774, fifty-six delegates from twelve colonies met at Carpenter's Hall in Philadelphia as the First Continental
Congress. (Georgia sent its regrets, citing the ongoing conflict with the
Creek tribes as a more pressing priority.) Unlike poor Gage, who was
receiving his marching orders from civilian superiors at the top of a
political hierarchy an ocean away, the delegates in Philadelphia were
guided by a directive coming from the ground up in all the provincial
precincts up along the Atlantic coast. Though no one used such words
at the time, the Continental Congress was functioning as a republican
government that derived its authority from the people at large.[41]

That context is crucial to comprehend because it shaped the framework for the deliberations in Philadelphia over the ensuing seven weeks. Unfortunately, much of the scholarship on the First Continental Congress has been burdened by the insistence on two misleading categories that distort the true terms of the debate and thereby obscure the reasons the outcome took the shape it did. The chief culprit was Joseph Galloway, a rogue delegate from Pennsylvania who subsequently became the most outspoken loyalist in London during the war. Galloway claimed that the delegates in Philadelphia were divided into two factions: moderates, who sincerely sought reconciliation with Great Britain; and radicals, who yearned for American independence. In fact, no delegate to the congress advocated independence. As George Washington, the least talkative member of the Virginia delegation, put it, independence meant war, and war was "a dernier resort," adding that "I am as well satisfied as I can be of my own existence, that no such thing is desired by any thinking man in North America."[42]

Any attempt to color the different camps within the Continental Congress cannot be done in black and white, but in multiple shades of gray. While the middle colonies, chiefly New York and Pennsylvania, tended toward more cautious articulations of American rights, and the delegations from Massachusetts, Virginia, and South Carolina were more ardently outspoken, there were exceptions to all generalizations. More important, the delegates were keenly aware of the need to project a unified front, which put enormous pressure on all concerned to lean toward the center, even if it meant compromising their fondest convictions. The Common Cause refrain became much more than a slogan.

Samuel Adams set the standard for conspicuous accommodation at the first session of the congress. John Jay of New York had observed that the diversity of religious preferences among the delegates made it impossible to select a minister who might bless the proceedings with a prayer. Although Adams was a rock-ribbed Puritan, known to regard Anglicans as watered-down papists, he rose to recommend Jacob Duche, the most prominent Anglican minister in Philadelphia. The symbolic gesture captured everyone's attention, as the delegates smiled and nodded toward Adams throughout Duche's prayers. Three years later, when Duche fled to London as a loyalist, no one saw fit to remember the earlier infatuation with his eloquence.[43]

Through the early weeks of September, the entire Massachusetts delegation chose to remain in the background. "We have been obliged to act with great Delicacy and Caution," John Adams reported, "to keep ourselves out of sight, to feel Pulses and sound the Depths, to insinuate our Designs and Desires by means of other Persons." Although this was an unnatural act for John, who customarily regarded silence as a mortal sin, he and his Massachusetts colleagues were well aware that they represented the epicenter of the American resistance movement. Delegates from beyond New England, especially more moderate members from the middle colonies, wanted to show their support, but they also dreaded the prospect of being dragged over the abyss into war with Great Britain by a few overly zealous patriots in Boston. The Massachusetts representatives needed to offset such apprehensions with conspicuous deference to the other delegations. Leadership at this moment meant listening.[44]

The deference strategy paid dividends on September 17, when Paul Revere delivered copies of the Suffolk Resolves to congress. Drafted by Joseph Warren, a rising star within the Sons of Liberty in Boston, the Suffolk Resolves were a radical manifesto that, upon arrival in London, were described by the North ministry as a de facto declaration of independence. Warren denounced the Coercive Acts as unconstitutional, sanctioned civil disobedience by all residents of Massachusetts as a patriotic obligation, proclaimed that all courts in the colony would remain closed, and announced the calling of a Provincial Congress in Concord as the new, extralegal government. Most ominously, the Suffolk Resolves required all militia to disavow their loyalty to the existent

British government, take an oath to Massachusetts, and then "acquaint themselves with the art of war as soon as possible." Almost deliberately provocative, the resolves seemed almost designed to divide the delegates in Philadelphia.[45]

The exact opposite happened. The vote to endorse the Suffolk Resolves was unanimous. Although at least half the delegates were known to harbor serious reservations, in unrecorded, behind-the-scenes conversations the Adams team provided assurance that they would exercise restraint over Warren and his radical compatriots. Letters quickly went back to Boston from the Adamses urging caution, discipline, and a wholly defensive posture. Conversations also began in congress about the possible evacuation of Boston in order to reduce the likelihood of a violent clash with British troops that might ignite all the combustible materials.

In his diary, John Adams proclaimed September 17 "one of the happiest days of my Life" because it showed that "all America will support Massachusetts or perish with her." In a letter to his beloved Abigail, he sounded the same note about his colleagues in congress: "They all profess to consider our Province as suffering in the Common Cause, and indeed they seem to feel for her, Us, as if for themselves."[46]

While Adams's joy was wholly justified, the more mundane reality was that the delegates in Philadelphia endorsed the Suffolk Resolves, despite reservations, because they believed they had no choice. And the endorsement had to be unanimous because anything less would let the cracks show in a resistance movement that must, above all, project a united front. There is reason to believe that behind the scenes, in ways that left no historical record, Samuel Adams was busy assuring his more nervous colleagues that Massachusetts would not betray their trust. Word was going back by courier to Joseph Warren in Boston to tighten control over the rowdier patriots who might provoke an explosive incident. If war was to come, history must show that the British fired the first shot.[47]

FROM THE VERY START of their deliberations, the delegates knew
they had a mandate to impose a boycott on British imports, and that
some colonial legislatures had also recommended a boycott on American exports as well. With surprising speed a consensus formed around
an embargo of both imports and exports and, with equivalent ease,
that the boycott of imports would include "any Goods, Wares, or Mer-
chandizes from Great Britain or Ireland"—in effect, everything—and
would begin on December 1.

A separate paragraph, almost presented as a brief aside, announced
the wholly unexpected inclusion of all African slaves on the boycott list.
It declared in a subdued tone "that we will not import or purchase any
slave imported after the first day of September next, after which time
we will wholly discontinue the slave trade." In one nonchalant sentence,
the delegates seemed to succinctly resolve a problem that was destined
to bedevil their successors in the Second Continental Congress, then
surface again as a divisive issue eleven years later in the Constitutional
Convention. What had just happened?[48]

The short answer is that we do not know. Neither the documentary
record, nor the correspondence of the delegates, provides any account
of the deliberations on the slave trade. Indeed, the silence is probably
the strongest evidence that the issue was too controversial to permit
exposure in a deliberative body that needed to conceal any divisions
that undermined the Common Cause. We know that Virginia supported ending the slave trade, not because the planter class harbored
moral reservations, but because their plantations were overstocked. We
also know that South Carolina and Georgia strongly opposed any policy that imposed limits on slave imports. Georgia, of course, was not
present in Philadelphia, though South Carolina was. We also know that
rice was the one commodity conspicuously removed from the boycott
list of exports, and that South Carolina was the chief exporter of rice.

So, it is plausible to speculate that the rice exception was a political reward to South Carolina for joining the consensus on ending the slave trade. But we are only guessing.[49]

The debate over the boycott on exports became an argument over Virginia's addiction to tobacco. As the largest delegation from the largest colony, the Virginians felt empowered to plead for special treatment, requesting an extension beyond the December 1 deadline so that the Tidewater planters could harvest and sell their tobacco crop before the boycott went into effect. After much back-and-forthing, the congress voted to extend the embargo on all exports until September 10, 1775, thereby joining Virginia rather than making her an exception.

In order to enforce the two-pronged embargo, most especially to prohibit the consumption of commodities on the nonimportation list, the congress created the Continental Association. The animating idea was elegantly simple: namely, to delegate the implementation of an intercolonial policy to the people on the ground. The congress specifically recommended:

> That a Committee be chosen in every County, city and Town by those who are qualified to vote for Representative in the Legislature, whose business it shall be attentively to observe the conduct of all persons touching the Association; and when it shall be made clear to a satisfaction of the majority of such Committee that any person within the limits of their appointment has violated this Association, that such majority do forthwith cause the truth of the case to be published in the Gazette, to the end that all such foes of British America may be publickly known, and universally condemned as the enemies of *American* Liberty; and thenceforth we will break off all dealings with him or her.[50]

This was a document with revolutionary implications that most members of the Continental Congress did not fully foresee. It transformed

the entire American countryside into a political arena in which everyone was required to play a role, and no one could remain a neutral spec-
tator. For, as it turned out, everyone was "touched" by the Association.
What clothes you wore, what food you ate, whom you sat next to at
church, what prices you charged if you were a merchant or grocer, all
became political statements for which all were held accountable. It was
as if all America had become a large church in which the congregation
was assuming the obligation to separate the saints from the sinners.[51]

The sprawling scale of the local enforcement networks, what one
historian has called "the infrastructure of revolution," defied reliable
modes of measurement. In the months following the adjournment of
the Continential Congress, it is estimated that 1000 Committees of
Safety or Committees of Inspection were appointed in the American
colonies, each committee containing between twenty and two hundred
members. Massachusetts, for example, appointed 160 town committees
with ten members each. Virginia allocated twenty committee members
for each of its 61 counties. Philadelphia's Committee of Inspections and
Observation divided the city into twelve districts, which were policed
by subcommittees of varying sizes. Although surviving records permit
only glimpses of the enforcement network, the overarching pattern
seems reasonably clear.[52]

First, unlike subsequent revolutionary movements in France and
Russia, there were no guillotines or firing squad walls. Violence was the
exception rather than the rule, a last resort after nonviolent forms of
intimidation had failed. True enough, stubborn dissenters could expect
to be threatened with bodily harm. Daniel Dunbar in Salem, Massachusetts, for example, was required to "ride the wooden horse" for two
hours after refusing to resign his royal commission in the militia. But
the enforcement of the Association was more like a religious revival in
which the sinners were urged to repent. Being marked by your neighbors as a traitor usually sufficed to produce a conversion. Outright loyalists were ostracized, humiliated, banned from attendance at dances,

funerals, or church services until they either joined the Common Cause or moved away.[53]

As a result, within a matter of months after the Continental Congress adjourned in late October 1774, the entire American countryside had been politicized. Apart from Boston and New York, where the British army and navy maintained garrisons, almost every county, town, and hamlet from Massachusetts to Georgia had come under the control of local associations and militia units opposed to any projection of British authority. In effect, what Gage had witnessed occurring throughout New England in the summer of 1774 spread like a political wildfire throughout all the American colonies. When the delegates in Philadelphia enacted the Continental Association, their goal was to establish the framework for an economic boycott designed to pressure British merchants, who would then generate political pressure on Parliament to repeal the Coercive Acts. As it turned out, they had also created a political machine operating at the neighborhood level that forced the vast majority of Americans to join the resistance or suffer the consequences. And once in place during the winter of 1774–75, the machine ran itself.

WHILE THE ASSOCIATION PROCEEDED to grind away at the ground level among ordinary colonists, the designated elite in Philadelphia were grinding away behind closed doors to craft the updated constitutional argument. As noted earlier, several pamphlets had appeared by the time the First Continental Congress convened, all arguing that there was no longer any middle position on the question of Parliament's sovereignty, because the distinction between Parliament's right to tax and right to legislate had been obliterated by the Coercive Acts.

The logic of the new American position, then, was to claim that the only remaining link with the British Empire was the king. And beyond that link lay American independence. It soon became clear that a significant number of delegates in the congress were finding it difficult to digest the implications of that logic. They were searching for language to frame the argument in a way that maximized the prospects for reconciliation, a way to extend a hand rather than toss down a gauntlet.

The most venerable but controversial of the forms to which the colonists were accustomed were the Navigation Acts. The logic of the American constitutional argument by 1774 was to repudiate Parliament's authority altogether, but half the delegations in the congress wished to make the Navigation Acts an exception to that principle, thereby making a clear statement of their desire to remain within the British Empire. By accepting Parliament's authority to regulate all trade, the Americans would also undermine the accusation of the British ministry that their ultimate goal was independence.[54]

The same moderate mentality shaped the decision to supplement the official report of the congress to the American people with additional statements to the British people and the king. This was a tactical decision to make their case against Parliament's authority to a larger British audience, in effect going over the head of the North ministry with appeals targeted at popular constituencies in England capable of forcing changes in the current course of the British government.

This tactical maneuver followed naturally from another all-important decision the delegates made about the message they intended to send. After wandering for several weeks through the complicated constitutional history of Great Britain and its American colonies, the delegates came to the realization that they had entered a legal maze with multiple twists and turns that varied from colony to colony. Every colony had its own story to tell. What they all shared in common, and what had brought them all together in Philadelphia, was opposition to the doctrine of parliamentary sovereignty that had launched the imperial crisis of the past decade. And once they confined their focus chronologically to the decade following the Treaty of Paris, they all shared a common experience, and could therefore tell together a single story that pivoted on 1763. Moreover, it was a story that invited Britons and Americans alike to realize that they were living through an unprecedented aberration in Anglo-American history.[55]

The most dramatic version of this narrative appeared in *An Address to the People of Great Britain*. The opening paragraph defined the theme and set the tone:

> Friend and Fellow Subjects: When a Nation, led to greatness by the hand of Liberty, and blessed by all the Glory that heroism, munificence, and humanity can bestow, descends to the ungrateful task of forging chains for her friends and children, and instead of giving support to Freedom, turns advocate for slavery and oppression, there is reason to suspect that she has either ceased to be virtuous, or been extremely negligent in the appointment of her Rulers.[56]

The *Address* then proceeded to describe the long-standing support throughout the American colonies for British values and institutions, culminating in complete commitment to the glorious victory over France in the Seven Years' War. The triumph achieved in the Treaty of Paris was a joyous occasion for all British-Americans: "We looked to you as our parent state, to which we were bound by the strongest ties and were happy in being instrumental to your prosperity and grandeur." But then, without warning, everything changed, for reasons that continued to baffle all Americans: "To what causes, then, are we to attribute the sudden change in treatment," the *Address* asked, "and the system of slavery which was prepared for us at the restoration of the peace?"[57]

The answer to that question, according to the anonymous author of the *Address*, was that a small cabal of British ministers, led initially by George Grenville and more recently by Lord North, had chosen to transform the colonial relationship from a connection based on mutual affection and consensus to one based on mistrust and coercion. There was no obvious explanation for this abrupt shift, except perhaps the misguided fear that the colonists were contemplating independence and therefore needed to be deprived of the freedom to consider such a course. If so, the groundless fear of that outcome had ironically produced the possibility it was designed to avoid.

The *Address* did not attempt to chronicle the offensive acts of Parliament that caused the current crisis. Instead, it focused on the underlying principles that the new imperial policy had violated, all of which came back to the core principle of consent: the right to be taxed; the right to trial by a jury of one's peers; the right to protest occupation by a standing army. The *Address* described all these rights as the inviolable rights of Englishmen that no British subject, whether resident in Great Britain or America, could possibly do without, warning their British brethren that the unwarranted restrictions imposed on Americans might soon be imposed on them.

The solution to the current impasse was obvious: "Place us in the same situation that we were at the close of the last war, and our former harmony will be restored." It was that simple. Elaborate arguments were unnecessary. The answer lay back there for all to see and remember before the hostile takeover of the British Empire in 1763. The *Address* concluded with regrets for the recent boycotts "so detrimental to our fellow Subjects in Great Britain and Ireland," vowing to end them as soon as the British electorate did its duty by removing "those wicked Ministers and evil Counsellors that enslave us all."[58]

Upon reading the *Address*, William Pitt apprised an American visitor that "such wisdom, moderation, and manliness of character would have done honor to Greece and Rome in their best days," going so far as to describe its author as "an American Thucydides."[59]

The author of the *Address* was John Jay, a previously obscure twenty-nine-year-old lawyer from New York. Jay became a stellar example of the way in which the American Revolution brought latent talent to the surface, talent that would have otherwise remained dormant and invisible. Born into a prominent family with roots in the earliest Dutch founders of New York, Jay was educated at King's College (later Columbia) and then, like John Dickinson, at the Middle Temple in London, where he also acquired an admiration for the trappings of British culture and a personal style of quiet confidence. What happened to Jay during the First Continental Congress proved a preview of what would happen over the course of his distinguished career as a diplomat, statesman, and jurist: his peers recognized him as a conspicuously competent colleague, articulate on his feet and on paper, sufficiently confident to lead by listening, therefore the obvious choice whenever an important task needed doing. Jay was among the most reluctant revolutionaries in the congress, but proved the most eloquent spokesman for the story the congress wanted to tell.[60]

THE OTHER TWO official statements of the congress, *A Memorial to the Inhabitants of the British Colonies* and *The Petition to the King*, were written by John Dickinson. Unlike Jay, Dickinson was already famous as "the Pennsylvania Farmer," indeed the most prominent critic of British policy in America. For that reason, he was given the assignment, even though Dickinson was a latecomer to the deliberations in Philadelphia.[61]

Like Jay in the *Address,* Dickinson in *A Memorial* imposed a tight focus on the preceding decade as the critical period when British policy toward the colonies took a decisive and disastrous turn. But whereas Jay opted to tell a story, Dickinson chose to make a legal case that quickly became a detailed chronicle of Parliament's offensive legislation from the Sugar Act to the Coercive Acts. This was familiar territory for many American readers, but Dickinson saw his task as providing a concise summary of the evolving American argument against Parliament's purported sovereignty, much like a prosecutor summing up his case to the jury at the end of a trial. As a result, *A Memorial* lacked the compelling voice that Jay projected in the *Address,* and the verbal flair that Dickinson himself had brought to his *Farmer* essays.

And because he was addressing an American audience, Dickinson felt obliged to rally the undecided around the banner of the boycott as a patriotic cheerleader—not a rhetorical pose that came naturally to Dickinson's Quaker temperament, whose style was not to have one. In the end, he urged his fellow Americans to suffer through the sacrifices that would be necessary to bring Great Britain to its senses and that, so he hoped, would eventually produce "a hearty reconciliation with our fellow-citizens on the other side of the Atlantic." All in all, it was a highly competent but uninspired performance that preferred to smooth down the sharp edges of American defiance in favor of a more subdued voice of almost studied moderation. No member of Parliament or the North ministry could read Dickinson's words and plausibly claim that the American colonists were being led by a band of radical zealots bent on independence.[62]

Dickinson's voice in *The Petition to the King* was moderation carried to self-conscious deference. His goal was to distinguish between America's firm but reasoned repudiation of Parliament's claim of sovereignty and its abiding loyalty to the Crown. That loyalty, in Dickinson's telling, defied merely legal or constitutional rationales; it was rooted in the emotional bond between loving children and an equally loving parent that could never be erased. Given the sheer potency of that mutual affection, any claim that the colonies aimed at independence was a preposterous libel manufactured by the king's devious and disloyal ministers.

This emotionally defined framework then became the foundation for a preposterous conceit, Dickinson's claim that George III was wholly unaware of the offensive legislation passed by Parliament over the last decade. Dickinson presented the recent history of British policy toward the colonies as the work of ministers acting without the king's knowledge, since he never could have endorsed such misguided attacks on his own loving children. The British occupation force in Boston should therefore not be described as royal troops, but as "ministerial troops," acting in George III's name but without his approval.[63]

This piece of fiction, which Dickinson surely recognized as such, became the central pretense of *The Petition*: the presumption that George III was poised to become the American savior once apprised, as Dickinson was now doing, of the ill-fated course that Parliament had taken his beloved empire. As a political tactic in the current context, it made sense, first by painting a plaintive face on the American position that British pundits had described as grimly defiant; second by maximizing whatever prospects that existed for a change in heart within the upper reaches of the British government, most especially the king himself. On the other hand, by making George III the designated solution to the imperial crisis, Dickinson was investing American hopes in the most hopeless imperialist of all, a risky act of appeasement that came back to haunt Dickinson's reputation as a staunch leader of the American resistance over the ensuing months. As it turned out, George III never read *The Petition*. Lord North chose not to bother the sovereign with any missive from an illegitimate body. Not that it mattered.[64]

WHICH WAY WAS history headed, toward reconciliation or war? Dickinson brooded on that question after attending the last session of the Continental Congress in late October. If his fellow Englishmen were well advised—and Dickinson believed they had been advised well by the congress—the way forward was backward, to the arrangement that had existed before a few misguided souls in Westminster had driven the empire onto the shoals of its own ruin. "I grieve for the Fate of a brave and generous Nation plung'd by a few profligate Men into such scenes of unmerited and inglorious Distress," he wrote to Arthur Lee. "Let her rouse her natural Noble Spirit—be true to herself, and of course be true to Us."

Otherwise, Dickinson was convinced that the British Empire was on a collision course with catastrophe. "Any effort to reinforce General Gage this Winter or next Year," he predicted to Lee, "will put the whole Continent in Arms from Nova Scotia to Georgia." And all those retired British officers sipping gin in their London clubs while holding forth on Britain's military invincibility were only indulging in senile delusions. "What can she effect at 3000 Miles Distance," Dickinson asked rhetorically, "against at least four hundred thousand Freemen?"[65]

In fact, much as he dreaded the thought of a civil war within the imperial family, Dickinson believed that the operative question was not whether the Americans could win, but rather how they could possibly lose. His mind was already racing ahead to the next chapter, after America had won its independence, and the horrific problems accompanying America's existence outside the protective canopy of the British Empire began to fester: "A multitude of Commonwealths, Wars and Calamaties, Centuries of mutual jealousies, Hatreds, Crimes, and Calamities—centuries of mutual Jealousies, Hatreds, Wars, and Devastations, until at last the exhausted Provinces shall sink into Slavery under the yoke of some fortunate conqueror."

The problem, then, was not to win the war, but to survive its aftermath. The vastly more sensible course was to allow American independence to occur gradually, over the course of the next century, in the way that Franklin had always envisioned. Dickinson clung to the conviction that only a deranged king and a willfully suicidal British ministry could remain blind to the brilliant prospects of an Anglo-American empire.[66]

Of course, they could, and did. Some observers might have described Lord North as a floating cloud of comfortable banalities, but no one accused him of suicidal tendencies. At least in retrospect, the blindness within Britain's governing class was not a function of idiocy but certainty. It knew it was right to insist upon Parliament's sovereignty as a nonnegotiable principle. It knew that the North ministry commanded comfortable majorities in both branches of Parliament that rendered all debate perfunctory. It knew that the British army and navy, taken together, was the most potent military power on the planet. And it therefore knew that any compromise with its upstart cousins across the Atlantic was unnecessary.

In order to convey these certainties with the proper tone of condescension, North commissioned a response to the resolutions of the Continental Congress from England's most acerbic wit and literary lion. Samuel Johnson took up the task with his customary gusto in a pamphlet entitled *Taxation No Tyranny: An Answer to the Resolutions and Address of the American Congress,* which appeared in March 1775. There is one justifiably famous line in Johnson's essay, coming near the end: "Why is it that we hear the loudest yelps for liberty among the drivers of negroes?" The fact that the American argument against British policy was littered with analogies to enslavement strikes most modern observers as a massive piece of hypocrisy, and of course it was. Johnson was the first writer to cite it as one more charge in his case against the colonists as duplicitous traitors.[67]

Otherwise, *Taxation No Tyranny* is a relentlessly sarcastic polemic designed to demonize the American cause to a British audience presumably prepared to smile at references to Americans as "a race of rattlesnakes" and "ungrateful wretches." Apparently even the North ministry found several passages excessive, deleting before publication Johnson's claim that he would burn down the houses of all colonists who refused to quarter British troops.

For literary scholars of the Johnson corpus, *Taxation No Tyranny* is an excellent sample of the great man's verbal dexterity and impassioned defiance of traditional codes of etiquette. For historians of the American Revolution, it is a document that displays the presumptive sense of superiority, indeed arrogance, that informed British policy on the eve of the American rebellion, verbal wit weaponized on behalf of stupefying hubris. In that sense, Johnson's pamphlet exposed the reason Dickinson's fond hope that the British government would surely come to its senses was doomed, and why John Adams was proven right a few months later, when he apprised Abigail that hopeful souls like John Dickinson were "waiting for a Messiah who will never come."[68]

IF THERE WAS A Messiah anywhere in England, it was William Pitt, by all accounts the most distinguished, if ailing, statesman in Great Britain, indeed, the conspicuous creator of the expanding British Empire in America. On January 15, 1775, Pitt rose to speak in the House of Lords. He asked his colleagues to excuse his somewhat disheveled appearance, which was somewhat concealed by the overlapping red robe he wore as a peer and the wig that covered his balding head. He had crawled out of his sickbed to address them, Pitt explained, because he had come to believe that the current ministry under Lord North's leadership was carrying the empire he so loved into an unnecessary war. Pitt spoke for over an hour, his dramatic pauses somewhat extended by his eroding memory, and a few years later, when every dire consequence he warned against came true, no penitent figure in the British government could plead ignorance as a defense.

Pitt claimed that he had listened with a growing sense of horror at what he called "your vain declarations of the omnipotence of Parliament, and your imperious doctrines of the necessity of submission." Was it possible, he asked rhetorically, that his erstwhile colleagues had fallen victim to some sudden lapse of memory? Had they somehow forgotten "that there is no such thing, no such idea in this Constitution, as a supreme power operating upon property?" Where was it written—he could not find it—that "an Englishman can be deprived of the bread he eats without his consent?" How had it happened that a small group of colonists, gathered in Philadelphia, "seemed more alive to the true spirit of English liberty than the Lords of the realm gathered in these hallowed halls?"

Indeed, Philadelphia now seemed to be auditioning for the role of the new Athens. All could see that the recently arrived resolutions from the Continental Congress were quite sensible. The Americans recognized both their rights and their obligations. They thereby offered a clear path forward and out of the present morass: "Taxation is theirs; commercial regulation is ours." And by reiterating their abiding loyalty to the king, they effectively exposed the ludicrous claim that Americans aimed at independence.

These were important concessions, so it was now Parliament's turn to follow suit by offering to withdraw all British troops from Boston. Repudiating the Coercive Acts would then come next. Pitt was sure that his fellow Lords need not be reminded of the gentlemen's code: "Concessions come with better grace, and more salutary effect, from the superior power." Indeed, such grace was the ultimate measure of superiority.

Pitt then criticized the shabby treatment recently accorded General Gage, a wholly accomplished and loyal British officer who was being recalled for speaking the truth about the intractable military challenges that any war with the Americans posed. As commander of His Majesty's forces in the last great war, Pitt's military credentials were impeccable, and he felt no compunction at trading on the credibility they carried to contradict the conventional wisdom currently circulating within both branches of Parliament. In effect, Pitt insisted that Gage's realistic assessment of the American resistance movement in New England would prove equally accurate for the entire American theater.

The belief that two or three British regiments could control the New England countryside beyond Boston was always a pipe dream. Ten, twenty, or thirty regiments would also find themselves drowning in what Pitt described as "a dominion of eighteen hundred miles of Continent, potent in valor, liberty, and resistance." This was not to

mention that these "true sons of the soil all believed with complete conviction, that their cause was just." And so did Pitt: "I tell you plainly,
my Lords, no son of mine, nor anyone over whom I have influence,
shall ever draw his sword upon these fellow Englishmen."[69]

After Pitt sat down to only scattered applause, the House of Lords
proceeded to vote on his motion to remove British troops from Boston,
which Pitt had described as the first step back from the precipice. The
vote was 18 aye, 68 nay. The next day Lord North reported to George
III that the ministry's majority in Parliament was holding firm. The
king was relieved to hear North's splendid news, for it confirmed his
unwavering conviction that "America must be a colony of Great Britain or treated as an enemy." He then offered a succinct summary of
his imperialistic agenda: "Distant possessions standing upon equality
with the superior state is more ruinous than being deprived of such
connections." Rather than consent to Pitt's policy of appeasement,
George III preferred to teach the Americans a lesson they would never
forget. This was the reason that, many years later, when asked who
deserved the greatest credit for making American independence happen, John Adams loved to confound his questioners by giving the award
to George III.[70]

More immediately, by early 1775, whatever prospects that had once
existed for a political solution to the imperial crisis were fading even
further into the mists of the middle distance. To be sure, the outbreak
of hostilities at Lexington and Concord was four months down the
road, but that was now the only remaining road on the political map.
All alternative routes were now blocked. The delegates at the Continental Congress had done their best, Pitt had done his best, but in the wake
of their failure, both sides were now operating on the assumption that
war was looming.

In London, Lord North grudgingly embraced the earlier recommendation of Gage to bolster the overall size of the British army by
recruiting twenty thousand European mercenaries. The House of Com-

mons, by a 296–106 vote, declared New England to be in a state of rebellion that required prompt military subjugation. In order to oversee the new military initiative, North appointed the controversial George Germain, a notorious hard-liner, to replace Dartmouth as American Secretary.*

In Massachusetts, the first order of business for the Provincial Congress, meeting in closed session at Salem, was the procurement of essential weaponry: 16 cannons; 20 tons of grapeshot and round shot; 1000 barrels of powder; 500 muskets and bayonets; and 75,000 flints. The congress also ordered an upgrading of all militia units to assure that they would be "completely armed and otherwise prepared to march to such place or places as events shall deem necessary."[71]

Coincidentally, the first such place turned out to be the place where the provisional government was meeting at Salem. In February 1775 an undersized British regiment under the command of Colonel Alexander Leslie was ordered to seize the arsenal there. Living up to their subsequent reputation as Minutemen, four thousand militia from surrounding towns converged on a bridge leading to the Salem arsenal. Leslie halted his troops upon encountering this vastly superior force, saluted the militia commander, and explained that he had orders to cross the bridge. The militia commander granted Leslie permission to do so, but only if he then marched his troops back again without entering the arsenal. Otherwise, he nonchalantly observed, "Everyone of you will be a dead man." With corresponding nonchalance, Leslie led his men across the bridge, back again, then filed through the rows of smiling militia on his return to Marblehead. A young nurse, Sarah Tarrent, leaned out her window as the British troops marched past. "Go home," she shouted, "and tell your master he has sent you on a fool's errand."[72]

It was a minor episode that fully exposed the military dilemma the

---

* Germain's appointment provoked behind-the-scenes opposition from the army. He had been tried for treason and narrowly avoided execution for alleged cowardice at the Battle of Minden, in Prussia, during the Seven Years' War.

British army faced in New England whenever venturing beyond Boston. Despite the peaceful ending, the incident also provided a preview of the decidedly less peaceful fate awaiting British troops less than two months later, after the engagement at Lexington and Concord. Looking even further ahead, what we might call the Encounter at Salem Bridge offered a glimpse at the strategic problem, which was inherently insoluble, that confounded the British army throughout the war whenever the military campaign moved inland, beyond the protection provided by the British fleet. With a few important exceptions, the entire American interior was hostile territory under the political and military control of residents loyal to the goals of the American Revolution.

How did that happen? The answer is gradually but relentlessly, starting in May 1774, when committees of correspondence created an intercolonial communications network in order to share information about the Common Cause in response to the Coercive Acts. By the fall and winter, albeit at different speeds, most colonies had adopted the model of the Provincial Congress—Virginia called it a Convention—which became the extralegal legislative bodies that replaced the sanctioned British government. Royal governors were isolated, then ostracized, with many fleeing to British ships off the coast—a flight pattern that began in the winter of 1774–75 and continued apace through the spring. By then the majority of colonial governments were under the control of the resistance.[73]

Even more consequential than the capture of all basic institutions of government, the local enforcement mechanisms of the Continental Association kept grinding away. Every hour of every day in multiple towns, hamlets, and farming communities, all doubters, temporizers, and recalcitrant patriots were forced to face the same kind of intimidating choice that Colonel Leslie faced at that Salem bridge.

A few patches of loyalist sentiment remained alive in New York, New Jersey, and western regions of the Carolinas, but the battle for hearts and minds throughout most of the American countryside was effectively won before independence was declared. From the British perspective, all the ground on the far side of the Rubicon within the American interior was hostile territory, and would remain so for the next seven years of war. Even before the American Revolution officially began, or even had that name, The Cause had become more fully American and implacably revolutionary, making the British prospects for success, as Pitt had predicted, remote in the extreme.[74]

PROFILE

JOSHUA LORING

The mobs that gathered around his handsome home in Jamaica Plains left Joshua Loring with little choice. In August 1774 he moved his entire family—father, mother, wife, and child—to the safety of the British garrison in Boston. As his father explained the decision, "the Loring family has always eaten the King's bread, and always intended to."

All members of the Loring family survived the smallpox epidemic raging in Boston, then joined the loyalists who evacuated the city with the British army in March 1776. By then Elizabeth (Betsy) Loring had become the constant companion of General William Howe. It was a blatantly open affair, duly reported in both the British and American press as an updated version of Marc Antony and Cleopatra.

It was also a political arrangement. In return for lending his attractive young wife to Howe, Joshua was made Commissary General of Prisoners, a lucrative post that he retained until the end of the war. From the perspective of the Loring family, the arrangement made eminent sense as a bargain that ensured its status as a beneficiary of British patronage. From Howe's perspective, such affairs were commonplace among senior officers stationed abroad during wartime. Most wives realized that fidelity was a frequent casualty of war, not to be mentioned when their husbands returned.

Joshua's job as superintendent of prisoners of war in New York also afforded him the opportunity to avenge the abuse he and his family had suffered at the hands of those Boston mobs. As the officer in charge of the notorious "ghost ships" in the East River, he was responsible for overseeing eighteen thousand American prisoners, who suffered conditions comparable to Japanese prison camps in World War II. Approximately eleven thousand prisoners died of disease or malnutrition. No loyalist inflicted as much damage to The Cause as Joshua Loring.

He joined his family in England after the war and resumed his marriage with Betsy, who promptly produced three more children before Joshua died, quite suddenly, in 1789. Mrs. Loring was granted a lifetime pension from the British government and was able to witness three of her sons enjoy successful careers in the British army and navy, one rising to the rank of admiral. Her highly personal investment in the British cause had paid dividends. She died at eighty-three in 1835.

Joshua Loring, Jr., by John Singleton Copley, date unknown. There is some dispute about the accuracy and the artist of this likeness.

CHAPTER TWO

Prudence Dictates

Whot has the negros the afracons don to us that we shuld takt ham from thar own land and mak tham sarve us to the da of thar deth. . . . God forbid that it shuld be so anay longer.

—"Humanity" to John Adams, January 23, 1776

It is not the kind of statement customarily found in a revolutionary manifesto. And yet, there it is, in what is arguably the most famous revolutionary manifesto in modern history. Here are Thomas Jefferson's most forgotten words:

Prudence, indeed, will dictate that Governments long established should not be changed for light and transient causes; and accordingly all experiences hath shewn, that mankind are more disposed to suffer, while evils are sufferable, than to right themselves by abolishing the forms to which they are accustomed.[1]

In drafting these words, Jefferson was not indulging in a philosophical meditation on the virtue of prudence. He was describing the cautious diplomatic posture of the Continental Congress and the provisional governments of all thirteen colonies for the preceding fifteen months.

His words serve to remind us of a chronological anomaly: the war for American independence began in April 1775 with the outbreak of violence at Lexington and Concord, but the American colonies did not declare their independence until July 1776.

For over a year an undeclared war was going on. In fact, the bloodiest battle of what proved to be an eight-year war, Bunker Hill, occurred in June 1775; and the British were already calling the ongoing conflict the American rebellion. But throughout this extended year, the colonists refused to acknowledge that they were rebels, or that they were leaving the British Empire. And no one on either side used the term "American Revolution."[2]

The operative term from the summer of 1775 to the summer of '76 was The Cause, an abbreviated version of Common Cause, which had come into existence to describe the united response to the Coercive Acts. It combined a clear sense of commitment with a conveniently obscure reference to the goal of that commitment. Before April 1775 it had a mostly political meaning—that is, collective opposition to British oppression in Massachusetts.

After that date a military dimension was added to the meaning, most conspicuously in the appointment of George Washington to command the New England militia units gathered around Boston, soon to be called the Continental Army. Less conspicuously, it referred to the mobilization of militia throughout the colonies as a police force that implemented the political agenda of several hundred Committees of Safety. Throughout what we might call the Strange Year, loyalists were being purged and reluctant patriots were being required to pledge themselves to The Cause.[3]

While The Cause provided at least a measure of verbal focus before "War for American Independence" or "American Revolution" became viable labels, the fundamental ambiguity of The Cause is symptomatic of the inherently elusive character of American resistance to British rule in 1775–76, which simultaneously embraced the sword and the olive branch. The Cause had, in effect, stalled on the far side of the Rubicon to catch its breath and assess the paths forward into unmarked territory.

To further complicate the nomenclature problem, the Continental Congress was attempting to function as a provisional national government, despite the fact that no such thing as an American nation existed. Ironically, the political temperature of American patriotism, called *rage militaire*, reached the highest (or hottest) level of the entire eight-year war before there was any agreement on how and where to direct it.[4]

Three prominent American leaders—John Dickinson, John Adams, and Thomas Paine—provide the clearest windows into the full spectrum of alternative visions. On the British side, the two equivalent figures were George III and George Germain, who afford access to a much more controlled, decisive, but tragically myopic machine for making war and, ultimately, losing an empire. Finally, there are several thousand less prominent and less visible Americans going house to house, enforcing allegiance to The Cause and its various manifestations. They need to be noticed, in part because they are the power source for the entire resistance movement, in part because they became the ultimate arbiters of what The Cause had come to mean by the summer of 1776.[5]

IF THESE WERE the major players, the script they had all been handed in the late spring of 1775 after what Longfellow called "the shot heard 'round the world" initiated a new chapter in an ongoing story. Edmund Burke had glimpsed the plot of the story seven years earlier, in 1768: "The Americans have made a discovery, or think they have made one, that we mean to oppress them. We have made a discovery, or think we have made one, that they intend to rise in rebellion. We know not how to advance; they know not how to retreat. Some party must give way." The clash at Lexington and Concord confirmed the conspiratorial mentality on both sides: for the British, that the Americans were in open rebellion; for the Americans, that the British were fully pre-pared to impose their imperial agenda with military force. The interac-tive dialogue between the two conspiratorial mentalities had become a death spiral.[6]

When the Continental Congress reconvened in early May, no one was prepared to advocate American independence, and no one dared even suggest conceding Parliament's authority over the colonies. The dominant posture was best articulated by the newest delegate from Virginia, the tall, angular, freckle-faced young man from Monticello, Thomas Jefferson: "We have not raised armies with ambitious designs of separating from Great Britain. We still wish for reunion with the parent country and would rather be dependent on Great Britain, prop-erly limited, than any other nation on earth. But rather than submit to British demands, I would rather sink the whole island in the ocean."[7]

Jefferson's opposing impulses matched up nicely with the two-track policy the congress officially adopted on May 26: on the diplomatic side, send another petition to the king requesting his intervention on their behalf; on the military side, prepare for war by raising a Continental Army of twenty thousand troops and appointing George Washington as commander in chief. This double-track strategy accurately reflected the competing priorities within the congress as a whole, even within the minds of most delegates. In early July, the congress issued two official resolutions, *The Olive Branch Petition*, requesting George III to end the ongoing war and initiate negotiations for a peaceful settlement; and *A Declaration of the Causes and Necessity of Taking Up Arms*, describing the American military initiatives as justifiable responses to the British buildup in and around Boston. Both the *Petition* and *Declaration* were written by John Dickinson.[8]

If there were a singular embodiment of The Cause, Dickinson was it. He was the rock-ribbed patriot who could be trusted to "do the right thing, rightly." And the right thing was to sustain an unequivocal commitment to American sovereignty while simultaneously urging the

British government to come to its senses. Much like Benjamin Franklin, Dickinson believed that the Anglo-American empire was destined to dominate the world, if only a few misguided ministers in London did not kill it in the cradle.[9]

Based on notes that Dickinson recorded in late May, we know that he saw himself as the major advocate for the diplomatic side of the two-track strategy. There was unanimous consent for a vigorous military response, less support for another appeal to the king. Dickinson rallied the more hesitant delegates behind the diplomatic option. His major argument was that nothing would be lost by making the effort, and even if it failed, "it may convince the World that we have done everything possible to avoid the War." Moreover, such an appeal would defer any decision on independence until support for that ultimate commitment congealed in more reluctant colonies, chiefly Pennsylvania and New York. It was the course that prudence dictated.

Dickinson harbored deeper doubts that he kept to himself. He did not really believe that the king was oblivious to the aggressive course his ministers were pursuing. But he was unsure how enthusiastic George III was about the direction of British policy. Dickinson did know beyond any doubt that Parliament's posture was overwhelmingly hostile. (Records of the debates in Parliament lay on his desk.) There was no way to change so many minds, but perhaps the mind of George III could be persuaded to see the light. There was, in fact, no other diplomatic option. Dickinson privately referred to *The Olive Branch Petition* as "a prayer."[10]

He also had begun to harbor serious reservations about whether the current level of American patriotism was sustainable in a protracted war: "We have not yet tasted deeply from the bitter cup called Fortune of War. . . . A bloody battle lost. . . . Disease breaking out among our troops unaccustomed to the Confinement of Encampment. . . . The Danger of Insurection by Negroes in the Southern Colonies. . . . False hopes and selfish Designs may all operate hereafter to our Disadvantage."[11] Dickinson was concerned that, even if The Cause triumphed, postwar America was likely to dissolve into a collection of regional confederations. Once a common enemy was removed from the American political equation, Dickinson worried, there was nothing to hold the former colonies together, prompting him to imagine "an Ocean perpetually tempestuous without Bottom and without Shore." If forced to choose between such an uncertain future and remaining in the British Empire, Dickinson preferred the latter, even if it meant living "in a State of Dependence upon and subordination to our Parent State." The same farmer who had carried The Cause all the way to the edge of the abyss, for realistic reasons that all proved prophetic, found himself unable to jump.[12]

Dickinson was the epitome of the moderate mentality that flourished in the middle colonies, where the population was more diverse ethnically, religiously, and demographically than New England, more a political stew in which Germans, Scotch-Irish, and French Huguenots coexisted alongside a Quaker elite to create a social chemistry that put a premium on live-and-let-live tolerance. As a result, the political as well as the seasonal climate was milder southwest of the Hudson, where moderation was the presumed posture and prominent leaders like Dickinson tended to resemble smooth stones that skipped across the surface of troubled waters. More basically, thus far the war had not touched their daily lives; the full wrath of British policy had been directed at Massachusetts. Dickinson spoke for that segment of the American population that regarded war as an unconscionable and unnatural act, and who were perfectly willing to wait and see.

JOHN ADAMS WAS the epitome of an edgier mentality that flourished in New England, with roots in the Puritan tradition. His Puritan ancestors had not bowed to British monarchs; they made Charles I kneel at the block before chopping off his head. Dickinson's Quaker ancestors, on the other hand, had done their best to sit out the English

Civil War. Dickinson was tall, gaunt, and cultivated polite conversation at his dinner table. Adams was short, stout, and regarded argument as the highest form of discourse. Both men were conservatives in the Burkean tradition, meaning they preferred evolutions to revolutions.

Dickinson believed that the diplomatic track offered the best opportunity to end the impasse. Adams believed that pleading with George III was both hopeless and unbecoming a proud people who were, after all, the aggrieved party. But he supported the diplomatic initiative because it bought time for independence to ripen out there in the countryside. "We cannot force events," he explained to a friend, "so must suffer People to take their own Way and at their own speed." In the end, however, Adams believed that Dickinson and his fellow moderates in the congress were destined to discover that "the cancer is too deeply rooted, and too far spread, to be cured by anything short of cutting it out entirely." For Adams, The Cause had become synonymous with American independence.[13]

Adams himself had become the chief voice for New England in the congress. Previously he had served as the junior partner to his cousin Samuel Adams, whose specialty was covert maneuvering behind the scenes. After Lexington and Concord, New England needed a greater public presence. The clear signal that the torch had been passed occurred on June 15, when John Adams nominated a Virginian, George Washington, to head the army encamped in Boston.

Given Adams's more prominent role, the rupture in his relationship with Dickinson had troubling implications for the political posture of unity within the congress. The occasion was a speech Dickinson delivered in early July, shortly after Adams had read the after-action reports on Bunker Hill, where British regulars, distraught at watching so many of their fellow soldiers go down, proceeded to bayonet many of the wounded Americans and desecrate their bodies. Adams stood up and walked out as Dickinson was speaking. In his diary that night, he recorded his version of what happened next: "Mr. Dickinson observed

me, and darted out after me in a most abrupt and extraordinary manner, in as violent a passion as he was capable of feeling, and with an
air, countenance, and gestures, as rough and haughty as if I had been a
school-boy and he the master. He vociferated, 'What is the reason you
New Englanders oppose our measure of reconciliation?' "[14]

Matters between the two men went downhill from there. In a letter to his friend James Warren three weeks later, Adams spat out his
invective against "a certain great Fortune and piddling Genius whose
fame has been trumpeted so loudly, and who has given a silly cast to
our whole doings." British officials in Boston intercepted the letter, then
released it to the press as evidence of a split in the Continental Congress
symptomatic of a larger division within American ranks. Who spoke
for The Cause, Adams or Dickinson? Was the proper symbol an olive
branch or a sword? Throughout the remainder of the summer, those
questions hung in the air as British and American troops in and around
Boston began a long staring match called the Boston Siege.[15]

THE ANSWER TO that question, oddly enough, resided across the
Atlantic in London in the person of George III. A merely symbolic
embrace of *The Olive Branch Petition* by the king at this early stage of
the war possessed the potential to change the political chemistry everywhere outside New England. Dickinson was presenting George III with
a splendid opportunity to exploit the split between avid and reluctant
believers in The Cause. Indeed, anyone familiar with the history of
George III's reign might very well describe him as the ideal American Messiah.

From the time he ascended to the throne in 1760 at the tender age
of twenty-two, George III cultivated the image of a vigorous, well-read,
conspicuously sociable monarch who took his duties seriously, all qual-
ities that contrasted sharply with his Hanoverian predecessors. Tall,
with auburn hair and blue eyes, he was physically impressive if not

quite handsome, graceful in his gait and on a horse, a serious dabbler in music, astronomy, and mechanical gadgets of all kinds, a faithful patron of the theater and—a rarity within the upper reaches of the British aristocracy—a faithful husband to Queen Charlotte, who was perennially pregnant. Samuel Johnson described him as "the only British king in recorded memory to genuinely care about his subjects." In short, before Thomas Jefferson demonized him as the quintessential tyrant, George III was generally regarded as the epitome of the benevolent monarch.[16]

Something snapped in George III in 1773, after he learned that a gang of Boston rabble disguised as Mohawk Indians had tossed a valuable cargo of British tea into Boston Harbor. He took the outrageous act personally, as if they had thrown him into the water to rot with the tea. He now realized that his previous efforts at generosity had been misguided. The children in his imperial family had shown themselves to be prodigal sons who must no longer be indulged. Moreover, as he now sniffed the air floating from across the Atlantic, he smelled an American conspiracy that was just as diabolical as the conspiracy the colonists had described in the alleged British plot to enslave them.

By the summer of 1775 George III had embraced the British side of the conspiratorial narrative with a vengeance. Probably influenced by interviews with loyalist refugees in London, chiefly Thomas Hutchinson, he began describing the American resistance movement as an ill-designed campaign for independence hatched by a small coterie of radical extremists. The chief villain was Samuel Adams, who had successfully duped the king's previously loyal subjects, the vast majority of whom would return to the fold once those diabolical demagogues were eliminated. Terms like "deluded multitude" became a repeated refrain in the monarch's conversations. It was his responsibility—indeed, it was his duty as their king—to rescue these misled subjects from their true oppressors and restore the natural order of peace and harmony to his American empire.[17]

If King George failed at that task, a whole new vista of apocalyptic scenarios began to crowd into his mind, all amplifying his sense of horror, since nothing less than the survival of the entire British Empire was at stake. For the loss of the American colonies was likely to set off a chain reaction. Canada was sure to go next, then Jamaica and other lucrative British possessions in the Caribbean. Who knew how far the virus would spread? Not even India would be safe. (It was an early version of the "domino theory.") There was also a sharp personal edge to George III's new understanding of the challenge he faced, for he had come to the throne at the same moment when the British Empire had stepped onto the world stage as the dominant European power. What would history say if the same monarch who brought the British Empire into existence, after a very short reign at the top, oversaw its premature demise?

In the late summer and fall of 1775, George III stepped out from behind the scenes to become the public face for a wholly punitive, nonnegotiable policy toward the colonies. In August he issued a proclamation declaring the American colonies to be in "a state of rebellion," urging Parliament "to prosecute with vigor every measure that may tend to force the deluded People to Submission." In a speech before Parliament in October, he announced his repudiation of *The Olive Branch Petition*. He had felt no need to read it, he explained, since he was certain it was just another American exercise in duplicity, "meant only to amuse, by vague expressions of attachment to the parent state, and the strongest protestations of loyalty to me, whilst they are preparing for a general revolt."[18]

Then, in November 1775, he opened Parliament with a speech identifying New England as the cradle of the rebellion and reporting that the British navy had already begun to bombard coastal towns. (Though he did not know it, the town of Falmouth—now Portland, Maine—with three hundred families and two hundred buildings, had already been burned to the ground by the British navy.) He also reported on recent discussions with Lord North about recruiting foreign mercenaries from Russia and Germany and opening negotiations with tribes of the Iroquois Confederacy as prospective allies in the war. Shortly thereafter, he announced the appointment of Lord George Germain to the newly created post of Secretary for the American Colonies, making a long-standing advocate for more punitive measures the de facto secretary of war. Germain was on record as believing that the American colonies were "over-indulged children" who would only respond to "a more manly method than that in which we have hitherto trifled." He began his new job by declaring that "the whole power of the British state should be exerted to win the war with one decisive blow."[19]

Taken together, these public announcements, which often took two months to reach American shores, exposed the useful fiction that George III was oblivious to the ongoing war as a complete delusion. Moderates in the Dickinson camp could and did retain their reticence toward American independence, but banking on George III as a savior was no longer tenable. Not only was the British monarch unwilling to play that role, he was the most ardent enemy of reconciliation in the entire British government.

John Jay remembered that word of George's repudiation of *The Olive Branch Petition* had a discernible impact on the delegates in congress because of its dismissive tone, much like a slap in the face to a loving child. Others, including Adams, thought that the revelation that foreign mercenaries were being hired had greater influence on conversations in City Tavern, where delegates mixed with local residents and talk was freer. "By Intelligence hourly arriving from abroad," Adams noted at the time, "We are more and more confirmed, that a Kind of Confederation will be formed among the Crowned Skulls, and numbskulls of Europe, against Human Nature."[20]

Dickinson was understandably silent, since the diplomatic path forward he had hoped to blaze had become a dead end. And the person standing there to block the way was the very man he had hoped would open the gate. He had invested his enormous prestige as America's most eloquent farmer in a prayerful plea, and George III had not even shown the courtesy of a response. It was depressing to realize that The Cause had come to mean lingering in some political version of limbo. By the late fall of 1775, Dickinson had become the chief spokesman for those reluctant American patriots who did not know what to do.[21]

A DISTINCTLY DIFFERENT VOICE, supremely confident about the proper course forward, arrived on the scene in January 1776. His name was Thomas Paine. His vehicle was a pamphlet entitled *Common Sense,* which became the most influential journalistic performance of the revolutionary era as well as the quintessential example of an idea whose time had come.

Paine himself was a highly improbable candidate for political stardom. In America for less than two years, he arrived in 1774, carried off the ship on a litter with a serious case of typhus. He bore a letter of recommendation from Benjamin Franklin, describing him as "an ingenious young man." Just what kind of genius Franklin was referring to in the not so young man—Paine was thirty-seven—could not be discovered in his résumé, which revealed a knack for failure as a husband, shopkeeper, corset maker, and part-time privateer.[22]

Beneath that unimpressive veneer, however, Paine carried two talents that merited Franklin's description and soon bloomed luxuriously in American soil: first, a passionate sense of social justice based on his experience in the urban working class of Lewes and London; second, a gift for crafting prose that was simultaneously electric and seductively simple. True to its title, *Common Sense* used the idiom of ordinary conversation to convey an extraordinary message: that American independence was inevitable, for all the reasons an island could not rule a continent.

Common Sense began as a frontal attack, not just on George III, but on the very idea of monarchy itself, which Paine described as a "mere absurdity" akin to believing in childish fables. Did anyone seriously believe that kings spoke directly to God? A history of the British monarchy revealed its origins in a "French bastard," William the Conqueror, who invaded England with his "gang of armed banditti." Afterward the royal lineage became a rogues' gallery of crowned criminals, a legacy that George III had continued by recruiting Hessian mercenaries to kill and rape on his behalf. Trusting in King George was "like shaking hands with the murderer of men, women, and children."

After killing kingship, describing the last remaining link with the British Empire as a privileged barbarian, Paine proceeded to reframe the central American argument for armed resistance. Given his depiction of British history as an unending tale of corruption, it made no sense to connect The Cause with some purported era of peace and harmony before 1763. The colonists were not fighting for their rights as British subjects, but for their natural rights as Americans. They should not look backward to some mythical past, but forward to a glorious future as free and independent residents of an enormous continent with unlimited horizons. "The cause of America is in great measure the cause of all mankind," Paine rhetorically shouted at the end. "We have it in our power to begin the world over again. The birthday of a new world is at hand." A recently arrived English immigrant was telling his American readers that, whether they knew it or not, they were launching an American Revolution.[23]

Paine was sounding a new note—in fact, a new chord of several notes that redefined The Cause as the opening shot in a radical transformation of political institutions throughout the world. It represented a visionary way of thinking with mostly French origins, soon to be called the Enlightenment, and destined to find its fullest expression over a decade later in the French Revolution. According to this utopian school of thought, once the despotic institutions imposed on mankind during the Dark Ages were toppled, and the last king was strangled with the entrails of the last priest, then the latent potential for self-government inside all human beings would flow forward to create a wholly harmonious society requiring only a minimum supervision by government.

In the Americans' case, there was no need to strangle George III, only to repudiate him as a despot, unworthy of their attention or affection. Once his armies were defeated and dispatched with only their humiliation intact, the Atlantic Ocean would make the separation complete. As for the postwar American government, Paine envisioned a national assembly with elected representatives from all the newly created states, no fewer than 390 delegates, who would meet annually to pass all laws on the basis of a three-fifths majority. The beauty of Paine's revolutionary agenda was that it was self-enacting. No orchestration was required. Once America renounced its ties with British monarchy, the revolutionary energies would be released and flow freely into the new natural order, making America "the asylum for mankind."[24]

Common Sense was a sensation, selling 150,000 copies in three months, the modern equivalent of 50 million copies, placing it at or near the all-time best-seller list for nonfiction. Because the author remained anonymous for several months, and because Adams was regarded as the most prominent critic of reconciliation in the congress, he was initially named as the author in several newspapers. "I am as innocent of it as a Babe," Adams told friends, adding that "I could not reach the strength and Brevity of his style, Nor his elegant Simplicity, nor his piercing pathos." He was obviously pleased to learn that *Common Sense* was generating a dramatic shift in popular opinion toward independence and, not so incidentally, delivering a devastating blow to any belief in George III as a possible savior.[25]

But by shifting the emphasis from British rights to natural rights, Paine vastly expanded the meaning of The Cause and the prospective American agenda beyond independence. Because he was sitting in the middle of the wind tunnel in the congress, Adams found himself swamped with correspondence from previously silent constituencies

now speaking out for the first time about their proper place in an independent America. If Paine was the prophet of the American promise,
and the war for independence was also an American Revolution about
actualizing that promise, the expectations were almost endless.

THE LONG-STANDING American claim that Great Britain was plotting to enslave them prompted several protests about the obvious hypocrisy of it all. An anonymous writer from Virginia minced no words: "Is
it not incompatible with the glorious struggle America is making for
her own Liberty, to hold in absolute Slavery a Number of Wretches?"
Another correspondent, signing as "Unknown," suggested that it was
obvious that, once the war was won, emancipation should be the first
item on the political agenda. Once the slaves were freed, the owners
should be compensated by the profits acquired in selling land in Canada, which would presumably be acquired and annexed to the union.[26]

In the same vein, but with a more compelling voice, came the following questions from "Humanity": "Whot has the negros the afracons don to us that we shuld takt ham from thar own land and mak
tham sarve us to the da of thar deth. . . . God forbid that it shuld be so
anay longer. I hear the gentleman that heads the army [i.e., Washing-
ton] holds 700 of them in bondeg."* In a letter forwarded to Adams by
Samuel Hopkins, a Rhode Island minister, a rhetorical version of the
same question was raised. "But if the slave trade be altogether unjust,
as we all agree, is not slavery not equally unjust? What do we mean by
Liberty?"[27]

As it turned out, that question had all kinds of broader implications
beyond the obvious analogy of slavery. Elbridge Gerry, an old Massachusetts friend, forwarded to Adams a recent letter from another New
England stalwart for independence, James Sullivan, who appeared to be

---

* At the time Washington owned about two hundred slaves.

experiencing a political epiphany. "Laws, and Government are founded on the Consent of the People," wrote Sullivan, "and that consent should be held by each member of Society as a right. Why a man is supposed to consent to the acts of a Society in which he is an absolute excommunicate, none but a lawyer well versed in the feudal Sistem can tell."[28]

Sullivan was arguing for the abolition of the property requirement to vote in Massachusetts, but as Adams pointed out to him, his argument had the potential to destroy *all* distinctions for citizenship: "There will be no end to it," Adams warned. "New Claims will rise—Women will demand a Vote. Lads from 12 to 21 will think their rights not attended to, and every man who has not a Farthing, will demand an equal Voice with any other in all Acts of State." Taken literally, what Sullivan was proposing amounted to a recipe for anarchy: "I am grieved to hear of this Rage for Innovation," Adams reported to John Winthrop, a professor of astronomy and physics at Harvard. "These ridiculous Projects are not repairing, but pulling down the Building when it is on Fire, instead of laboring to extinguish the Flames. These radical Projects being bandied about in County Assemblies and town meetings tend directly to Barbarism."[29]

They were also being bandied about in his own family, initiated by his ever "saucy" Abigail, who was not someone Adams could dismiss as an anarchist or a barbarian. "And by the way," she began what has become the most famous letter in the *Adams Family Correspondence*:

In the new Code of Laws which I suppose it will be necessary for you to make I desire you would Remember the Ladies, and be more generous and favourable to them than your ancestors. Do not put such unlimited power into the hands of the Husbands. Remember all Men would be tyrants if they could. If perticuliar care and attention is not paid to the Laidies we are determined to foment a Rebelion, and will not hold ourselves bound by any Laws in which we have no voice, or Representation.[30]

In a subsequent letter she apprised her husband that she and Mercy Otis Warren, her best friend, were planning to write the Massachusetts legislature to protest the fact that they were being taxed without their consent.*[31]

John initially believed that Abigail was being playful, not really serious, and he responded with his own playful effort at mockery, claiming that everyone knew that women were the true tyrants within the household, and that he had no intention of exchanging "the tyranny of George III for the despotism of the petticoat." Bantering in this fashion was a fixed feature in their correspondence, but in this instance Abigail wanted him to know that she could banter and still be deadly serious. In order to make herself clear, there was nothing playful in the next back-of-my-hand letter:

> I can not say that I think you very generous to the Ladies, for whilst you are proclaiming Peace and good will to all Men, Emancipating all Nations, you insist upon retaining an absolute Power over Wives. But you must remember that Arbitrary power is like most things that are very hard, and not withstanding all your wise Laws and Maxims, we have it in our power not only to free ourselves, but to subdue our Masters, and without violence throw both their Natural and legal authority at your feet.[32]

Adams regarded these words as a warning shot across the bow of everything he was working to achieve in Philadelphia, delivered by no less than his ever loyal but equally liberated wife. Abigail's brief for women's rights was only one manifestation of the more expansive political agenda with truly revolutionary consequences most fully framed in *Common Sense.* The Cause, it turned out, became a prospective Ameri-

---

* For more on Mercy Otis Warren, see the profile at the end of this chapter.

can Revolution once you crossed the line from rights as Englishmen to natural rights. Or, in Abigail's version of the hidden American promise, the broader implications had always been lurking in the language her husband had hurled at British tyranny ever since the Stamp Act crisis. However one explained the sudden awakening, in the winter and spring of 1776, the entire reform agenda for the next century of American history bobbed to the surface.

BY THE SPRING OF 1776, the man who had earned a reputation among his colleagues in congress for his vesuvial outbursts had reached the surprising conclusion that his highest priority was to control the explosive energies bubbling up from below: "There is one Thing, my dear sir, that must be attempted and most Sacredly observed," Adams wrote James Warren. "There must be a Decency and Respect, and Veneration introduced for Persons in Authority of every Rank, or we are all undone." For Adams, the core meaning of The Cause must remain nothing less but also nothing more than independence. Whatever inspirational meanings the term had acquired must be deferred, for they would undermine the unity necessary to fight and win the war. And if that happened, all egalitarian dreams about a future American society became irrelevant.[33]

And so, if The Cause was evolving into the American Revolution, Adams assumed that his chief obligation was to make it happen in slow motion. "The Management of so complicated and mighty a Machine as the United Colonies requires the Meekness of Moses, the Patience of Jobe, and the Wisdom of Solomon," he observed. Any attempt to accelerate the pace of progress was likely to produce "Discontent and Convulsions that destroyed the entire enterprise." "I have ever thought it the most difficult and dangerous Part of the Business," he confessed to Mercy Otis Warren, "to contrive some method for the Colonies to glide insensibly from under the old Government, into a peaceable and contented submission to a new one." If Dickinson was an enlightened conservative, Adams was a conservative revolutionary.[34]

While Adams could not control events, he could control his way of thinking about how they should happen. By May 1776 he had developed a clear picture of how an orderly march toward independence ought to proceed: "The Colonies should all assume the Powers of Government in all its branches first," he explained. "Then they should confederate with each other, and define the Powers of Congress next. They should then endeavor to form an Alliance with some foreign State. When that is done a public Declaration [of Independence] might be made." He was describing a step-by-step process that established the political institutions for a postindependent America *before* taking the last step toward independence. American colonies should not leap until they knew where they were going to land. Over the next three months events would make a shambles of this neat scenario, but the scenario itself provides a revealing look at the conservative cast of Adams's mind.[35]

He assumed personal responsibility for implementation of the first step in his grand plan. Delegates from New York, North Carolina, and Pennsylvania had approached him in March, deferring to his acknowledged authority as a student of government, asking for advice about how to revise their respective colonial constitutions. After drafting several letters offering guidance, Adams decided to publish a single document that any or all colonies could consult. He gave it the modest title *Thoughts on Government,* and it appeared in the *Pennsylvania Packet* on April 22. Although he subsequently described *Thoughts* as "a mere scrap, done in haste," at the time he let Abigail know that he was deeply moved at the opportunity to influence history as it was happening: "When I consider the great events which are passed, and the greater which are rapidly advancing, and that I may have been instrumental in touching some springs and turning some small wheels, which have had and will have such effects, I feel an awe upon my mind which is not easily described."[36]

Thoughts provided Adams's blueprint for republican government at the state level. He wanted the new state constitutions to feel like familiar adaptations of the old colonial governments rather than jarringly novel innovations. He recommended three branches of government— executive, legislative, and judicial—in which the principles of separation of powers, a bicameral legislature, and an independent judiciary were the salient features. He made a point of insisting that one size would not fit all the states, but instead urged the lawmakers in each colony to modify his model to fit their own experience. A great experiment in republican government was being launched, and the colonies were a diverse collection of laboratories, where one should expect different variations on his framework to emerge.[37]

Thoughts was also the Adams response to Paine's prescription for the proper shape of republican government in *Common Sense*. He rejected one of Paine's fundamental assumptions, which had also led the British ministry astray for the past decade. It was the assumption that sovereignty in any government must be indivisible. So, according to Paine, when you moved from a monarchy to a republic, you replaced an omniscient king with an equally omniscient and sovereign source of authority called "the people." (Rousseau would call that collective wisdom "the general will.") Adams insisted that the belief in an omniscient entity called the people was every bit as fictional as the belief in a divinely inspired king.

A new and thoroughly modern idea was entering the political conversation at this moment, the idea of multiple or shared sovereignties. Franklin had glimpsed it much earlier, and had devoted much of his time in London trying to make members of the British government embrace it. And once they did, the intractable argument over Parliament's authority became easily negotiable, because sharing authority with the colonial legislatures became possible. It was a visionary version of the British

Commonwealth. But no one, not even his good friend William Pitt, could see it. Down the road, James Madison would see it, and called it "federalism"—that is, shared authority between the federal government and the states. The French philosophes could not see it, which was one reason that, over a decade later, Adams warned anyone who would listen that the French Revolution was doomed to end in dictatorship.

But in May 1776 the French Revolution and the British Commonwealth were both mere specks on the horizon. The more immediate and pressing matter in the Adams scheme was his resolution recommending that every colony draft a new constitution to replace the existent British charters of governance. It passed on May 10. Five days later, Adams stepped forward to present another resolution, designed to serve as a preface to the previous recommendation. He would go to his grave claiming that he had drafted the real declaration of American independence on May 15, that the lightning had truly struck on that day, and that Jefferson's later draft in July was merely a thunderous aftermath.

Though the claim has always sounded self-serving, it possessed more than a kernel of truth. After a series of "whereas" sentences that documented the king's failure to answer America's humble petitions for reconciliation, the conclusion followed that George III had effectively declared independence of his former American subjects, who were now on their own.

> Resolved, that it be recommended to the respective Assemblies and Conventions of the United Colonies, where no Government sufficient to the exigencies of their affairs has been hitherto established, to adopt such Governments as shall in the opinion of the Representatives of the People best conduce to the happiness and safety of their Constituents in particular, and Americans in general.[38]

Adams immediately described these words to a friend as "the most important Resolution that ever was taken in America." For in the

Adams formulation the act of creating their own state governments was the ultimate act of American independence. Formally repudiating George III was not necessary, since he had already repudiated them. All the multiple meanings of The Cause had finally come down to one word, "independence." Americans should now prepare to live the full meaning of that word in their own republican governments.[39]

One collateral consequence of the Adams resolution was to prompt a widespread series of public meetings throughout the colonies at several levels—colony, county, town, village—to decide whether to draft state constitutions in place of their old colonial charters. The contrast with the British way of proceeding was dramatic. The British government had made an imperial decision in an imperial way, top down from George III, deciding to subdue the American rebellion by force. The Continental Congress was making a parallel decision in a republican way, bottom up from all the communities along the Atlantic coast.

Adams was extremely nervous about surrendering control to such a vast congregation of ordinary citizens. But he had no choice, because this was the acid test that any putative American republic must pass if it were to remain true to its principles. Leadership meant waiting and listening for those voices from below, not natural acts for Adams. Keenly aware, as he put it to an old Boston friend, that "we are in the midst of a Revolution," he felt like a conductor forced to stand still at the podium while the orchestra played on without his direction.[40]

If he could not control events, he could exercise some control over how they would be remembered by posterity. "In all the Correspondencies that I have maintained," he wrote Abigail, "I have never kept a single Copy. I have now purchased a Folio Book, in the first page of which I am writing this letter, and intend to write [i.e., copy] all my Letters to you from this time forward." He urged Abigail to do the same, "for I really think that your Letters are much better worth preserving than mine."[41]

Worrying came naturally for Adams, and his chief worry was that popular opinion could swerve in two wrong directions. The delusional prospect of a diplomatic resolution might still command a majority in the middle colonies, where the war had not yet touched daily life and Dickinson's influence remained a potent threat. In the other direction, the influence of *Common Sense* and its radical implications could not be calculated. Like a virus, it could easily spread, infecting The Cause with utopian schemes that would kill any prospect for a united front on independence. That was especially troubling if slavery entered the conversation, which would put all the colonies south of the Potomac at risk as dependable allies in the looming war. Only a middle course would work, at once sufficiently courageous to carry The Cause forward, yet sufficiently pragmatic to go only so far. It was a lot to ask the gods, even more to ask that moving target called the people.

Adams's fondest hopes enjoyed an improbable ally across the Atlantic. Shortly before the referendum on independence was launched, word reached the colonies that Great Britain was gathering the largest amphibious force ever assembled by any European power, more than 400 ships to transport 32,000 soldiers, to include 8,000 mercenaries from several German principalities, along with 10,000 sailors. American intelligence sources in London had known for several months of British plans to stage a major invasion at New York, then march its army up the Hudson corridor to join forces with an army coming down from Canada, thereby sealing off New England by land and sea. Now that plan was actually being implemented under the leadership of George Germain, who made no secret of his intention to end the American rebellion with one massive blow. It was clear that such a blow should be expected within a matter of weeks. Ordinary Americans were being asked to deliver their opinion on American independence just as the largest armada ever to cross the Atlantic was coming to render those opinions irrelevant.[42]

இஇ

As British military power was converging, American political power was spreading out. There was no precedent for the far-reaching mandate the Continental Congress was requesting, a full-scale popular referendum—aye or nay—on the question of independence. Several colonies forwarded the question to local governments at the county or town level. Massachusetts, for example, requested and received fifty-eight responses from towns in late May and June, all answering the question "Do said Inhabitants solemnly engage with their Lives and Fortunes to support the Congress in the Measure?" There was something almost elegiac about ordinary farmers, accustomed to gather in order to pass regulations about roaming cows or pigs, meeting now to debate the fate of America's role in the British Empire.

The residents of Topsfield were properly impressed by the seriousness of the occasion, observing that "it is the greatest and most important question that ever came before this town." Only a few years earlier, they explained, "such a question would have put us into surprise, and would have been treated with the utmost contempt." Topsfield was typical of many towns in describing the conversion to independence as a recent development, forced upon its citizens by the policies of George III and his ministers. Several towns mentioned the rejection of *The Olive Branch Petition* as a decisive turning point. Others identified the hiring of foreign mercenaries as the ultimate betrayal. Whatever the specific reasons, the accumulation of evidence rendered the old constitutional arguments irrelevant now that their former patriarch had decided—the patriotic rhetoric was florid, but not merely rhetorical—to send the flower of the British army and navy to murder their men and rape their women.[43]

A few pockets of reticence remained on Cape Cod and Nantucket, apparently wary of their vulnerability to retaliation by the British navy. Otherwise, the returns from Massachusetts were the most fully recorded, succinctly expressed repudiation of the last link holding the colonies in the British Empire. The overwhelming verdict throughout all New England seemed to be that they were only recognizing a reality that already existed, created by none other than George III himself, who had within the past year apprised them in no uncertain terms that they were no longer members of his family. If The Cause had a temperature, and the referendum of May and June was the thermometer, New England had the highest fever.[44]

The returns from Virginia were nearly as resolute as those from New England, though the voices came from counties rather than towns, and they were more expansive, almost oratorical performances, unlike the legal briefs submitted by New England towns. Virginia clearly regarded itself as the most important player in this political crisis, and sent its resolutions to other colonies on the presumption that they set the standard for others to follow, especially their neighbors to the south. Given the primacy of Massachusetts in the struggle to date, this was a rather inflated posture, but it came to the Virginians naturally. (It was the major reason Adams was later to joke that "in Virginia all geese are swans.") Here is a sample of the Virginia style, from the Buckingham County resolution of May 21:

The unhappy dispute between Great Britain and These United Colonies seems now arrived at a crisis, from whence events ought to take place which, at the beginning, we believe, were in contemplation but by a few, and even by them viewed at a much greater distance. When discussions first arose, we felt our hearts warmly attached to the King of Great Britain and the Royal family; but now the case is much altered. At the time we wished to look upon the Ministry and Parliament as the only foundations from which the bitter waters flowed; and were therefore led to think that the King, long deceived by his councellors, might open his eyes, and become mediator between his contending subjects. The measures, however, still pursued against *America* leave no room to expect such an interposition. Our enemies announce our ruin, and the King's Speeches, addresses, and proclamations are evidently concerted efforts to carry their favorite point.[45]

In part because Virginia wanted to lead the pack, the delegates to the Virginia Convention—the name they had adopted for the provisional government—delivered their decisive commitment on independence to the Continental Congress on May 15, even before reviewing the county resolutions. The Virginia report also cataloged the list of oppressive policies imposed by George III and his ministers in recent months, culminating in "the dispatch of Fleets and Armies and the aid of foreign troops engaged to assist these destructive purposes."[46]

There was one distinctive feature in Virginia's list of grievances that somewhat awkwardly raised the forbidden subject of slavery: "The King's representative in this colony [Lord Dunmore] hath not only withheld all the powers of Government from operating for our safety, but having returned on board an armed ship, is carrying on a piratical and savage war against us, tempting our slaves by every artifice to resort to him, and training and employing them against their masters." Governor Dunmore had in fact issued a blanket offer of emancipation to all Virginia slaves owned by rebels who joined him, thereby igniting the primal fear of slave insurrections harbored by the planter class. Subsequent resolutions from provincial governments in both Carolinas picked up on this theme, as did Thomas Jefferson a few weeks later in his draft of the Declaration of Independence, which echoed the charges against Lord Dunmore almost word for word.[47]

Early reports from Delaware and New Jersey seemed to indicate that the looming invasion had converted reluctant patriots to The Cause in the middle colonies. Delaware altered instructions to its delegates in Philadelphia to permit a vote on independence if a majority of other colonies concurred with that verdict. New Jersey, apparently influenced by the Virginia resolutions, elected a new slate of delegates to the Continental Congress favorably disposed toward independence. The legislature also called for the arrest of their loyalist governor, William Franklin. Despite appeals from his daughter-in-law, Benjamin Franklin refused to intercede on his son's behalf.[48]

Both New York and Pennsylvania remained wedded to a diplomatic solution, no matter how doubtful and unlikely it now seemed. The Pennsylvania delegation in congress was still under orders "to dissent from any notion leading to the separation from the Mother Country." Before it called itself the Keystone State, Pennsylvania had earned the reputation as the cornerstone of caution in the middle colonies. Pennsylvania, in short, was still Dickinson country.[49]

The only way to bring Pennsylvania in line was to change the proprietary government, which was controlled by Quaker pacifists and wealthy merchants with a vested interest in reconciliation. And the only way to change the government was to revise the Pennsylvania constitution so that excluded constituencies who strongly supported independence, chiefly the artisan class, were allowed to vote. This new version of Pennsylvania, in short, would become Paine country.[50]

It was purely coincidental, but extremely fortuitous, that the Continental Congress met in the Pennsylvania State House, the same building where the Pennsylvania legislature convened upstairs. Samuel Adams made several trips up and down the stairs on May 15, calling attention to the fact that his cousin's resolution, endorsed that day by the congress, rendered inoperative any constitution that required its officials "to take oaths and affirmations for support of any government under the crown of Great Britain." Since the Pennsylvania constitution fit that description, it obviously must be replaced. Five days later, a mass meeting of four thousand previously disenfranchised voters occurred within the brick-walled yard behind the State House. By a voice vote it adopted the outlines for a new Pennsylvania constitution that expanded the electorate by nearly 90 percent, virtually all of whom favored American independence.[51]

Neither John nor Samuel Adams favored the elimination of the property qualification to vote. But both men deeply believed that this was the climactic moment when the question of American independence would be decided, and bringing Pennsylvania into the fold was worth the cost of an otherwise cherished political principle. The trade-off paid dividends in late June, when the newly elected Pennsylvania legislature registered its willingness "to concur in a vote of the Congress declaring the United Colonies free and independent States." True to his reputation as America's most adroit behind-the-scenes operative, Samuel Adams left no fingerprints on the State House banister, but the deft management of the Pennsylvania conversion to The Cause bore all the marks of his handiwork. It was also the culminating triumph for the Adams team in mobilizing support within the Continental Congress for what had begun, two years earlier, as a New England agenda.[52]

By mid-June it was clear that the referendum on independence was going to be a landslide. The overwhelming response validated the John Adams strategy of delay while the fruits of independence ripened on the imperial vine. It was the accumulation of evidence during the previous year about the belligerent intentions of George III that wore down old allegiances and made the decisive difference among most colonists. Reading the resolutions that poured into the colonial legislatures was like harvesting a crop of anti-British sentiment that had been planted and nourished by King George himself. In one sense, the colonists were saying that the question of American independence had already been decided, so their only task was, albeit sadly, to register their recognition that the king had banished them from the British family.

What had not happened was just as politically revealing as what had. Beyond the precincts in and around Philadelphia, neither *Common Sense* nor Thomas Paine was mentioned. The forbidden topic of slavery had come up awkwardly in Virginia, and the removal of the property qualification to vote had earned its way into Pennsylvania. But otherwise the prospects for dramatic social change were silently deferred for another day.

Especially in New England, the residents of all those towns and villages had stayed on script. Just as Adams had hoped, the core meaning of The Cause was nothing less, but also nothing more, than American independence. Unity behind that banner trumped all the other political diversions. From Adams's prospective, that often confounding cohort called the people had behaved with remarkable restraint, more like an army than a mob. He could not have asked for more. Prudence had dictated, and the people had listened.

Dickinson had the much more difficult task, in part because his committee was so large, one delegate from each of the thirteen colonies, in part because no model for a nation-sized republic had ever been contemplated. (The three-branch framework Adams had proposed in *Thoughts on Government* was aimed only at the states.) While the Continental Congress had been functioning as a provisional national government for the past year, its authority to manage a collective response to the ongoing imperial crisis was presumed to be a temporary improvisation, not a permanent government. Abigail Adams raised the obvious question, more presciently than anyone else, in a letter to her husband:

> If we separate from Brittain, what Code of Laws will be established? How shall we be governed so as to retain our Liberties? Can any government be free which is not administered by general stated laws? Who shall frame these Laws? Who shall give them Force and Energy? Tis true your Resolutions as a body [i.e., the Continental Congress] have hitherto had the force of Laws. But will they continue to have [after independence]?[53]

The charge to Dickinson's committee provided the first clear hint at an answer to Abigail's questions. The committee was asked to draw up "Articles of Confederation," strongly suggesting that, after independence, the term "United States" should refer to a voluntary union of mini-republics called states. The Virginia resolution implicitly endorsed a framework in which the term "United States" would become a plural noun by declaring that the former colonies were departing the British Empire as "independent states." They would presumably remain united under the banner of The Cause to win the war, then go their separate ways, only loosely united in a confederation of sovereign states. The Cause clearly meant independence, but just as clearly independence did not mean the creation of a nation-sized republic destined to assume a prominent place in the world of nations. The model was a refurbished version of the Continental Congress.[54]

The debate over the Dickinson Draft was like an airburst in the night that exposed the deep divisions that had previously managed to coexist comfortably under the broad tent of The Cause. The delegates could not agree on the central question of federal versus state authority, how to resolve the claims of states like Virginia with ill-defined western borders, how to count slaves for the purposes of representation, and more generally whether they wished to create a national government at all. Adams was especially distraught to discover that the unity afforded by common resistance to British rule apparently dissolved as soon as the debate focused on what an independent American republic should look like: "We are sowing the Seeds of Ignorance, Corruption, and Injustice," he lamented, "in the fairest Field of Liberty ever appeared on Earth, even in the first attempts to cultivate it." Americans were united—or at least mostly united—in opposition to the imperial agenda of George III and the British ministry. But they were divided along sectional and state lines once their common enemy was taken out of the equation. They knew what they were against, but not what they were for.[55]

ENTER THE GENIUS OF Thomas Jefferson, who possessed the verbal skills and mental instincts to pitch The Cause, already an elusive term, at a sufficiently higher altitude that it floated above the divisive disputes into a region where all could gather in apparent agreement. How Jefferson did that is a story that, for obvious reasons, has not escaped the attention of historians ever since. *American Scripture* by Pauline Maier announces in its title the interpretive challenge posed by a man and a moment that occupy a semi-sacred region of the American soul inherently immune to secular assessment.[56]

Myth trumps truth in all the popular polls that matter, so it has become almost obligatory to imagine Jefferson sitting at his portable desk in his second-floor apartment at Seventh and Market Streets in mid-June 1776, meditating in a solitary séance as tongues of fire appeared over his head, guiding his quill pen to scratch onto parchment the magic words being dictated to him from above. What William James called "the will to believe" must never be underestimated, much less discounted, most especially when it provides the mythological foundation emerging nations apparently require. But even if truth be treason, at some point in time after the mythology has served its purpose history must prevail. Here, then, is a succinct and unadorned historical account, with common misconceptions noted and supernatural explanations banned from consideration, of how the Declaration of Independence happened.

On June 11 the Continental Congress appointed a five-man committee to draft a document to announce American independence, pending a positive vote on the Virginia resolution sometime on or after July 1. The committee consisted of Adams, Franklin, Jefferson, Robert Livingston of New York, and Roger Sherman of Connecticut. None of them regarded the assignment as particularly important. Depending on where you stood, the chief business was going on elsewhere: in the still-divided Pennsylvania and New York delegations; in the Dickinson committee's deliberations on the shape of the new government; in the state conventions drafting new constitutions; and on the shoreline of Long Island, where sentinels watched for the approaching British fleet.

The significance we bring to the moment was not present for the Committee of Five.

The committee met later that day or the next—we don't know for sure—in Franklin's quarters out of deference to the senior statesman, who was laid up with a bad case of gout. They then discussed the framework for the desired document, concurring that its central feature must be a bill of indictment against George III, enumerating the multiple ways he had violated their rights as Englishmen.

Adams and Jefferson had different memories of what happened next. In the Adams version, there was a discussion about who should draft the document, with Franklin the unspoken favorite based on his international stature and his reputation as America's preeminent prose stylist. But Franklin demurred, citing his current physical condition and his long-standing refusal to draft any document that would be edited by a committee. Adams then declared himself inappropriate, saying he had become "obnoxious" to more moderate delegates by arguing so strenuously for independence. Jefferson, on the other hand, recalled that it was assumed from the start that he would draft the declaration, based on his previous role as a "penman" who had drafted several resolutions and statements for the congress.

Much later, after the historical significance of the Declaration had begun to emerge, Jefferson claimed that he "had turned to neither book nor pamphlet while writing," nor had he "copied from any particular or previous writing." While true, it was not the whole truth, and fed the mythology of a solitary Jefferson communing with the gods. In fact, he had before him his own draft of a new constitution for Virginia, which contained a long list of grievances against George III that replicated a shorter list he had written for his *Summary View of the Rights of British America* (1774). Jefferson had in effect been practicing the grievances section of the Declaration for two years. In that sense, he was the most experienced prosecutor the congress could have appointed to make the case against George III. His task in mid-June was made much easier, because he was copying himself.[57]

Jefferson completed his draft of the Declaration during the third week of June. (Adams remembered, probably exaggerating, that it took him "only a day or two.") He then shared his draft with Adams and Franklin, whose judgment he trusted. They suggested only one change. Instead of "We hold these truths to be sacred and undeniable," probably Franklin suggested "self-evident," an alteration that Jefferson accepted as an improvement. The full committee then placed the document before the congress on June 28, a scene depicted in John Trumbull's painting *The Declaration of Independence* that most viewers think depicts the signing ceremony on July 4, which in fact never occurred.

It was an extremely crowded moment. On the same day Jefferson's draft was submitted to the congress, the first wave of the British fleet, 113 ships carrying General William Howe and nine thousand troops, was sighted off the Long Island coast. On July 2, by a vote of 12–0, with New York abstaining, the congress approved the Virginia resolution and thereby declared American independence.*

Over the next two days, as General Howe's army landed on Staten Island, the congress made eighty-five specific changes in Jefferson's draft, revising or deleting slightly more than 20 percent of the text. (At some point Franklin leaned over to console the sullen and silent author, reminding Jefferson that this was the reason he never wrote anything that would be edited by a committee.) On July 4 the congress completed its work and sent the final version of the Declaration to the printer, who put that date on the top of the published version. There was no signing ceremony on that day. Most delegates signed on August

---

* Adams delivered the speech endorsing independence without notes. Though it was the most significant speech in his life, there is no record of what he said. Dickinson delivered the speech opposing a decision on independence. The notes for his speech, not discovered until 1944, indicate that he no longer harbored any faith in George III, but urged delay until a French alliance could be negotiated and a stable American government be firmly established. Dickinson suffered under the stigma of being "the Man Who Would Not Sign the Declaration" for the rest of his life.

2, but there was no single day when all the delegates stepped up to affix their names to the parchment copy.

All the editorial changes occurred in the lengthy grievances section of the document, the delegates apparently regarding the earlier paragraphs as a rhetorical overture of minimal significance. They found three of the charges against George III either too Virginian or too Jeffersonian for their taste.

First, they deleted Jefferson's long paragraph accusing George III of refusing to end the slave trade and implicitly blaming him for slavery itself. Jefferson had also included Virginia's condemnation of Lord Dunmore for offering emancipation to Virginia's slaves, which appeared to contradict his earlier criticism of slavery. The delegates deleted the entire paragraph, presumably preferring that slavery remain the unmentionable elephant in the room.*58

Second, they deleted a somewhat shorter paragraph in which Jefferson claimed that the original English immigrants to America came "at the expense of their own blood and treasure; unassisted by the strength of Great Britain," which meant that the colonists had always been independent of British rule. This was a preposterous rewriting of American colonial history, and congress struck it out as an embarrassing fiction.

Third, the end of Jefferson's draft featured a melodramatic paragraph charging George III with abdicating his role as an affectionate parent: "The facts have given the last stab to agonizing affect," he lamented, "and manly spirit bids us to renounce forever these unfeeling brethren." This was the reified Jeffersonian style, levitating into a sentimental cloud bank. The delegates found it inappropriately emotional for a diplomatic document and edited it out.59

---

* The deleted paragraph is perhaps the most dazzling incoherent piece of prose that Jefferson ever wrote. The convoluted syntax suggests that Jefferson was struggling to make slavery itself, not just the slave trade, one of George III's crimes, imposing it on the innocent colonists against their will. This was patriotic fiction, but since they were blaming the king for everything else, why not add slavery to the bill of indictments, thereby laying the political foundation for emancipation?

THERE IS A BROAD CONSENSUS among historians that the editorial changes made by the delegates in Philadelphia improved the cogency and clarity of Jefferson's draft. It is difficult to imagine any similarly sized legislative body in contemporary America even attempting the task, much less performing it as well, most especially while the country was being invaded by a foreign power. It is also understandable that the delegates focused their attention on the grievances against King George, since he was the last remaining link with the British Empire that, until this moment, the Continental Congress had sought to sustain. Before American independence could be officially declared, the king needed to be indicted. Small wonder that Jefferson's editors devoted their fullest energies to that culminating act, or that they did so by documenting in detail George III's violations of their rights as Englishmen under the British constitution.

As a result, they ignored altogether the following words, which had nothing whatsoever to do with the king, or the rights of Englishmen, or British law. These are the words that Abraham Lincoln was referring to in a speech delivered on the eve of the Civil War: "All honor to Jefferson—to the man who, in the concrete pressure of a struggle for national independence by a single people, had the coolness, forecast, and capacity to introduce into a merely revolutionary document, an abstract truth, applicable to all men and all times, and so to embalm it there, that to-day, and in all coming days, it shall be a rebuke and a stumbling block to the very harbingers of reappearing tyranny and oppression."[60] These are the words fated to become the seminal statement of the American Promise:

> We hold these truths to be self-evident; that all men are cre-
> ated equal; that they are endowed by their Creator with certain
> unalienable Rights; that among these are life, liberty, & the pur-
> suit of happiness; that to secure these rights, governments are insti-

tuted among men, deriving their just powers from the consent of the governed.[61]

The entire history of liberal reform in the United States can be written as a process of discovery, within Jefferson's words, of a mandate for ending slavery, providing the rights of citizenship to Blacks, women, and gays, and protecting a full range of individual freedoms. Three of the most iconic expressions about human rights in American history refer back to Jefferson's elegiac words: the demand for women's rights at Seneca Falls (1848), Lincoln's condemnation of slavery in the Gettysburg Address (1863), and Martin Luther King's "I Have a Dream" speech (1963). What has come to be called the American Dream, then, is the Jeffersonian dream writ large, a utopian vision of the ideal society that can never be fully achieved, but the goal that each generation aspires to approximate and more closely approach.

During the summer of 1776, none of the delegates in Philadelphia who edited and then endorsed the Declaration of Independence, including Jefferson himself, foresaw the expansive implications of its language. Within the context of their own moment, what Jefferson had deftly done was provide a lyrical tribute to natural rights that preceded his narrower and more legalistic defense of English rights. He had thereby smuggled the radical agenda of Thomas Paine and his political disciples into the founding document, effectively hiding it in plain sight until the infant American republic had survived its fragile infancy, when its revolutionary implications could slowly and more safely seep out.

One of the greatest advantages of The Cause had always been its inherent ambiguity, which allowed it to expand or contract according to the exigencies of the moment. The more expansive Jeffersonian version would find its place in the future, most conspicuously in the mind of Abraham Lincoln.

On July 9, 1776, New York made the vote on independence unanimous. John Jay drafted the resolution, declaring New York's commitment to The Cause, adding "we lament the cruel necessity which has rendered this decision unavoidable." Jay was surely referring to the imminent arrival of Admiral Richard Howe's enormous fleet, more than two hundred ships, sighted on the horizon that day and headed toward a rendezvous with his brother on Staten Island. The Cause now needed to contract into its military mode, in order to avoid losing the war in the first battle after declaring independence. If that happened, all versions of The Cause would be rendered irrelevant.[62]

PROFILE

MERCY OTIS WARREN

Two months after Boston staged its Tea Party, John Adams wrote a friend for assistance. "I require a certain pen, which has no equal that I know in this country, to describe a late frolic among the sea nymphs." Shortly thereafter Adams received a long political poem, patriotic propaganda in classical verse, celebrating the courage of "Mohawk warriors" and demonizing Governor Thomas Hutchinson as the cause of the carnage. The poem ran in the *Massachusetts Spy* under the signature "Anonymous."

A few weeks later, a satirical play appeared entitled *The Adulterer* in which Hutchinson was vilified as a corrupt demagogue called "Rapatio," a play on rapist. Three more political dramatizations followed: *The Defeat* (1774), *The Group* (1775), and *The Blockheads* (1776). All were thinly veiled polemics against the British occupation of Boston. All appeared in the Boston press under the same silent signature.

"Anonymous" was Mercy Otis Warren. She was the best friend of Abigail Adams and the younger sister of James Otis, a prominent early critic of British imperial policy. By the mid-1770s Otis had fallen victim to dementia, and several observers claimed that he had passed the patriotic torch to his precocious sister.

She was also married to James Warren, a leading figure in the

Massachusetts provisional government as well as the Sons of Liberty, which met frequently to discuss political strategy in the Warren house in Plymouth, where Mercy was not shy about sharing her opinions.

The Copley portrait captures her as an attractive, elegantly attired young woman, sufficiently self-confident to look us squarely in the eye. Like Abigail, she had been homeschooled by her father. In Warren's case, she was also tutored alongside her brothers, who were preparing for admission to Harvard, which meant she was fluent in Latin and Greek. Both Abigail and John regarded Mercy as the best-read woman in New England.

She gave The Cause an operatic voice. All her poems and plays have an arched tone and an unrelenting moralistic message. Great Britain is the Evil Empire and America is a woman risking rape and death if she succumbs. There are no hues or shades in her patriotic story, no appeals to moderation or compromise. She preached The Cause in its purest form.

Long after the war, when journalists and historians expressed disbelief that a woman had written all those anonymous poems and plays, Adams relished apprising them that they were wrong, and that Mercy Otis Warren was that woman.

She confirmed her writerly credentials with the publication of a *History of the Rise, Progress, and Termination of the American Revolution* (1805) under her own signature. When Adams

Mrs. James Warren (Mercy Otis) by John Singleton Copley, 1763.

complained in a barrage of letters that she had failed to give him the credit he deserved in her history, she wrote back, describing his complaints as "the most captious, malignant, irrelevant compositions that have ever been seen." Even old friends did not duel with Mercy Otis Warren.

PART II

Arms and Men, 1776–1780

CHAPTER THREE

The Escape

We expect a bloody Summer of it at New York, as here I expect
the grand efforts of the Enemy will be aim'd; and I am sorry
to say that we are not, either in Men or Arms, prepared for it.
—George Washington to George Augustine Washington, May 31, 1776

The scene is iconic. George Washington stands squarely in the prow
of the boat, leaning into the wind, as soldiers in the Continental
Army row him across an ice-choked river. The facial expressions of all
the passengers convey a shared sense of urgency, a visual rendering of
Thomas Paine's words at that same dramatic moment: "These are the
times that try men's souls." The fate of the American Revolution hangs
in the balance.

Not much imagination is required to conjure up the picture, which
is depicted in the painting by Emanuel Leutze, *Washington Crossing the
Delaware* (1851), arguably the most famous painting in American history. It describes Washington's daring attack across the Delaware River
on Christmas night in 1776, which led to the capture of a Hessian garrison in Trenton.

To say that it turned the tide of the war for American independence
would be an exaggeration. Much like the Doolittle raid on Tokyo in the
wake of the devastating defeat at Pearl Harbor in World War II, Wash-

ington's bold crossing of the Delaware boosted American morale in the wake of several dispiriting defeats on Long Island and Manhattan three months earlier. In that sense, it was really the first uplifting moment in what would prove to be a six-year roller-coaster ride before the final victory at Yorktown. For the full historical context, and for those more verbally than visually inclined, David Hackett Fischer's authoritative account, *Washington's Crossing* (2004), is the place to begin.[1]

That could also be the title of an earlier, equally dramatic episode that no artist has seen fit to immortalize; and a story that only a few scholarly specialists in military history have chosen to tell, the story of Washington's earlier crossing of the East River. Most Americans alive at the time, in fact, were ignorant of its happening. Because it was a retreat rather than an attack, newspaper editors chose not to report it for fear the story would undermine popular support for the war. In a strange sense it is not a forgotten episode, because it was never remembered in the first place.[2]

In terms of historical significance, Washington's crossing of the East River actually deserves to rank ahead of his more famous crossing of the Delaware four months later: much more was at stake. If Washington and the bulk of the Continental Army had been killed or captured on Long Island, the fate of the war for independence would have become uncertain. The army was probably replaceable; Washington was not. The impact of the loss on hearts and minds out there in the countryside at that vulnerable moment adds another dimension of ominous ambiguity to the calculation. We can know beyond any doubt that once the British missed this opportunity to eliminate Washington and destroy the Continental Army, it would never come again.[3]

Given these quite daunting considerations, no succinct summary of this lost story, once found, will suffice. Certain obvious questions demand more detailed answers: How did Washington get himself marooned on a New York archipelago that was known to be indefensible? Given the manpower resources available to the American side,

why was he commanding an arm of only ten thousand regulars supported by twenty thousand undependable militia? Why was Washington so dangerously bold during the New York campaign and the British
commanders, William and Richard Howe, so inexplicably cautious?
(In retrospect, they should have changed places.) Why did Washington
linger on Manhattan, another water-laced trap, after the Great Escape
from Long Island? What impact did the near-death experience in the
Battle of New York have on American conduct of the war afterward?
The search for answers to these questions, for reasons that will quickly
become obvious, must begin slightly more than a year earlier at the misnamed Battle of Bunker Hill.[4]

ON JUNE 17, 1775, 2200 British troops made three frontal assaults
on New England militia units entrenched atop Breed's Hill in Boston.
Two incongruous facts leap out right away: the battle acquired its name
from the adjoining Bunker Hill; and the bloodiest battle of the entire
war for independence occurred over a year before American independence was officially declared. Although the British troops eventually
took the hill, in doing so they suffered more than a thousand killed and
wounded, nearly half the attacking force. When word of the casualties
reached London, several retired British officers were heard to say that
a few more such ruinous victories and His Majesty's army in America
would cease to exist. The shock waves from Bunker Hill also struck
His Majesty himself. As we have seen, George III launched a series of
punitive policies against American rebels whom he now regarded as
recalcitrant, effectively declaring his independence from them fully a
year before they responded in kind.

General William Howe experienced the shock waves more immediately. Howe's reputation for personal bravery was well earned; he had
led the "forlorn hope" assault (i.e., suicide mission) on the Plains of
Abraham at Quebec in the decisive battle of the Seven Years' War. At

Bunker Hill he also led from the front, marching ahead of the lead column with conspicuous nonchalance, trailed by members of his staff, one of whom carried a wine decanter on a silver tray, a visible statement of preternatural poise calculated to convey a message that the assault against undisciplined militia would be a waltz. The silver tray, wine decanter, and Howe's entire staff were blown away by the initial volleys of musket fire from above. Howe spent the most dangerous two hours of his life climbing over dead and wounded British soldiers piled up in mounds of blood and gore. By all rights, he should have gone down with his troops.

Howe never forgot the scene. "The sad and impressive experience of this murderous day sunk deep in to the mind of Sir William Howe," one American officer later recalled, "and it seems to have had its influence upon all his subsequent operations with decisive control." As a man, he began consuming ungodly amounts of alcohol; he also initiated an openly scandalous relationship with Elizabeth Loring, the young wife of Joshua Loring, a prominent loyalist who apparently smiled at the liaison. He never again ordered a frontal attack against entrenched American troops.[5]

Meanwhile, on the American side, another lesson from Bunker Hill was sinking in: namely, that militia fighting for a cause they deeply felt and freely embraced could defeat disciplined British mercenaries. What the militia lacked in experience, so the argument went, was more than offset by the conviction they carried in their hearts. The conviction even had a name, *rage militaire*, a French term that described an inspirational affinity for combat by volunteers driven by a passionate commitment instead of the mercenary motive of mere money.

Bunker Hill also provided the first American martyr to this inspirational ideal in the person of Joseph Warren. A prominent Boston physician and charismatic leader of the Sons of Liberty, Warren suddenly became General Warren, the hero who stood his ground on the redoubt atop Breed's Hill when the third assault wave of British troops overwhelmed the surviving remnant of militia after they had exhausted their ammunition. The orders that Warren obeyed when he went to his glorious death did not come from superior officers, but from inside himself. If the militia was the collective expression of *rage militaire*, Warren became the singular embodiment of the same revolutionary spirit in almost perfect form. The recovery of his body became a sacred obligation; and the discovery that it had been desecrated with multiple bayonet wounds after his death provoked a flood of sermons and speeches demonizing British savagery.[6]

The belief in a militia-based army made perfect sense in New England, where local militia had served as the chief source of security against Indian attacks for over a century. In the wake of the British occupation of Boston after passage of the Coercive Acts, it soon became obvious to General Thomas Gage that British troops venturing beyond Boston were at risk of being overwhelmed by militia units from adjacent towns and counties. On two occasions, the sheer scale of the numerical superiority enjoyed by New England militia became visible: in September 1774, approximately fifty thousand militia marched on Boston in response to a false alarm that British warships were bombarding the city; then in April 1775, British troops returning from skirmishes at Lexington and Concord found themselves moving through a gauntlet of citizen-soldiers who were, in the phrase of the day, "numerous and armed."[7]

It seems clear, at least in retrospect, that the chief advantage enjoyed by New England militia in these early encounters with British troops was captured in the first word of that phrase. The militia were invincible because there were just so many of them. But in the emerging revolutionary rhetoric, the militia advantage was described as the outcome of a deeper wellspring of political conviction.

Simply put, it was a matter of consent versus coercion. An American army of militia was superior to a British army of professionals because the principle of consent was inherently more powerful than any involuntary obedience to superior authority. For the same reason that American colonists could not be taxed without their consent, any American army defending that principle could not take the British army as a model without violating the values it was purportedly fighting for.

ON JUNE 15, 1775, two days before Bunker Hill, the Continental Congress voted unanimously to appoint George Washington as commander in chief of the fifteen thousand militia currently surrounding Boston. John Adams, who nominated Washington, subsequently claimed, only partially in jest, that Washington was the obvious choice because he was a full head taller than anyone else in the room. He was also a Virginian, by far the largest colony, which needed to assume its rightful leadership role in the undeclared war.

He was also the only delegate wearing a military uniform, a sartorial reminder of his military experience as commander of the Virginia Regiment during the Seven Years' War. Compared with the British officers he would soon be facing in Boston, however, he was a rank amateur, and he knew it: "I am embarked on a tempestuous ocean from whence, perhaps, no friendly harbor is to be found," he confessed to his wife's brother-in-law, adding that "it is an honour I wished to avoid." Before departing Philadelphia, he purchased a tomahawk, several cartouche boxes, and five books on the military art. He was preparing to give himself a crash course on how to run an army.[8]

Washington assumed command of "the Troops of the United Provinces of North America" at Cambridge on July 3, 1775. They were called "United Provinces" because almost all the soldiers were New Englanders from militia units in Massachusetts, Connecticut, New Hampshire, and Rhode Island; nor were they, in any meaningful sense of the term, an army.

That distressing fact consumed Washington's attention for virtually every minute of every day for the next seven months. During the first week, the general orders flowing out from headquarters conveyed his incredulity at the scene he was seeing: soldiers urinating and defecating whenever the spirit moved; engaging in brawls with militia from other colonies in juvenile disputes about honor and bravery; insulting their officers, whom they had elected, when ordered to drill at an inconvenient time; bathing naked in a local stream while embarrassed women walked by; firing muskets in the air to scare the sleeping horses.

If the upside of a militia-based army was its volunteer spirit, the downside was that the free-flowing energies released by that spirit were incompatible with conventional forms of military discipline. Poised to assume command of an army, Washington discovered he was overseeing a tentatively organized mob. "I have often thought how much happier I should have been." he lamented to his aide, "if, instead of accepting a command under such circumstances, I had rather taken my Musket upon my Shoulder & entered the Ranks, or had retired to the backcountry and lived in a Wigwam."[9]

The Boston Siege, as noted earlier, soon turned into a marathon staring match. Approximately six thousand British regulars and a large complement of loyalist refugees were barricaded in Boston while more than twice that number of American troops hovered beyond musket range in trenches and makeshift redoubts. In February Washington ordered his staff to draw up a plan for a surprise attack across Boston Harbor at night. (One version of the plan featured a reconnaissance patrol on ice skates.) The general orders on the day of the proposed attack played all the patriotic chords: "It is a noble cause we are engaged in, the Cause of Virtue and Mankind; our posterity depends on the Vigor of our exertions; in short, Freedom or Slavery must be the result of our conduct." Whether Washington actually believed such rhetoric, which was written by an aide, is unknowable. He unquestionably believed in these final words: "Anyone attempting to retreat or desert will be instantly *shot down*." At the last minute he decided to cancel the attack on the grounds that the troops lacked the discipline to conduct such a complicated offensive operation.[10]

As the siege around Boston hardened into a stalemate, two frustrating convictions hardened in Washington's mind. He had become increasingly impatient with the moderate faction in the Continental Congress, who continued, as he put it, "to feed themselves on the dainty food of reconciliation." The official claim that the British army he was facing was not His Majesty's troops, but "ministerial troops," might have once been a convenient fiction that left the door open for George III to reach his senses and end the imperial crisis. But for Washington the line had been crossed when he read the after-action reports on Bunker Hill, which described British soldiers bayoneting all the American wounded on the ground. He did not believe he could ask brave men to go to their own deaths in an undeclared war for any cause less than American independence.

His letters to John Hancock, president of the Continental Congress, were also filled with a litany of lamentations about the current condition of the newly named Continental Army. His chief complaint was the inherently transitory character of any militia-based army, which became a fluctuating flow of inexperienced amateurs, coming and going like tourists as one set of enlistments ended and another began. "It is not in the pages of History, perhaps, to furnish a case like ours," he apprised Hancock, "to maintain a post within Musket-Shot of the Enemy for Six Months together, and at the same time to disband one Army and recruit another." Every report he submitted on the status of the Continental Army was a temporary snapshot of an ever-moving picture.[11]

Washington was trying to tell his civilian superiors that they had overlearned the lessons of Bunker Hill. The chief mistake was the seductive illusion that a volunteer army of militia, all fighting for a cause they believed in deeply, could defeat an army of seasoned professional soldiers. The illusion was understandable, given those British bodies lying on the slopes of Breed's Hill. But the conflict with Great Britain was entering a new phase in which the old lessons would no longer suffice. As the designated commander on the ground, he needed to convey the more relevant lessons of the Boston Siege as he now understood them.

Succinctly put, America could not win the war until it replaced its current militia-based model with a professional force of veteran soldiers capable of competing on equal terms with British regulars—in effect, "a permanent standing army." Washington was well aware that his recommendation was likely to fall on deaf ears: "It may be said, that this is an application for powers that are too dangerous to be entrusted," he acknowledged to Hancock. "I can only add that desperate diseases require desperate remedies, and with truth declare that I have no lust for power, but declare with so much fervency as any man upon this wide extended Continent for an opportunity of turning the Sword into a ploughshare."[12]

He was also fully aware that proposing the British army as a model might have an almost treasonable ring, since it contradicted the patriotic assumption, itself rooted in revolutionary principles, that the British army embodied all the coercive values Americans were purportedly fighting against. Washington's rebuttal was brutally realistic: the only way to assure the triumph of revolutionary principles was to win the war; and the only way to win the war was to create a professional force capable of besting the British army. "To expect the same service from Raw and undisciplined Recruits as from Veteran Soldiers," he concluded, "is to expect what never did, and perhaps never will happen."[13]

This was an idea whose time had not yet come, and in a very real sense never would. Just as Washington's mind was running ahead of popular opinion on the independence question, it was also early in its anticipation of the military liabilities posed by a militia-based army once the *rage militaire* phase of the conflict evolved into a protracted war. During the siege, Washington conducted several councils of war in which his two most experienced subordinates, Horatio Gates and Charles Lee, both veterans of the British army, argued for a defensive strategy designed to avoid engaging British regulars on their own terms. This quasi-guerrilla approach, called a "war of posts," presumed that the militia-based Continental Army would never be capable of winning a conventional battle, so American strategy should adapt to that reality.

Washington preferred to change that reality. Given the size of the American population, he estimated that America could easily put a Continental Army of sixty thousand troops in the field, more than sufficient to overwhelm any force the British could carry across the Atlantic. All enlistments should last "for the duration," which he estimated at no more than two years. He was less interested at this stage in strategies designed to avoid losing the war than winning it outright. He wanted a Continental Army that was a projection of his own decisive, controlling personality. It all made perfect strategic sense. Unfortunately, it was politically impossible.

THE BRITISH ARMY in Boston was eventually placed in an untenable position when a battery of cannons hauled on sleds from Fort Ticonderoga in upstate New York was placed on Dorchester Heights. After lingering in Boston Harbor for a week, the British fleet evacuated the city on March 17, 1776, sailing to a British naval base in Halifax, Nova Scotia. Though there had never been a major battle, the American press reported the evacuation as a crushing defeat for the British army. And the Continental Congress regarded it as clinching evidence that the Continental Army, as currently constituted, was fully capable of vanquishing the British leviathan. "Under your Directions," wrote President Hancock, "an undisciplined Band of Husbandsmen, in the Course of a few Months, became Soldiers, defeating an Army of Veterans, commanded by the most experienced generals." The congress ordered a gold medallion cast in Washington's honor, the first official step toward the creation of an otherworldly American icon. The Cause would not require a large standing army, it was now clear, because it possessed a singular figure who was the one-man solution to all the glaring military deficiencies of the current militia-based army.[14]

Two weeks later, Washington received orders to take the Continental Army—actually the surviving remnant of ten thousand troops who had chosen not to return to their families and farms—and proceed with all due speed to New York. Intelligence reports indicated that a British invasion force of considerable size was expected to land there within the next two months. Washington was assured that his army would be supplemented, probably doubled or tripled in size, by militia units from nearby colonies on the eve of the battle. This proved to be the strategic framework for all major military actions throughout the remainder of the war: a hard core of veteran troops (though in this case the veterans averaged only six months experience), reinforced by local militia from the surrounding region in a kind of "balloon effect" before each battle.

Whatever one might choose to call this hybrid creation, it was not a "standing army."[15]

Just a few days before he headed south with his makeshift army, Washington received a report from Charles Lee, who had been sent down to New York to cast his seasoned eye on the looming battlefield. Lee endorsed the intelligence estimates that, for two overlapping reasons, New York was the likely British target. First was its strategic location. "The consequences of the Enemy's possessing themselves of New York," he warned, "have appeared to be so terrible that I have scarce been able to speak." As the gateway to the Hudson corridor, New York provided a launching pad for a British campaign that would link up with another army coming down from Canada through Lake Champlain, thereby sealing off New England.

Second, and more ominously, because greater New York was an archipelago comprised of three islands—Staten Island, Long Island,

and Manhattan—it would prove either difficult or impossible to defend. "What to do with this city, I own, puzzles me," Lee wrote, "since it is so encircled with navigable water that whoever commands the sea commands the town." There was no question that the British navy, the most formidable force of its kind in the world, would command the sea. It would also provide the British with tactical supremacy throughout the battle, to include the mobility to insert troops wherever it chose, and platforms of artillery at the point of attack. (Lee did not mention that New York also contained the highest percentage of loyalists of any American colony.) All in all, New York was probably the worst place on the North American continent for any American army, much less the untested Continental Army, to make a stand.[16]

Meanwhile, up in Halifax with his army and the loyalist refugees from the Boston Siege, William Howe was speculating that the proposed British invasion of New York would probably be unopposed. Writing to George Germain, Howe relished the opportunity to "rough up" the American army on such favorable terrain, and by so doing put a quick end to a conflict he considered senseless. But he doubted that the Americans would accommodate him. "I confess my apprehensions that such an event will readily be brought about," he apprised Germain, "for the rebels, knowing their advantage in having the whole country, as it were, at their disposal, will not readily be brought into a situation where the King's troops can meet them on equal terms." He expected Washington to burn the city of New York to the ground, then take his army inland to Connecticut or New Jersey. "Their armies retiring a few miles back from the navigable rivers," Howe observed, "ours cannot follow them from the difficulties I expect to meet with in procuring land carriage." As Howe saw it, the decisive battle that both he and Germain were hoping for was unlikely to happen.[17]

Howe's letter to Germain essentially replicated the same strategic assessment of the New York theater that Lee had provided to Washington a month earlier. Knowing as we do the catastrophe about to befall the Continental Army once Washington decided to defend New York, it is impossible to avoid asking the obvious question: What was Washington thinking as he marched south from Boston with ten thousand troops that he knew to be untested amateurs, toward a destination he knew to be indefensible? Was he experiencing a temporary lack of judgment? Momentarily caught up in the patriotic exuberance of *rage militaire* that his more sober self regarded as delusional? Distracted by the sheer logistical challenge—he had never done it before—of transporting so many men, horses, cannons, and inevitable hangers-on that accompany an army on the march? Temporarily dazzled by the huzzahs from ecstatic crowds gathered in all those New England towns?

The short, historically correct answer is none of the above. Washington was not choosing to defend New York. He was obeying an order from his civilian superiors to do so. There was no established procedure within the American government for making such a decision, because there was as yet no such thing as an American government. The Continental Congress was functioning as a provisional confederation of colonies, about to make the all-important decision on American independence. In this crowded moment, confronted with reliable intelligence that a British invasion at New York was looming, the delegates in congress ordered Washington to oppose it. Nothing that could be called strategic thinking went into the decision. American strategy was being dictated by British strategy.

In addition to the civilian orders from above, there were voices inside Washington that echoed those orders with the authority of a command. Like many officers in both the British and American armies, he harbored a quasi-chivalric code that imposed mental and even emotional constraints on his behavior. It was the reason that officers expected their troops to remain at attention rather than lie down or take cover before receiving a volley of musket or cannon fire from the other side; or the reason why ordering a retreat, even a strategic retreat when facing overwhelming odds, was frowned upon and risked accusations of cowardice. Within this honor-driven world, the call to battle was like a summons to duel. It could not be refused without inviting criticism of one's character. As Washington approached New York in early April 1776, then, he was poised to defend the indefensible with an army he knew to be inferior because, quite literally, he thought and felt he had no choice.

WHILE WASHINGTON'S amateur army was trudging south toward New York, the British war machine was gearing up at lightning speed. In a burst of logistical energy, the British ministry assembled nearly 400 ships equipped with 1200 cannons to transport 32,000 soldiers and 10,000 sailors; it was the largest armada ever to cross the Atlantic. (That record stood until the American Expeditionary Force crossed going the other way in World War I.) By European standards, the British army worldwide was small, about 45,000 troops. Over half of them were now being deployed to the American theater, supplemented by 12,000 mercenaries recruited at considerable cost from several German principalities. The top echelon of the British government had decided that half measures were no longer sufficient, that nothing less than the retention of its North American empire was at stake. The moment had arrived to smash the incipient American rebellion in one massive blow.[18]

The architect of this unprecedented projection of British military power was George Germain. By appointing Germain as American Secretary, George III had decided to put the imperial face on the British Empire. Germain believed that the Americans who inflicted all those British casualties at Bunker Hill needed to be taught a lesson and brought an unblinkered focus to the task. As one British historian has described him, "there was no trash in his mind."[19]

Germain also saw more clearly than most other members of the British ministry that any war against the Americans posed enormous strategic and logistical challenges. He had read the letters from General

Gage about the overwhelming level of military resistance throughout the New England countryside as sobering reports by the most experienced British officer in the American theater. Instead of concluding that Gage had lost his nerve and was past his prime—the dominant opinion within the ministry—Germain concluded that Great Britain faced a formidable American adversary with resources that defied conventional measures of military effectiveness; even more ominously, the rebels had space, time, and numbers on their side; and a prolonged war of attrition would bring those advantages more and more into play. "As there is no common sense in protracting a war of this sort," Germain observed, "I should be for exerting the utmost force of this Kingdom to finish the rebellion in one campaign."[20]

His most controversial decision—less so at the time than ever after—was his choice of the Howe brothers to oversee the campaign. From a professional perspective, William and Richard Howe made perfect sense; indeed, were almost caricatures of the British officers as duty-driven aristocrats. They were connected by blood to the royal family, albeit awkwardly; their grandmother had been the favorite mistress of George I. Both brothers had attended Eton, the preferred gateway for the most privileged members of British society. Both occupied secure seats in Parliament, the older and titled Lord Richard in Lords, William in Commons. On the basis of merit and military experience, each had risen to the top of his respective field, William as the leading proponent of light-infantry tactics in the army, Richard as one of the ablest seamen in the world's greatest navy. As already noticed, William had somehow survived Bunker Hill without a scratch, supervised the evacuation of Boston, and was awaiting orders with ten British regiments in Halifax, the alluring Betsy Loring still at his side.[21]

In one significant sense, however, Germain's appointment of the Howes was strange, for both men were on record as believing that the American war was a massive mistake. William had vowed to his constituents in Nottingham that he would never take up arms against the

Americans, citing his affection for the residents of Massachusetts, who had commissioned a plaque in Westminster to honor his older brother, George Augustus Howe, who had gone down gloriously alongside Massachusetts militia at Ticonderoga in 1758. Lord Richard had hosted Benjamin Franklin at his home in 1775, working feverishly with the recently disgraced American sage to conjure up a last-minute compromise that avoided the looming abyss. Both Howe brothers were devoted Whigs, who believed that George III and Lord North were leading the British Empire into an unnecessary and misguided war.

In order to win the participation of the Howes, Germain found it necessary to propose an awkward arrangement: in addition to their titles as major general and admiral of His Majesty's forces in America, they would also have the title of peace commissioners charged with the task, as their instructions read, "for restoring peace to our colonies and plantations in North America, and for granting pardons to such of our subjects now in rebellion as shall deserve our royal mercy." During extensive negotiations with Germain in May 1776, Lord Richard insisted that he and his brother could undertake the military mission to invade and occupy New York only on the condition that they be granted the diplomatic authority to offer generous terms for reconciliation after delivering a sufficiently devastating military defeat to convince the Americans that their cause was hopeless.[22]

In truth, the terms that Germain was prepared to endorse virtually assured that the diplomatic side of the Howes' mission would prove hopeless. Nothing less than total abandonment of Parliament's authority to tax or legislate for the colonies would have sufficed as a starting point for negotiations. Moreover, Lord Richard's negotiations with Germain had delayed the departure of the British fleet until early June, so that its arrival in Long Island Sound occurred just after the official American declaration of independence, thereby rendering the proposal for reconciliation dead on arrival.

The divided loyalties of the Howe brothers have hovered over all appraisals of their military behavior during the New York campaign ever since. Tactical decisions by General Howe at several key moments in the battle become comprehensible only within a diplomatic rather than military context, which is to say that Howe's highest priority was to win battles without inflicting damage that might preclude the restoration of amicable relations once the senseless conflict was ended. He did not want to kill the Continental Army, only to wound it.

WASHINGTON ARRIVED IN New York on April 13, joined a few days later by his wife, Martha, who had come up from Mount Vernon with a small entourage of household slaves to handle domestic chores. After setting up his headquarters in the middle of Manhattan, Washington cast his own experienced eye—his first career was surveyor—on the terrain that Charles Lee had described in such ominous tones. It was now dotted with multiple forts, redoubts, barricades, and trenches, all being constructed by a small army of slave laborers and soldiers according to the engineering scheme Lee had devised. Lee's obvious goal was to transform a vulnerable archipelago into a multilayered version of Bunker Hill, where any British attack force could claim victory only at a very high cost.[23]

As that fatalistic scenario settled in Washington's mind, he ordered one of his brigadiers who had been born and raised in New York, General William Alexander, to oversee two full regiments, over a thousand men, to dig and build ten hours a day. (Alexander claimed descent from Scottish royalty, and although the House of Lords rejected the claim, he insisted on being called Lord Stirling, and Washington, then everyone else, somewhat strangely complied.) "We expect a very bloody Summer of it at New York," Washington wrote his brother, "as here I expect the grand efforts of the Enemy will be aim'd; and I am sorry to say that we are not, either in Men or Arms, prepared for it." To the extent that digging and piling up rocks counted toward preparations, Washington was determined to leave no stone unturned.[24]

He was also determined to make the surrounding water equally impassable, or at least to restrict British mobility in the Hudson and East Rivers. To that end, he requested the construction of six fireships to harass British traffic in both rivers, as well as several sunken ships, called *chevaux-de-frise,* to block the entrance to the Hudson and narrow stretches of the river, where American artillery could damage or sink British frigates as they maneuvered through the debris. He was open to any suggestion that might offset the naval advantage the British enjoyed, to include a recommendation from Benjamin Franklin for what he called a "submersible vessel" capable of attacking British warships from beneath the surface of the water. The inventor of this vessel, David Bushnell, turned out to be a visionary who was slightly more than a century ahead of his time.[25]

Washington gave responsibility for planning the defense of Long Island to another brigadier, General Nathanael Greene, who proceeded to impress all concerned with his calm but conspicuous competence. Without any previous military experience or training, Greene designed a necklace of five forts across Brooklyn Heights, all connected by trenches and further fortified with well-spaced redoubts that afforded defenders with "killing zones" all the way down to Gowanus Heights. Later on, when Hessian officers filed their after-action reports, they made a point of praising the defensive scheme on Long Island, claiming that it was capable of stopping a frontal attack by fifty thousand troops.[26]

Known as "the fighting Quaker," Greene had joined Washington's army during the Boston Siege as a former private in the Rhode Island militia. By the end of the siege he was a major general, one of Washington's discoveries whose rise in rank would have been unimaginable in the British army, an advertisement for the way the American Revolution pushed latent talent to the top. At New York, Greene's confident presence, despite a chronic limp, became fully visible for the first time, immediately recognizable as a distinctive voice within Washington's general staff.[27]

Greene was also extremely realistic. He was at pains to insist that New York was not Boston, either geographically or politically. "The Fortifications in and about this city are exceedingly strong and strengthening every day," he wrote his brother. "But the New England colonies without the least fortification are easier defended than this Colony, owing to different dispositions of the People. Tories here are as plenty as Whigs with you." All assumptions about popular support for resistance to Great Britain's imperial agenda based on recent experience in New England were likely to prove misguided. According to Greene's assessment, a majority of the farmers on Long Island were loyalists, or at least British sympathizers, poised to welcome the British invasion force as liberators. Among all the reasons New York would prove difficult to defend, perhaps the most worrisome was that a substantial portion of the residents did not wish to be defended.[28]

Washington did not need to be reminded that the war was about winning hearts and minds as much as winning battles. But as the weather warmed, he was processing that point at a higher altitude. It was already clear that the military side of the strategic equation was affecting the political side; the looming British invasion was ramping up the vote for independence, for the elemental reason that it seemed almost designed by George III and the British ministry to eliminate any hope for reconciliation. It was less clear what effect, if any, a positive vote on independence would have on the posture of the Continental Army at New York. At least on the face of it, the sudden surge of patriotism should embolden the troops to defend The Cause with greater energy and conviction once it was officially declared. On the other hand, how would it look if, in the immediate wake of the long-delayed decision on independence, the military embodiment of The Cause in the form of the Continental Army was annihilated? This was the hearts-and-minds question that Washington carried with him in a hastily arranged trip to Philadelphia in late May 1776.[29]

The question was not answered because it was never asked. Washington had brought Martha along in order to undergo inoculation for smallpox, and she required his attention during the recovery phase, which occurred at Thomas Jefferson's quarters. Although this was the first summit meeting between Washington and his civilian superiors about overall American strategy for the conduct of the war, it was an extremely crowded moment for the delegates of the Continental Congress. Their minds were less focused on the British fleet approaching New York than the looming vote on independence.[30]

As a result, all of Washington's substantive discussions about military strategy occurred with John Adams. As far as Adams was concerned, the decision to defend New York was a settled matter, so his chief duty as de facto secretary of war was to assure Washington that he would do all in his power to provide him with the resources required to perform that mission. He himself planned to reread Thucydides on the Peloponnesian War.[31]

In that overheated moment, as the political commitment to The Cause was reaching a climax, even to mention a strategic withdrawal of the Continental Army would have sounded unpatriotic. So Washington never raised the issue. If there was ever an opportunity to avoid making the biggest strategic blunder of the entire war, this was it. The fatal decision was made by default—that is, by not being faced. Neither Adams nor Washington knew it, but they had just decided, at the very moment that the American Revolution was aborning, to put its success at greater risk than it would ever encounter again during the entire war.

BASED ON CORRESPONDENCE over the ensuing weeks, we know that Washington was promised an injection of militia from New Jersey, Delaware, Maryland, and Connecticut, thereby raising his strength to twenty-five thousand troops. He was authorized to round up and arrest all known loyalists on Long Island, thereby ending the pretense that they could not be touched until independence was officially declared. He was directed to construct "as many fire rafts, row gallies, armed boats, and floating batteries as necessary," a final gesture at impeding British naval access up the Hudson and East Rivers.[32]

These were all tactical adjustments within an overall strategy that now enjoyed the presumptive advantage of being unquestioned. Washington took refuge in the Bunker Hill syndrome and the spiritual potency of The Cause. "If our troops will behave well," he confided to Hancock, "the enemy will have to wade through much blood & Slaughter before they can carry any part of our Works, If they carry 'em at all. May the sacredness of our cause Inspire our Soldiery with sentiments of Heroism, and lead 'em to the performance of noblest exploits." He was counting on a miracle.[33]

On July 12, just as the forward element of Richard Howe's fleet appeared on the horizon, Washington convened a council of war in order to propose a surprise attack on Staten Island before the full complement of Howe's force arrived. The draft for a complicated, three-pronged assault in Lord Stirling's hand was circulated among the general officers, who then voted unanimously to reject the plan. Their troops, they all agreed, were too inexperienced to carry out any offensive operation, much less the kind of coordinated attack Stirling described.[34]

Just a few hours later on the same day, Admiral Howe ordered two of his largest warships, the *Phoenix* and *Rose*, to stage a display of British naval supremacy. The two ships swept past American shore batteries on southern Manhattan, opened fire on dwellings and military installations all along the west side of the island, proceeded past Fort Washington (in present-day Washington Heights), where American batteries inflicted minimum damage, then continued all the way to Tappan Zee thirty miles north of the city.[35]

Howe intended this display of British naval supremacy as a demonstration designed to make Washington fully aware that his situation on the New York archipelago was hopeless. If he harbored any hopes about restricting the mobility of the British fleet, they were now exposed as pipe dreams. Howe gave Washington one day to digest the implications of his tactical predicament, then sent him a letter proposing a meeting. "I trust that a dispassionate consideration of the King's benevolent intentions," Howe observed, "may be the means of preventing the further Effusion of Blood and become productive of Peace and lasting Union between Great Britain and America." Howe hoped that he could assume his preferred role as peace commissioner, put down his sword, pick up his olive branch, and effectively end the battle for New York before it ever began. He addressed his letter to "George Washington, Esq. &C&C&C."[36]

This designation posed a problem when Howe's emissary met with Washington's adjutant general, Joseph Reed, in rowboats between Staten Island and Governor's Island. (Reed was another one of Washington's gifted amateurs, the product of a prominent Philadelphia family who had studied law at the Middle Temple in London, served as Washington's aide during the Boston Siege, and only recently been persuaded to rejoin Washington's staff as adjutant general, a position for which he declared himself wholly unqualified.) Reed's legal training came in handy as he shouted above the waves that his client, General Washington, could not possibly receive a letter addressed to some unknown ambiguity entitled "&C&C&C." All the world knew General George Washington to be the commander in chief of the Continental Army. If Lord Howe could not address him as such—and he could not without violating his orders—then the letter could not be delivered.[37]

Undaunted, a week later Howe tried again. This time he sent his own adjutant general, James Patterson, to Washington's headquarters in Manhattan, carrying a deferential cover letter. "Ld. How and General How did not mean to denigrate the Respect or Rank of General Washington," it began; indeed, "they held his Person & Character in the highest Esteem." After exchanging a few pleasantries, Washington read Howe's proposal for peace negotiations, then apprised Patterson to convey his regrets to Lord Howe. What the good lord had described as his "great Powers" were sadly deficient, for he was only authorized "to grant pardons—and those who have committed no Fault wanted no Pardons." If Howe wanted Washington to realize that his precarious position left him little room to negotiate, Washington wanted Howe to realize that his instructions as peace commissioner left him with virtually nothing to offer short of surrender. As he put it to another officer, Howe was only proposing "Pardons for Penitent Sinners."[38]

Two weeks later Howe described his attempted overture to Washington as "more polite than interesting; however it induced me to change my superscription for the attainment of an end so desirable." This was Howe's elliptical way of saying that he must put his peace commission back in his pocket. It was now clear to both Howe brothers that they needed to deliver a humiliating defeat to Washington and his amateur army before resuming their preferred role as diplomats.[39]

Preparations for the invasion began in earnest on August 8, when the fleet carrying the advance party of Hessians finally arrived. A week later Nathanael Greene reported that lookouts had witnessed Hessian troops landing on Staten Island. "I have the pleasure to inform you," Greene wrote Washington, "that our Troops appear to be in exceedingly good Spirits, and make no doubt that if they should make their attack here, we shall be able to render a very good account of them." Just in case that effort proved inadequate, Greene had ordered all livestock on the island rounded up and slaughtered, so it would not fall into British hands.[40]

Shortly after writing these words, Greene came down with a life-threatening fever, probably malaria, and Washington ordered him back to headquarters at Manhattan for treatment. He replaced Greene with General John Sullivan, who had only recently arrived from serving with General Gates near Lake Champlain, and therefore lacked any knowledge of the terrain or the network of defenses Greene had so diligently constructed. Upon learning of a British landing at Gravesend Bay on August 22, Washington had second thoughts about leaving Sullivan in sole command on Long Island, and granted the request from General Israel Putnam, a legendary warrior who was said to find gunfire almost musical, to join Sullivan. "The brave old man," reported Joseph Reed, "was quite miserable at being kept here." If the plan was to make Long Island another Bunker Hill, it made sense to put a hero of Bunker Hill like Putnam in charge.[41]

But Washington initially believed that the landing at Gravesend Bay was probably a feint. He expected the main British attack to come in northern Manhattan, and he placed the bulk of his army in that location. Why would General Howe choose to come up from Long Island, when by coming down from King's Bridge at the Harlem River, he effectively blocked any escape route onto the mainland?

This was not a rhetorical question. From the American side it was the existential question. Charles Lee had mentioned it glancingly in his original scan of the terrain back in February, but then it had somehow dropped out of the strategic equation. The central idea that had come to dominate Washington's thinking, and what went for thinking in the upper reaches of the Continental Army, was the Bunker Hill model. But not even Nathanael Greene seemed to ask, at least out loud, the obvious questions: at Bunker Hill, once the American troops were overwhelmed, they retreated down the hill, then walked home. Where did they go after inflicting massive casualties on the British on Long Island or Manhattan? Perhaps it had become unpatriotic even to ask the questions, because there was no answer. All visions of the post–Bunker Hill scenario were a nightmare. By deciding to defend New York, not only had Washington decided to defend the indefensible, he had put the Continental Army in a water-ringed trap from which there was no escape.

The strategic predicament of the Continental Army was quite obvious, so it was not surprising when the British general Henry Clinton proposed a feint at Long Island, then the major attack at King's Bridge in northern Manhattan, thereby "corking the bottle" and closing the trap around the Continental Army, which could then be gradually eroded and, if necessary, annihilated. It *was* surprising that William Howe rejected Clinton's advice, indeed threatened Clinton with a charge of insubordination for making his argument with such intensity.* Howe rejected Clinton's advice not just because he loathed him, but chiefly because he did not want to destroy the Continental Army. He wanted to defeat it, to be sure, but to do so with a minimum of bloodletting, in a measured way that left room at each stage for the leaders of the misguided American rebellion to reconsider the error of their ways. He sought to avoid total destruction of the Continental Army because that would inflict a wound on the Anglo-American relationship that might never heal. He wished to avoid an American version of the Scottish massacre at Culloden (1746).

For all these reasons, and a few others, Long Island made perfect sense as the point of entry. It was crawling with loyalists, who would rally to the British banner and thereby expose the purportedly bottomless devotion to The Cause as fiction. It would provide Howe's artillery units with a platform on Brooklyn Heights from which to render southern Manhattan and New York Harbor indefensible, so they probably could be occupied without a fight. It would inflict sufficient losses on the Continental Army to make its survival highly problematic, permitting Washington and his civilian superiors to digest the full implications of their intractable predicament and, sooner or later, come

---

* There had been bad blood between Howe and Clinton ever since their disagreement over tactical decisions at Bunker Hill. More generally, Clinton was infamous within the British army for being insufferable, most especially for picking fights with his superiors. He always knew he was right. (In this instance, he was.) William Willcox, Clinton's biographer, thinks that he was probably bipolar and concludes that, despite his considerable gifts as a strategist and tactician, "he carried failure within himself." See William B. Willcox, *Portrait of a General: Sir Henry Clinton and the War for Independence* (New York, 1964), 492–524.

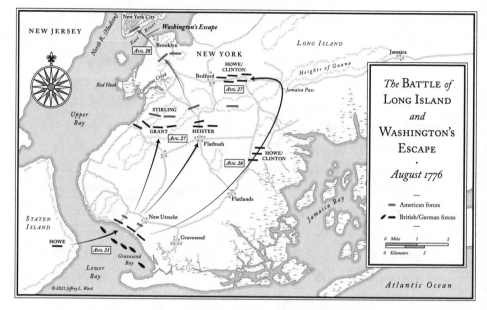

Long Island, August 1776

to their senses at the negotiating table. Then William Howe and his brother could revert to their roles as peace commissioners and return to England in triumph as the soldier-diplomats who ended an unnecessary war.

As Howe looked up the slope toward Gowanus Heights, he saw thick woods riddled with layers of trenches and moundlike barricades all the way up to Brooklyn Heights, where a line of forts and redoubts formed a crescent across the rim of the Brooklyn peninsula. Several passes snaked up the slope, too narrow for artillery or massed troops, obviously designed as killing zones, to include range markers for the riflemen above. It was clear that Greene had performed his customary magic and designed a formidable set of interlocking death traps. Although Howe possessed two-to-one superiority in troop strength, he never gave a thought to mounting a frontal attack against such concentrated firepower.

Patrols sent out to probe for possible flanking routes reported that all paths were either impassable or heavily defended. All but one, it turned out. Far to the east, nearly seven miles from the American center on Gowanus Heights, known only by local farmers (who just happened to be loyalists), lay Jamaica Pass. Upon learning of this neglected path, Clinton immediately recognized it as the key to the battle for Long Island. He proposed a flanking maneuver up Jamaica Pass that would place British troops behind American entrenchments on Gowanus Heights, thereby cutting off their retreat to the forts on Brooklyn Heights. He also proposed a diversion by British and Hessian troops that engaged the right and center of the American defensive front until they found themselves surrounded. It was a simple but brilliant plan, the obvious solution to Howe's tactical dilemma. Howe's initial instinct was to reject it, as he did everything proposed by the obnoxious Clinton. But after Clinton persuaded a junior officer to suggest the same plan, Howe nodded in agreement and embraced it as his own idea.[42]

Clinton led the vanguard, Howe the main body, as 10,000 British troops marched up Jamaica Pass all through the night, emerging behind American lines in the early morning of August 27. The fact that they were not detected was a testament to the largely loyalist population on Long Island, where the British enjoyed an intelligence advantage never again duplicated in the war. Approximately 3000 American troops were now surrounded, vastly outnumbered, and quickly began to retreat across Gowanus Creek toward the forts on Brooklyn Heights. Many were gunned down while crossing the creek, which was soon covered with their floating bodies. Efforts to surrender in some quarters proved equally fatal, as Hessian and Highlander troops massacred whole clusters of prisoners, pinning some of them to trees with bayonets.[43]

Bravery was also on display, especially on the right flank of the

American line, where Lord Stirling led his Maryland regiment of continentals, an elite unit, on three suicidal charges—400 against 2000—that provided cover for the other American troops fleeing to the forts. The Marylanders suffered 90 percent casualties, though Stirling miraculously survived. Stirling's biographer described him as "an overweight, rheumatic, vain, pompous, gluttonous, inebriate." On this day, however, he "fought like a wolf." Stirling surrendered his sword to the Hessian commander before he could be executed by the surrounding troops.

It was all over in two hours. Washington, who had watched the debacle with his spyglass from Brooklyn Heights, at one point was heard to murmur "Good God: What brave fellows I must this day lose." American losses totaled 1100 killed, wounded, or captured. British losses were about one-third that number. Approximately 2000 Americans made it back to the forts, where 6000 troops were waiting to receive them.[44]

Howe then faced a decision. His regulars were moving toward the forts on their own initiative, feeling the momentum on the battlefield push them onward. The British troops below Gowanus Heights had by now come up to join the fight, giving Howe's army a three-to-one superiority in numbers over the entrenched but dazed Americans. All the energies in play had converged behind one great surging line of redcoated professionals with fixed bayonets, leaning forward, all knowing without any orders from superior officers what they had to do. Only an unexpected command to halt in midflight could have stopped the inexorable flow of the British advance.

When Howe gave that order, his staff was understandably surprised. Clinton was astonished. In his memoir, he recalled the moment. "Complete success would have most likely been the consequence," Clinton claimed with considerable evidence to support the claim. Then he added, with all the retrospective wisdom of hindsight, "For there is no way of saying to what extent the effect resulting from the entire loss of the [American] army might have been in that early stage of the rebellion, or where it would have stopped." (It is easy to understand why Howe despised Clinton.) William Willcox, Clinton's biographer, whose analysis of Clinton's emotional handicaps defies comparison in the scholarship on British conduct of the war, ended up endorsing Clinton's verdict that, by stopping the attack on Brooklyn Heights, "Howe lost as good a chance as Britain ever had of winning the war in a stroke."[45]

That was also the verdict of Israel Putnam. "Old Put" was looking down from the trenches of Brooklyn Heights, fully expecting, as the warrior he was, to go down fighting when overwhelmed by the advancing British wave. When that did not happen, Putnam observed that "General Howe is either our friend or no general," for there was no doubt in Putnam's mind that "Howe had our whole army in his power. Had he instantly followed up his victory, the consequences to the cause of liberty must have been dreadful."[46]

Howe's response to these hostile verdicts need not be conjured up. (He defended his conduct before Parliament soon after his return to England three years later.) Howe fully acknowledged that his troops were eager to advance on the American defenses, "and had they been permitted to go on, it is my opinion they would have carried the redoubt." Without mentioning the memory of Bunker Hill, Howe explained that a frontal attack against the formidable network of American forts and trenches would have generated considerable casualties "and I would not risk the loss that might have been sustained in the assault, so ordered them back." Moreover, again as Howe explained, a frontal assault was unnecessary, "because it was apparent the [American] lines must have been ours by regular approaches within a matter of days." By "regular approaches" Howe meant a tactical siege using angled trenches that eventually squeezed the beleaguered rebel force into submission. Howe was also at pains to remind his London critics that the troops under his command were a precious commodity, not easily replaced from across the Atlantic, so that limiting his losses had always been his professional priority. All those second-guessers on the back benches of Parliament who had never heard a shot fired in anger might wish to summon a decent measure of respect for an experienced officer's judgment, made in the heat of battle.[47]

What Howe's retrospective argument failed to address was the strategic context of his decision at the base of Brooklyn Heights. For one extended moment, so it seemed to all witnesses, the fate of the war for American independence hung in the balance, and in that moment, Howe hesitated. Clinton clearly saw the opportunity to end the war in one decisive battle that destroyed the Continental Army. Howe failed to see the opportunity because he was not looking for it. The annihilation of the Continental Army was never a picture Howe carried in his head. He and his brother harbored a more diplomatic vision in which the war ended with an embrace of Washington and his staff rather than a sordid saunter over their dead bodies. Even more specifically, when Howe halted the assault on Brooklyn Heights, he assumed that Washington and his army were trapped. For good reason, he gave no thought to the possibility they might escape.

It took a full month for Howe's report of the British victory on Long Island to reach Germain, who could not wait to apprise George III. "Indeed the leaders of the rebellion have acted as I could have wished," Germain observed—that is, they attempted to defend New York—"and I trust that the deluded people will soon have recourse to your friendship for mercy and protection, leaving their chiefs to receive the punishment they deserve."* His strategy for ending the rebellion decisively with a full commitment of Britain's military resources had apparently proved successful. It would be remembered as a one-battle

---

* Lord Germain's vision was less amicable than Howe's. He presumed that the leaders of the rebellion would be brought back to England, tried and convicted of treason, suffer a public hanging, then be drawn and quartered, their severed heads placed on spits as object lessons for the proper duration.

war. Germain began doing the paperwork for William Howe's elevation to a knighthood.[48]

Meanwhile, up on Brooklyn Heights, Washington was staring into the abyss. He was actually looking down the slope, where 25,000 British troops were encamped about six hundred yards away. A regiment of British engineers could be heard digging their angled trenches in a classic siege project. It began to rain heavily on August 28. As Washington rode along the American front, he could see the trenches in some sectors flooding, the sentries standing waist deep in water, tying their powder horns around their necks in order to keep their powder dry. Fatigued from lack of sleep, he inexplicably ordered another thousand troops over from Manhattan, thereby enlarging the size of his trapped army to almost 10,000 men. At this point, Washington believed he only had two options: surrender, or fight and face annihilation.

His initial instinct was to choose the second option. In the Washington calculus, retreat was not a viable choice, since it was blocked by an emotional wall separating honorable from dishonorable behavior. Surrender fell on the wrong side of that wall, thereby placing a permanent stain on his character that Washington regarded as worse than death itself. So the only choice was between death and dishonor, which in the Washington moral universe was really no choice at all.

Joseph Reed, his adjutant general, was the first person to challenge Washington's honor-driven impulses. In a letter to his wife, Reed seemed to indicate that he believed the original decision to defend New York had always been a mistake, placing the army "on this tongue of land, where we ought never have been." Now the full implications of that elemental blunder were looming large for all to see, and he pressed Washington to recognize that his highest obligation was not to his own code of honor, but to the survival of the Continental Army. In the present crisis, that meant getting off Long Island.[49]

On the twenty-ninth, Reed's recommendation received a strong endorsement from General Thomas Mifflin, who reported that troop morale in the trenches was low, with several units threatening to throw aside their muskets—the driving rain had rendered them useless—and surrendering en masse to British sentries. Mifflin then made a proposal calculated to override Washington's honor-driven mentality. If Washington were to convene a council of war, Mifflin volunteered to recommend an evacuation of the Continental Army across the East River to Manhattan. If and when the other general officers endorsed that recommendation, which seemed highly likely, Washington could embrace that judgment while preserving the pretense that he himself preferred to go down fighting. Mifflin would maintain his own honor by insisting that his Pennsylvania troops remain in the trenches until all other units had evacuated, and therefore run the greatest risk of being killed or captured.[50]

The council of war met that afternoon at Four Chimneys, a baronial estate with a panoramic view of the East River near the modern-day Brooklyn Bridge. The vote was unanimous, following precisely the script that Mifflin had proposed. Now, in a matter of hours, a group of inexperienced officers needed to plan and conduct one of the most difficult tactical retreats in military history. A recent Yale graduate, Major Benjamin Tallmadge, later remembered most vividly the challenge they faced: "To move so large a body of troops, with all their necessary appendages, across a river full a mile wide, with rapid currents, in face of a victorious well disciplined army nearly three times as numerous as his own, and a fleet capable of stopping the navigation, so that not one boat could have passed over, seemed to present most formidable obstacles."[51]

The tactical retreat of an army engaged with a larger enemy force is so difficult to orchestrate because units have to be removed piecemeal, in staged fashion, leaving a sufficient complement of troops to hold the perimeter. Timing, therefore, has to be precise, and the remaining troops need to spread out to replace those just evacuated. Most modern-day military manuals describe such a retreat as the most dangerous maneuver in warfare, only to be attempted by experienced troops in the most desperate situations. On Long Island that August night, desperation was present in great supply; experience was nonexistent.

There was one conspicuous exception, and his name was John Glover. Washington had first encountered Colonel Glover and his regiment of Marblehead fishermen during the Boston Siege, where their combination of military discipline and seasoned seamanship was put on display in the tricky currents of Massachusetts Bay. Since then, the so-called Marblehead Mariners had acquired a reputation as an elite unit of soldier-sailors who also looked the part. Their distinctive uniforms featured white caps, short blue coats, and canvas breeches waterproofed with tar. When they landed on Long Island and disembarked from their rowboats carrying their muffled oars like muskets, it was like watching the cavalry come to the rescue. "Now these were the lads," one soldier at the dock observed, "who might do something." What they were about to do was demonstrate how an experienced team of veteran seamen staged a rescue operation at night. They were a match for the best seamen in the British navy.[52]

Deception was the essential ingredient in the evacuation plan. Only a few of the officers and none of the enlisted men knew what was happening when the order to "go under arms with packs" came down the line. In many units, the soldiers assumed they were about to attack the British trenches and began to make out their wills in anticipation of certain death. Tench Tilghman, a young lieutenant soon to become one of Washington's most trusted aides, reported that whole regiments moved to the rear bewildered about their destination: "The thing was conducted with such secrecy that neither subalterns nor privates knew that the whole army was to cross back again to New York." Over fifty years later, Joseph Plumb Martin, a young private in the Connecticut line, remembered it as the only "whispering moment" in the war. "All orders were communicated to men in whispers," he recalled, "the troops forming various conjectures among themselves as to our destination."[53]

A military operation with so many moving parts was bound to generate unexpected mishaps. A potentially fatal blunder occurred when Mifflin received a misguided order to withdraw his Pennsylvania troops earlier than expected. Mifflin questioned the order, since the American front would be undefended once he ordered an evacuation, but reluctantly complied. While leading his troops to the river, Mifflin encountered Washington, whose astonished reaction was probably more colorful than the historical record provides: "Good God, General Mifflin, I am afraid you have ruined us!" Himself astonished, Mifflin tried to explain the mishap, then saluted and led his men back to their former positions. The American perimeter had been undefended for an hour, but the British had not noticed. Mifflin harbored a grievance against Washington—he felt his honor had been questioned—for the rest of the war.[54]

For those predisposed toward providential explanations, the gods seemed to be smiling on The Cause at dawn on August 30. Here is how Benjamin Tallmadge remembered the moment many years later:

> As the dawn of the next day approached, those of us who remained in the trenches became very anxious for our own safety, as the last to leave were more at risk. We also lacked the cover of darkness. At this time a very dense fog began to rise, and it seemed to settle in a peculiar manner over both encampments. I recollect this peculiar providential occurrence perfectly well; and so very dense was the atmosphere that I could scarcely discern a man at six yards' distance. . . . In the history of warfare I do not recollect a more fortunate retreat.[55]

While Tallmadge was being rowed across, one of Glover's seamen explained that, as a nor'eastern storm subsided, it not only produced the fog but also shifted the winds to the southeast, so the boats were now moving with, rather than against, the current. This weather change should have prompted the appearance of British warships, which would have transformed the American evacuation into a full-scale massacre, since the overloaded rowboats were defenseless. But Lord Howe, uncharacteristically, never noticed the wind shift and never brought the British fleet into play. As Tallmadge's boat approached the Manhattan shore, he looked back with his spyglass to see Washington stepping into the last boat to leave Long Island. It was the stuff of legend. In all, nearly 10,000 men were safely ferried to Manhattan with only three stragglers lost.*[56]

THE INITIAL BRITISH reaction was disbelief. Captain George Collier, commander of the warship *Rainbow*, spoke for his fellow officers in the Royal Navy:

> To my inexpressible astonishment and concern the rebel army have all escaped across the [East] River to New York! How this has happened is surprising, for had our troops followed them close up [at Brooklyn Heights], they must have thrown down their arms and surrendered; or had our ships patrolled the river, which we have been in constant expectation of being ordered to do, not a man would have escaped Long Island. Now, I foresee, they will give us trouble enough, and protract the war, Heaven know's how long.[57]

There had been muttered criticism of William Howe's decision to forgo an attack on the forts at Brooklyn Heights. (Henry Clinton was the chief mutterer.) Now that the Continental Army had somehow escaped its apparent fate in the forts, the criticism grew louder. Captain Collier added the voice of a naval officer to the rumor mill. In Lord Richard's case, how could he have possibly failed to deploy British warships in the East River? Why had both the Howe brothers missed such obvious opportunities to destroy the rebel army?

---

* For the nearly synonymous escape from slavery at Mount Vernon, see the profile of Harry Washington at the end of this chapter.

As far as Richard Howe was concerned, on the evening of August 30 his attention was elsewhere. He was dining on his flagship, *Eagle*, with two American generals captured on Long Island, Lord Stirling and John Sullivan. Howe was attempting to assess whether their recent humiliation had at least opened their minds to the terms he was prepared to propose again, not as an admiral, but as a peace commissioner. Although Stirling was unmoved, Sullivan found Lord Richard's personal sincerity compelling. He agreed to carry Howe's diplomatic message to the delegates in the Continental Congress for their consideration.

Both Howe brothers were once again thinking like diplomats rather than military officers. As commanders of His Majesty's forces, they had delivered a sufficiently potent blow to the Continental Army, enough to demonstrate the utter futility of the rebel cause. Based on the debacle on Long Island, it should be clear to any sensible set of American leaders that their army of rank amateurs had no chance against the experienced professionals of the British army and navy. One of William Howe's chief lieutenants, General Hugh Percy, confirmed that strategic assessment: "I may venture to assert," Percy observed, "that they will never again stand against us in the field. Everything seems to be over with them, and I flatter myself that this campaign will put a total end to the war." The almost inexplicable escape of the Continental Army demonstrated only that the Americans were most proficient at running away. But the will of the rebellion had been broken. It was now time, so the Howe brothers were thinking, to allow these hard facts to settle in, revert to the preferred roles as peace commissioners, and negotiate a speedy end to the senseless conflict. The iron fist had done its work. The Howes were again wearing their velvet gloves.[58]

When General Sullivan carried Howe's message to the Continental Congress on September 2, he received a decidedly cool reception. The overwhelming consensus was that Sullivan had allowed himself to be duped by Howe. Benjamin Rush, a Pennsylvania delegate, recalled that John Adams "whispered to me a wish that the first ball that had been fired on the day of the defeat of our army had gone through [Sullivan's] head." Adams then rose to describe Sullivan as an enemy agent, "a decoy duck whom Lord Howe had sent among us to Seduce us into a renunciation of independence." He reminded his colleagues that any proposal to retrace their steps must now be considered a treasonable act.[59]

John Witherspoon, president of the College of New Jersey (now Princeton), echoed the Adams assessment. "It is plain," said Witherspoon, "that absolute unconditional submission is what [Howe] requires," and that no man within earshot was prepared to contemplate that possibility. He also presumed that no delegate in the Continental Congress trusted the generosity of George III as much as Lord Howe apparently did. Despite these reservations, Witherspoon saw no harm in indulging the good lord's misguided fancies, going the proverbial extra mile in order to demonstrate due diligence to all concerned. The congress then voted to send a three-man delegation to confer with Howe "to hear any Propositions his Lordship may think proper to make." By choosing John Adams, Benjamin Franklin, and Edward Rutledge, a young but ardently patriotic South Carolinian, the congress virtually assured that Lord Howe's fondest hopes would be dashed. The only high-level conference between diplomatic representatives of both sides during the war occurred on Staten Island on September 11.[60]

Howe assured that all the civilities were conspicuously observed. Two rows of Hessian troops saluted the American delegation as it entered a large stone dwelling, ever after called Conference House. Howe had seen to it that the meeting room was decorated with green sprigs, moss, and flowers; a sumptuous spread included "claret, good Bread, Cold Ham, Tongues, and Mutton." The atmosphere was designed to convey a mood of mutual affection among members of the Anglo-American family, who had recently argued but were now coming together to patch up their differences. Howe was hoping to orchestrate a diplomatic breakthrough in the guise of a family reunion.[61]

In an effort to give diplomatic emphasis to that theme, Howe opened the discussion by declaring that he "felt for Americans as a brother, and if America should fall, he should lament it like the loss of a brother." Adams remembered to his dying days Franklin's deft response: "Dr. Franklin, with an easy air and collected countenance, a bow, a smile, and all the Naiveté which sometimes appeared in his conversation and is often observed in his writing, replied, 'My Lord, we will do our utmost to save your Lordship that mortification.' "[62]

In addition to expressing his deep affection for America, Howe had intended his opening remark as a thinly veiled reference to the humiliating defeat suffered by the Continental Army on Long Island. He assumed that the obvious superiority of British arms had created the context for the conference by casting a deep shadow over America's military prospects in the war. Instead, he quickly discovered that the American delegation seemed oblivious to the near-death experience of the Continental Army. The Howe brothers had staged a successful demonstration of British military invincibility, and the Americans did not seem to have noticed. Even if the Continental Army were completely destroyed, his guests seemed to believe, they would simply raise another army.[*]

Whether or not that belief was realistic or delusional, no one could say. The improbable escape of the Continental Army deferred that question at least temporarily. Howe had hoped to find—as he apparently found in General Sullivan—some flexibility in the American posture, some realization that they were holding a weak hand after Long Island. Instead, he discovered a negotiating team united on the principle of American independence. "Is there no way of treading back this Step

---

[*] Franklin had recently written a letter to Howe, but chose not to send it, describing the British cause as hopeless and predicting that the war would prove just as ruinous for Great Britain "as the Croisades [Crusades] formerly were to most of the Nations of Europe." In a subsequent letter to a friend he amplified his point. "For what have they done with their army and fleet? They have got possession of three small Islands on the coast of America, and yet if every Acre of American territory is contested the same proportion, the Conquest would ruin all Europe." See *The Papers of Benjamin Franklin*, 22:518–20, 575.

of Independence," Howe plaintively asked, "and opening the door to a full discussion?"[63]

There was not. Franklin, who did most of the talking for the Americans, reminded Howe that the colonists had proposed a new imperial framework in which they retained control over their own domestic affairs, including taxation, but George III had summarily rejected those terms, and there was nothing in Lord Howe's mandate as peace commissioner that permitted him to revisit the sovereignty question. The Americans had decided to answer that question for themselves, declared their independence, and there was no turning back. Near the end, Rutledge suggested that, since American independence was a nonnegotiable fact, perhaps Howe could persuade his friends back in London to embrace it, at which point all the mutual affection he remembered so fondly could be recovered in an Anglo-American economic alliance that offered commercial advantages to both parties. By now resigned to failure, Howe expressed his doubts that any of his superiors in London would find that idea attractive.

He undoubtedly shared his sense of disappointment with his brother, who was holding his troops in reserve on Long Island, hoping he would not need to fight another battle. But Lord Howe left no written record of his thoughts. His rather snobbish secretary, Ambrose Serle, did record his own thoughts later that night: "They met, they talked, they parted. And now nothing remains but to fight it out against a set of the most determined Hypocrits & Demagogues compiled by the refuse of the Colonies that were ever permitted by the Providence to be the Scourge of a Country." Serle's condescending presumption of British superiority provided a convenient reminder of the deeper reasons that American independence had become nonnegotiable.[64]

THE ONLY DOWNSIDE of the brilliantly conducted evacuation of Long Island was that it marooned the Continental Army on Manhattan, another island. Although initially dazed in the immediate aftermath of the Great Escape—he had not slept for forty-eight hours—Washington was soon apprised that he had only escaped into another trap. The New York Committee of Safety and General John Morin Scott both wrote the commander in chief on August 31 to warn that the only avenue off the island was King's Bridge, which crossed the Harlem River at the northern tip of Manhattan: "Should the Enemy occupy it, we have reason to dread the Consequences." General Scott was more specific. "By this Maneuver, we shall be encircled with the same Kind of danger that we had Reason to apprehend on the Other Side of the Water." Two days later, Colonel Rufus Putnam reported that his reconnaissance of the terrain around King's Bridge indicated there was no way to prevent a large British force from landing there, "placing the Continental Army in a Bad Box."[65]

In response to this intelligence, Adjutant General Joseph Reed concluded that, since the British were unlikely to allow another miraculous escape—this time across the Hudson—the goal of the Continental Army should be to delay the inevitable on Manhattan for as long as possible. "Our comfort is that the season is far advanced," he wrote his wife, "and if a sacrifice of us can save the cause of America, there will be time to collect another army before spring, and the Country will be preserved." For the moment, Reed was resigned to regarding the Continental Army as expendable.[66]

Meanwhile, over on Long Island, several British officers—Henry Clinton most vocally—were resigned to the realization that their commander seemed strangely uninterested in closing the trap at King's Bridge or, for that matter, doing anything at all. And they were right. William Howe was content to delay any military decision until he heard from his brother about the outcome of the conference on Staten Island. "For many succeeding days," Captain George Collier later recalled, "did our brave veterans, consisting of twenty-two thousand men, stand on the banks of the East River, like Moses at Mount Pisgah, looking at their promised land, little more than half a mile distant."[67]

It does not require hindsight to know what each side should have done in the strategic situation facing them in early September 1776. The British should have blocked the American exit off Manhattan. Henry Clinton made that argument in his customary fashion, which Howe, in his own fashion, dismissed as irrelevant. The Americans should have moved quickly to northern Manhattan and fought their way off the island before the full strength of the British army and navy could be brought to bear. The American officer most forcefully making that argument on the American side was Nathanael Greene, here emerging as the only senior officer prepared to confront Washington with advice he did not want to hear.

On September 5, now recovered from his bout with malaria, Greene wrote Washington, mincing no words: "The object under consideration is whether a General and speedy retreat from the Island is Necessary or not. To me it appears the only Eligible plan to oppose the enemy successfully and secure ourselves from Disgrace. I think we have no object on this side of King's Bridge. I would burn the City & suburbs."[68]

Greene's forceful recommendation faced two obstacles. The first was the standing order of the Continental Congress to defend the city and port of New York from British occupation. It was clear the delegates in Philadelphia did not appreciate the existential threat facing the Continental Army; it was also clear that following Greene's advice meant violating the principle of civilian control. The second obstacle was more intractable; it was Washington himself.

Put simply, Washington found it impossible to order another retreat. He had been persuaded, against his will, to order the evacuation of Long Island. Now that same will was reasserting control, telling him that retreat was defeat, which would leave a permanent stain on his reputation. In a long letter to Hancock on September 8, his honor-driven instincts took refuge behind his standing orders to defend New York. He also mixed together his personal reasons for rejecting Greene's advice and the likely impact another conspicuous failure would have on popular opinion out there in the countryside: "I am sensible a retreating Army is encircled with difficulties, that the declining an Engagement subjects a General to reproach, and that the Common Cause may be affected by the discouragement it may throw over the minds of many. Nor am I insensible of the contrary Effect if a brilliant stroke could be made with any probability of Success, especially after our loss upon Long Island." In effect, he could not order a retreat until he had fought and won a major battle that would redeem his honor and reassure wavering patriots.[69]

Washington's divided mind became the basis for the split-the-difference strategy adopted by the council of war. The Continental Army would be distributed across Manhattan in three groupings: 5000 troops would defend New York City at the southern tip of the island; 9000 would assemble at King's Bridge, poised to lead a breakout; the remaining 4000, the most inexperienced, would be stationed in the middle of the island, where a British attack was least expected. Though he believed he had no choice, by dividing his force to cover the entire island, Washington virtually assured that the British would enjoy overwhelming supremacy at whatever point of attack they chose. Not so incidentally, he was risking the loss of the entire Continental Army in order to strike some "brilliant stroke."

This was a recipe for catastrophe. The obligation to deliver that message to Washington fell to Greene, who called a covert meeting of the other general officers on September 11. The result took the form of a petition arguing that "the present Case is of such Magnitude and big with such Consequences to all America that a Breach of common Form is necessary." Washington could have rejected the petition outright as an act of insubordination, but coming as it did from Greene, whose judgment he had come to trust implicitly, Washington agreed to call another council of war on September 12.[70]

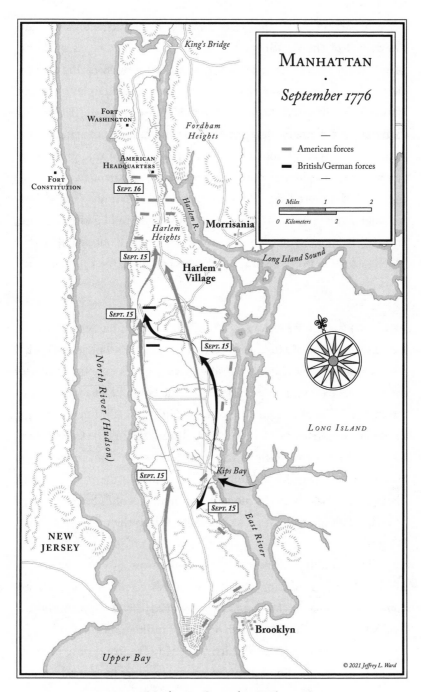

Manhattan, September 1776

By a vote of 10–3, the council of war recommended immediate withdrawal of the Continental Army from Manhattan. As on Long Island, Washington was able to preserve his honor by accepting the verdict while registering his personal preference to stay and fight. He wrote Hancock the next day, almost apologetically explaining the decision to abandon the defense of New York City. "But I am fully convinced that it cannot be done," he concluded, and "an attempt for that purpose, if persevered in, might and most certainly would be attended with consequences the most fatal and alarming in their nature." Greene had apparently convinced Washington that his highest obligation was not to retain his honor intact, but to avoid losing the Continental Army, which had become the institutional embodiment of The Cause itself.[71]

THE AMERICAN RETREAT up Manhattan began on September 14, the day after General Howe learned that his brother's diplomatic initiative on Staten Island had failed. Now that his hopes for a quick end to the war were dashed, Howe needed to decide how and where to resume the conflict. The obvious answer was to deploy his full force at King's Bridge at the northern tip of the island, thereby sealing the Continental Army in the same water-lined trap they had escaped on Long Island. Howe instead opted for an amphibious landing in the middle of the island at Kips Bay (between modern-day 32nd and 38th Streets), where he could deliver another punishing blow akin to the one delivered on Long Island.

Clinton led the advance party of 4000 troops, preceded by a massive bombardment during which five British warships unleashed an hour-long barrage that completely destroyed the shallow American trench line on the beach; the inexperienced militia units fled in horror. Clinton had orders to await the arrival of Howe's second wave of 9000 troops before proceeding across the island, an order he obeyed against his own instincts. If he had followed those instincts, the 5000 American troops under Israel Putnam coming up what is now West Street would have been trapped. Instead, Old Put, always at his best in a crisis, hurried his troops forward with encouraging expletives. Those troops included Alexander Hamilton and Aaron Burr, who twenty-eight years later would cross the same section of the Hudson River to fight the most famous duel in American history.[72]

It was Long Island all over again, though the American casualties were fewer because the militia ran away faster. Washington encountered the frantic troops in full flight while riding south to the sound of gunfire. One witness reported that "he struck several officers [with the flat of his sword], three times dashed his hatt to the ground" all the while cursing at the cowardice of the terrified troops who ran past him. The approaching British infantry came within fifty yards, but his staff could not persuade their commander to leave the field. Greene thought that Washington was deliberately exposing himself to danger, indeed was "so vext that he sought Death rather than life." Eventually someone, possibly his slave Billy Lee, grabbed the reins of his horse and led Washington to safety, protesting all the way. From that moment onward, Joseph Reed began to harbor doubts about Washington's fitness to command an army, when he could not command himself.[73]

The retreating troops began to reassemble again at Harlem Heights, just north of present-day 125th Street. It was a natural fortress with its south side protected by steep rocky bluffs nearly sixty feet high. Harlem Heights became the perfect place for the Continental Army to rest and restore its energy for the final race up Manhattan. Howe was leaving the escape route open by concentrating British troops on the southern tip of Manhattan, where they were being greeted as liberators by the loyalists in New York City. But instead of accepting Howe's invitation to escape, Washington issued orders to dig in atop Harlem Heights. Having discovered the perfect New York version of Bunker Hill, he abandoned his planned retreat and invited Howe to attack.

Rational explanations fail to do justice to Washington's thought process at the time, which was confused and deeply fatalistic. All his emotional baggage was fully exposed in a letter to Lund Washington, his manager at Mount Vernon:

> Such is my situation that if I were to wish the bitterest curse to an enemy on this side of the grave, I should put him in my stead with my feelings; and yet I do not know what plan of conduct to pursue. I see the impossibility of serving with reputation, or doing any essential service to the cause by continuing in command, and yet I am told that if I quit the command inevitable ruin with follow from the distraction that will ensue. In confidence I tell you that I never was in such an unhappy, divided state since I was born.[74]

His final words verged on the suicidal: "If I fall, it may not be amiss that these circumstances be known, and declaration made in credit to the justice of my character. And if the men stand by me (which by the by I despair of), I am resolved not to be forced from this ground while I still have life." He was preparing to join Joseph Warren on the list of American martyrs.[75]

William Howe was not disposed to accommodate Washington's quest for martyrdom. In fact, Howe was probably the last officer in the British army willing to consider a frontal assault on the cliffs of Harlem Heights. He was, however, disposed to dispatch reconnaissance patrols to locate the perimeter of the American defenses. At the same time, on September 16, Washington ordered Colonel Thomas Knowlton and his newly created band of Connecticut rangers, an elite unit, to locate the disposition of British troops to the south. What became the Battle of Harlem Heights began as an accidental encounter between Knowlton's 150 rangers and an undersized British regiment of 400 regulars near the present juncture of 107th Street and Riverside Drive.[76]

A fierce skirmish then ensued in which Knowlton's reputation as one of the most gifted combat commanders in the Continental Army proved justified. (A veteran of the French and Indian War, Knowlton's combat credentials became legendary after his heroics at Bunker Hill, subsequently immortalized in John Trumbull's painting of the battle, where Knowlton is the central figure.) Fighting behind a stone wall, Knowlton's troops inflicted heavy casualties on the fully exposed British soldiers, but were then forced to retreat when a full-sized regiment of Scottish Highlanders, the renowned Black Watch, came up to support their embattled comrades. Accustomed to seeing American soldiers in full flight, the poise of Knowlton's troops, who kept firing during their withdrawal, surprised the Highlanders. But their bugler defiantly sounded the signal used in fox hunts, when the fox is trapped.

In fact, it was the overconfident British and Scottish troops who were advancing into a trap. As they approached Harlem Heights, they found themselves enveloped by 5000 American soldiers coming down from the heights, their blood up because of the insulting British bugler. In the fierce fighting that ensued Knowlton went down, hit in the lower back while exhorting his troops from an exposed ledge. His purported last words, duly reported within weeks in most American newspapers, were the stuff of martyrdom: "I do not value my life if we do but get this day."[77]

Knowlton got his wish. Both sides threw more men into the action, transforming the skirmish into a small-scale battle involving 6000 soldiers. The British extricated themselves from the killing zone at the base of Harlem Heights, then made a stand in a wheat field just south of where Grant's Tomb is today. After two hours of furious fighting, having suffered 270 killed or wounded to 60 for the Americans, the redcoats were forced to withdraw. American troops, shouting "fox hunt," had to be restrained from pursuing the enemy beyond a safe range. It was the first occasion in the New York campaign when the British army experienced unequivocal defeat. In his general orders the following day, Washington chose to emphasize that very point: "The Behavior of Yesterday was such a Contrast to that of some Troops before, as must show what may be done when officers & soldiers will exert themselves."[78]

A strange interlude then ensued. The small but symbolic victory at Harlem Heights should have sufficed to restore Washington's wounded sense of honor, but it did not. The wound was too deep. Instead of resuming his retreat up Manhattan, he ordered his troops to deepen the trenches and strengthen the redoubts atop Harlem Heights. Having found the ideal defensive position, he chose to exploit it, hoping to entice Howe into another ruinous assault. For potent emotional reasons, he needed to win another battle, even if that meant risking himself and his army. But since Howe had no intention whatsoever of accepting Washington's offer, Washington was left to brood for three weeks about the reasons he found himself in the present predicament. Where had he failed? How much was he to blame for the debacles on Long Island and Kips Bay?

In a letter to Hancock, he deflected criticism from himself and located the fundamental flaw in a militia-based army: "When Men are irritated & the Passions inflamed, they fly hastily and cheerfully to Arms, but after the first emotions are over, to expect among such People as compose the Bulk of the Army that they are influenced by any other principles than those of Interest, is to look for whatever did, and I fear never will happen." He had been making a more restrained version of the same argument since the Boston Siege, but the headlong retreat of militia after Kips Bay enabled Washington to emphasize, in his most strident "I told you so" tone, the seriousness of the problem. "To place any dependence on Militia is, assuredly, resting upon a broken staff," he warned Hancock, "and will in my opinion prove the Ruin of our Cause."[79]

In one sense, Washington was looking backward, placing on the record his long-standing doubts about the reliability of militia. In case he went down, he wanted posterity to know his state of mind and his candid assessment of the weak hand he had been forced to play. In another sense, he was looking forward, projecting lessons of New York into the future. "It becomes evidently clear," he observed to Hancock, "that as this contest is not likely to be the work of a day, as the War must be carried on systematically, you must establish our Army on a permanent footing." The previous presumption (on both sides, in fact) that the war would be decided quickly, in one conclusive battle, was now exposed as an illusion. It was going to be a protracted conflict in which a passionate gush of patriotic energy (i.e., *rage militaire*) would not suffice, indeed would assuredly prove unsustainable.[80]

As if to make his point about the unreliability of militia, Washington allowed entire militia units to leave en masse, over 10,000 troops, effectively making them the first wave to evacuate Manhattan. This reduced his strength to 13,000 regulars, all dug in atop Harlem Heights, looking south, waiting for Howe to launch a frontal assault that would allow Washington to bloody Howe's army in one more battle before following the militia off the island.

By early October it had become obvious to the entire general staff that Howe had no intention of accepting the invitation to make Harlem Heights another Bunker Hill. At this point Joseph Reed began a whispering campaign against Washington, claiming that he was holding the fate of the Continental Army hostage to his own suicidal agenda. It was one thing for an honorable officer to risk death on the battlefield, quite another for a commander in chief to take the entire army with him. Reed argued that Washington was at least temporarily unfit to command and should be replaced by Charles Lee, recently returned from baffling the British in Charleston Harbor.[81]

It took two weeks for Washington to awake from his martyr complex. The awakening was prompted by intelligence reports that British transport ships were moving up the East River, presumably to block the exit ramp at King's Bridge. It was now obvious, even to Washington, that Howe refused to take the bait at Harlem Heights. On October 16 Washington requested a council of war to formulate an evacuation plan.[82]

Somewhat strangely, the council voted, with Washington's endorsement, to leave 2000 troops at Fort Washington. This made no tactical sense, since leaving a "castle in the rear" violated every principle of warfare. It did, however, make psychological sense in Washington's mind, as a statement that one part of him was not retreating. The statement proved costly when the entire garrison at Fort Washington, later reinforced to 2900 troops, was subsequently captured and imprisoned on the infamous ghost ships in New York Harbor, where the majority died of malnutrition and disease.[83]

Although William Howe harbored no martyr complex, he did retain his obsession with a diplomatic resolution of the war. And therefore, as he explained to Germain, instead of sealing the exit off Manhattan, he intended to leave the door ajar, then catch Washington's army in the open fields of the Bronx where he could "if possible bring him to action" on a conventional battlefield. His veteran troops virtually assured a decisive victory that would pave the way for a negotiated surrender and settlement.[84]

If the first escape across the East River was a dash, the second escape up Manhattan and across the Harlem River was a slog, requiring three days (October 18–21) to cover the twenty-one miles to White Plains. Fully a quarter of the 13,000 troops were sick or wounded; there were not enough horses to pull the wagons and cannons, which had to be hauled by hand; and food supplies were nonexistent, forcing troops to scavenge whatever they could find along the route. One soldier, Joseph Plumb Martin, remembered that he was required to carry a heavy iron cooking kettle, an ironic assignment since there was nothing to cook. The struggling parade of survivors was in no condition to fight, so if Howe had managed to catch them in full flight, the consequences would have been disastrous.[85]

Howe was in fact poised to do precisely that. On October 18, the same day the Continental Army began its evacuation, an invasion force of 4000 British and Hessian troops landed at Pell's Point in present-day Pel-

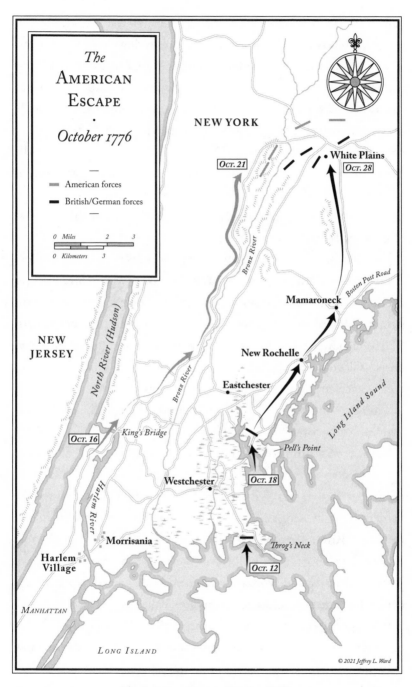

The American Escape, October 1776

ham. This was the advance party of a larger force Howe intended to lead across the Bronx River into the path of the retreating Continental Army.

Enter, once again, John Glover and his Marblehead Mariners, who had by chance been assigned to guard Pell's Point, this time coming to the rescue, with muskets rather than rowboats. Upon seeing a flotilla of two hundred British ships approaching his position, Glover remembered his hands were shaking: "Oh! the anxiety of mind I felt for the fate of that day." The anxiety was fully justified since he was outnumbered five to one. But Glover commanded some of the most disciplined troops in the Continental Army. He placed his 750 men behind a series of stone walls and invited an attack.

As the British and Hessian troops advanced, one row of Glover's men rose to fire, then retreated as the next row rose up to deliver another salvo, and so on from wall to wall. The net effect was a constant stream of lead providing no relief to the advancing columns of redcoats, who were mowed down before they came close enough to use their bayonets. (Glover later recalled that his men remained calm throughout the engagement, "almost as if they were shooting ducks.") The British lost more in one hour at Pell's Point than they lost in the entire New York campaign, over 300 dead and wounded, the Americans only 20.[86]

Howe was stunned when apprised of the unexpected setback. He ordered an immediate halt to the British advance inland. Glover's troops retreated to join Washington's army, which had just crossed the Harlem River at King's Bridge and was trudging up the west side of the Bronx River. They arrived at the hills of White Plains on October 21, two days before Howe's army was sighted on the southern horizon. The long-deferred and awkwardly executed second escape had just happened. Fortune or luck, what Washington called providence, had once again smiled upon The Cause, allowing it to survive an extended bout of honor-driven hesitancy that could have proven fatal. The window of opportunity for Great Britain to destroy the Continental Army had just closed.

PROFILE

HARRY WASHINGTON

In mid-August 1776, two weeks before Washington escaped across the East River, his enslaved namesake at Mount Vernon escaped down the Potomac. Harry Washington was not fleeing the British army, but seeking to join it. More specifically, he hoped to join what was called the Ethiopian Regiment recruited by the royal governor of Virginia, Lord Dunmore, who offered freedom to all Virginia slaves owned by rebels who joined his flotilla in the Chesapeake. When word spread through the slave community at Mount Vernon that Dunmore's ships were anchored at the mouth of the Potomac, it was all Harry needed to know. He commandeered a small skiff and sailed toward freedom.

The juxtaposition of the two Washingtons, each making bold dashes, one to escape capture or death, the other to escape enslavement, exposes the moral paradox that slavery posed for The Cause. For George Washington believed, with good reason, that he was fighting for American liberty from British tyranny. While Harry, for equally good reason, believed that Great Britain represented liberation from America's unique form of tyranny. Both men were acting on the same moral conviction about the primacy of independence.

Thanks to the prodigious research of the Australian historian Cassandra Pybus, we know what happened to Harry. It was a truly epic odyssey.

Dunmore's fleet deposited him in New York, where he was made a corporal in the Black Pioneers, a loyalist regiment attached to the Royal Artillery Department. He was in the British army that laid siege to Charleston in 1780 and remained with the British occupation there for two years before he returned to New York in 1782. On July 31, 1783, he boarded *L'Abondance* as part of the loyalist exodus bound for Nova Scotia.

Harry remained in the black loyalist community at Birchtown, Nova Scotia, for almost a decade. There he met and married Sarah, also a former slave, fathered three children, and worked a small farm. Conflicts with white loyalists in nearby Shelburne, plus the harsh Canadian winters, prompted an exodus of one thousand black loyalists to the British colony of Sierra Leone in 1792. Harry and his family joined the exodus. A year later he owned a small farm just outside the newly named Freetown.

The record goes quiet for eight years. Then, in 1800, the Freetown residents staged a protest against the Sierra Leone Company. (Intriguingly, they claimed they were being taxed without their consent.) As one had come to expect, Harry joined the protest, which was suppressed after considerable carnage by the British army. He appeared in the court records as one of the captured rebels. But instead of being executed for treason, he and his family were banished from Freetown.

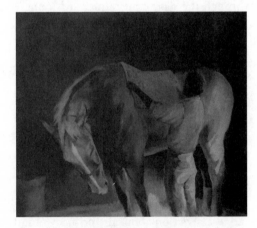

Harry Washington Saddling Nelson, a depiction by Marianne Miller, 2020. (Courtesy of Mount Vernon)

By then he was approaching seventy years, with multiple children and grandchildren. Most probably he lived out his life with the local Korya Temme tribe in the neighboring jungle. It was located only a few miles from the notorious prison camp where he had been held before boarding the slave ship that had carried him to Virginia fifty years earlier.

CHAPTER FOUR

The Few

We few, we happy few, we band of brothers;
For he to-day that sheds his blood with me
Shall be my brother.
—William Shakespeare, *Henry V*, Act 4

A mythical haze has settled over Valley Forge as the quintessential symbol of survival in the snow. There is even a painting entitled *Prayer in the Snow* done by Arnold Friberg for the bicentennial in 1976. It depicts Washington kneeling like a devout Christian, apparently asking for divine deliverance for his beleaguered troops at the winter camp. It never happened. Washington was a firm believer in providence, but he was never known to kneel, not even in church. Nor did he believe that God, if he did exist, ever saw fit to speak or listen personally to him.[1]

On the other hand, there really was blood on the snow, lots of it. Private Joseph Plumb Martin described the arrival of the Continental Army at Valley Forge on December 19, 1777, as "a cavalcade of wild beasts," twelve thousand barefoot soldiers trailing a ribbon of blood as

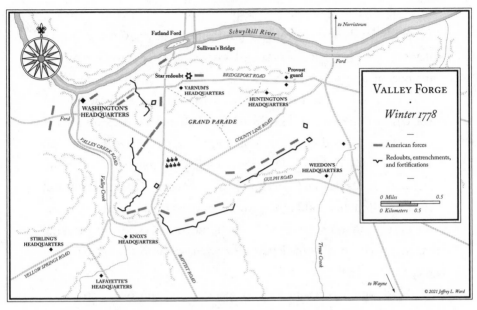

Valley Forge, Winter 1778

far behind them as the eye could see.* Washington himself confirmed the scene: "To see men without Clothes to cover their nakedness, without blankets, without shoes, by which their Marches might be traced by the Blood from their feet, is a mark of patience and obedience which in my opinion can scarcely be parallel'd."[2]

Floating above the blood on the ground was a palpable sense of desperation in the air. An army surgeon from Connecticut, Albigence Waldo, described a soldier named Will upon arrival at camp. He was without shoes, his breeches were no more than a loincloth, his hair was infested with lice, his body covered with sores. He kept repeating the lamentation, "I fail fast and soon I shall be no more."[3]

---

* Martin did not mention the "camp women" bringing up the rear. These were roughly five hundred wives, mothers, washerwomen, cooks, and prostitutes. Washington regretted their presence but admitted they performed essential services.

Will disappeared into the hospital system that, according to Dr. Benjamin Rush, was the rough equivalent of a death warrant: "I have made a discovery," Rush observed sarcastically, "a sure and certain method of destroying Howe's whole army without powder and ball. Lead them thro' any of the locations where we have a hospital, and I will ensure that in six weeks there will not be a man of them alive." One of the first recorded deaths at Valley Forge was a former slave named Jethro, one of 750 African American soldiers in camp, who was found facedown in his tent on Christmas Day, the victim of malnutrition and exposure. Roughly 2500 others would join Jethro in the hereafter over the next six months, along with five hundred horses, whose decaying carcasses generated a smell that grew even worse in the spring when they unfroze.[4]

Washington confirmed the desperate condition of his soldiers a week after arriving at Valley Forge in a letter to Henry Laurens, the new president of the Continental Congress. The miserable status of the army, he wrote, "must be seen to be believed," and was "beyond my power to relieve or prevent." He described the small huts the troops were beginning to construct, each sixteen by twelve feet, with a dozen men to a hut. Within two weeks there would be a thousand huts, the distinctive feature of the Valley Forge encampment that modern-day tourists tend to most remember.* Washington then concluded with an ominous warning: "I am now convinced beyond a doubt, that unless some great capital change takes place, this army must inevitably be reduced to one or the other of these three things: starve—dissolve— or disperse."[5]

Several historians have called attention to the fact that Washington's warning was only an updated version of his longtime refrain about lack of support for the Continental Army; also that such complaints

---

* When all the soldiers, camp followers, and family visitors were counted, Valley Forge temporarily became the third-largest city in America, after Philadelphia and Boston.

had become a winter ritual, when annual enlistments expired and, like an accordion, the army contracted, only to expand again in the spring when new enlistments arrived. During the winter encampment at Morristown, New Jersey, the previous year, so the argument goes, conditions were just as bad, and the threat of dissolution even worse, when the army contracted to fewer than three thousand men who were "fit for duty." Once placed in this larger perspective, Valley Forge loses its distinctive status as an American Gethsemane—Washington kneeling in the snow—and Washington's ominous warning that the Continental Army was about to dissolve on its own accord becomes just another case of Washington being Washington.[6]

One prominent eyewitness disagreed. Future Chief Justice John Marshall was a twenty-two-year-old lieutenant in an elite Virginia rifle company at Valley Forge. (He was nicknamed Silverheels for his prowess in athletic competitions.) In his multivolume biography of Washington, Marshall made a point of endorsing Washington's appraisal. "The representations made in this letter," Marshall insisted, "were not exaggerated." He went on to describe men cutting off their frozen fingers; the nightly cacophony of moaning from those thousand huts. You had to be there to believe the suffering and sense of desperation. And Marshall had been there. He wanted his readers to know that Valley Forge was not just another difficult winter encampment. It was different. Valley Forge was the nadir, when The Cause almost died.[7]

IT WAS A MOMENT as well as a location, the time when the deeper problems generated by a protracted war began to afflict the Continental Army, which had been built for a sprint, not a marathon. Unlike the British army, a century-old institution, the American army was a three-year-old improvisation. In the fall of 1777, the quartermaster department and its operational arm, the commissary system, both of which had been functioning on an ad hoc basis under Thomas Mifflin, com-

pletely collapsed when Mifflin abruptly resigned. As a result, the pipe-
line of food and clothing stopped flowing just when the Continental
Army arrived at Valley Forge. And no organizational framework existed
to solve the problem.

It was also highly unlikely that the Continental Congress would
be able to help. That November the delegates made their final revisions
of the document that John Dickinson had drafted two summers earlier, outlining the shape of a new federal government. (The delay was
understandable; a war was going on.) The revised draft of the Articles
of Confederation deleted all references to congressional authority over
domestic policy except control over the postal service and currency.
What Dickinson had proposed as the loose framework for a national
government had become a confederation of sovereign states that explicitly repudiated any national aspirations for the term "United States."
The emergency powers exercised by the Continental Congress in 1775–
76 were officially ended. Washington began the practice of writing
Circular Letters to the States, since that was the many-headed beast
where the future fate of the Continental Army, now the only remaining
embodiment of national unity, would be decided.[8]

The singular embodiment of national unity was Washington himself. On the eve of Valley Forge, even that previously impregnable fortress was under assault on its flanks. A frontal attack on Washington's
reputation still assured a one-way ticket to oblivion, but he was vulnerable to sniping in the congress because of his failure to prevent William
Howe from capturing Philadelphia. The defeats suffered by the Continental Army at Brandywine Creek in September, then Germantown
in October, raised questions about Washington's competence as a battlefield commander, questions amplified by the spectacular victory of
Horatio Gates at Saratoga in October, which resulted in the capture
of General William Burgoyne's entire army of seven thousand troops.
For the first time in the war, there was a shadow hanging over the man
leading all those shoeless men staggering into Valley Forge.[9]

Nathanael Greene worried about a different kind of shadow, an emerging shadow of doubt and despair the officers' corps was casting over the entire camp. Resignations were up sharply.* Greene tried to explain the drop in morale to Washington: "Everybody expected a short and speedy issue to the unhappy dispute, and everyone felt a perfect freedom to make the necessary sacrifices to bring about a proper reconciliation." But now, after three grueling campaigns and no end in sight, the bloom was off the patriotic rose: "People began to think cooly, they compare their condition in the field with that at home—the situation of their families, and their future prospects grow into objects of importance. Every officer sais he is willing to bear a part of the problem, but a very few have resolution to engage under such a hopeless project as the present institution exhibits to the view of everyone in the services."[10]

The "present institution" was the Continental Army. Unlike the British army, where officers were aristocrats pursuing a professional career, officers in the Continental Army lacked aristocratic bloodlines with family fortunes; they viewed military service as a temporary interlude of commitment to a virtuous cause. That had worked for a while. But virtue was a perishable commodity that could not survive what had become a protracted war. Looking at those starving soldiers in the huts, it was difficult to avoid the conclusion that the Continental Army, instead of being indispensable, had become disposable.

Beyond much doubt, Valley Forge was a survival story. But it was also a pivotal moment in the war. To say that patriotism was dying would be excessive. It was, however, receding from the national to the state and local level, where it resided in provincial legislatures, the Committees of Safety, and militia units. As the sole remaining national expression of The Cause, the Continental Army had become an invaluable anachronism, still essential, but a dangerous and even alien presence. It must be sustained, but just barely, because it epitomized the

---

* Eventually, 635 officers resigned at Valley Forge.

kind of consolidated power that defied the republican principles it claimed to be fighting for. The very fact that it was undergoing a near-death experience at Valley Forge was actually somewhat comforting to many delegates in congress.

THE COMMON REFRAIN in Washington's early letters was a version of "you have to see it to believe it." Henry Laurens decided that the Continental Congress, now ensconced forty miles away in York, Pennsylvania, needed to do just that. In early January Laurens appointed a five-man Camp Committee, which took up residence in Valley Forge on January 28.* One of the members, Gouverneur Morris, a New Yorker famous for his wit, his way with words (and with other men's wives), quickly summed up both the urgency and irony of the situation: "The American Army in the Bosom of America is about to disband for want of something to eat."[11]

The irony of the famine—ten to fifteen men a day were dying of malnutrition and exposure—was that it was occurring squarely in the middle of the most productive farming region on the Atlantic coast, the proverbial breadbasket for all the middle states, the major source of wheat and flour exports to Europe and the Caribbean. The irony went even deeper, since most of the food supply was not flowing into Valley Forge, but rather to the British army in Philadelphia.

Washington had hesitated to send foraging patrols into the countryside, concerned that confiscating the wheat and beef of local residents would, as he put it to Laurens, "spread disaffection, jealousy, and fear in the very people we are fighting for." General Howe was not burdened with such reservations, so British foraging teams had swept through the local farms and skimmed off the cream of the country.

---

* Strictly speaking, the committee occupied quarters three miles west of Valley Forge at Moore House, a six-hundred-acre estate and mansion. The committee did not share the suffering it was witnessing.

Once Washington realized that his starving troops left him no choice, he ordered "a grand Forage" led by Nathanael Greene. The results were meager: "All of the cattle and most of the best Horses have already been carried into the City," Greene reported. "We take all the Horses, Cattle, Hogs, and Sheep fit for use, but the Country has been so gleaned that there is but little left." Greene also noted that it was heartbreaking to watch entire families sobbing as his team of soldiers carried off their entire food supply for the winter.[12]

The British had not only gotten there first, they were able to offer payment to all farmers who carried their produce to Philadelphia for sale. And they paid in specie, or pounds sterling. Because American currency was vastly inflated—the phrase "not worth a Continental" had already become familiar—the certificates the Continental Army issued as payment were virtually worthless. As a result, a steady stream of wagons loaded with food supplies began to flow into Philadelphia. "I can assure your Excellency," wrote one officer charged with monitoring the traffic on the roads, "that not less Flour than is sufficient to maintain Eight or Ten Thousand men goes daily to Philadelphia."[13]

The local farmers knew all the back roads, and trapped as they were between armies waging a foraging war, selling to the British was less a political statement than the only way to sustain their families. When one American militia officer, acting on his own, had two wagon drivers shot, then left their bodies on the road as a warning to others, farmers began to enlist their wives and daughters as drivers, correctly assuming that women were less likely to be harmed or arrested.[14]

The flow of supplies into Philadelphia continued, and Washington did not know how to stop it without taking drastic measures that alienated the locals: "The situation in this state is melancholy and alarming," he acknowledged. "We have daily proof that a majority of the people in this quarter are only restrained from supplying the Enemy with Horses and every other kind of necessary thro' fear of punishment, and although I have made a number of severe examples, I cannot put a stop to the intercourse." (His examples were two known loyalists who were tried and hanged for smuggling.) Meanwhile, British troops were snug, warm, and eating well courtesy of American farmers, while American soldiers twenty-three miles away were freezing and starving.[15]

Eventually, Washington found a one-word answer to the supply problem, and his name was Greene. In the absence of any logistical framework in the quartermaster department, the only solution was superb leadership by a single man, prepared to exercise total authority and then perform miracles. Nathanael Greene was the obvious choice. (Washington had let it be known that, if he went down in battle, Greene was his preference as successor.) Greene did not want the job— he joked that "no one had ever heard of a quartermaster in History"— but a request from Washington, endorsed unanimously by the Camp Committee, was the equivalent of a command.[16]

A small army of purchasers, contractors, and wagon masters was necessary to operate the quartermaster and commissary departments, where corruption and profiteering were presumed privileges of the trade. Greene fired the whole lot, delegated the commissary department to a savvy Connecticut merchant named Jeremiah Wadsworth, and expanded the range of foraging teams into New Jersey, Delaware, and Maryland. Before the first daffodils appeared among the melting snow in April, a reliable supply of food was flowing into Valley Forge. Starvation ceased to be a threat to the survival of the Continental Army.

ANOTHER THREAT, less palpable than starvation but more politically troubling, had been brewing for several months before it reached a climax at Valley Forge. Historians have called it the Conway Cabal, although, as we shall see, it is somewhat misnamed, and there is even disagreement among scholars about whether it deserves to be called a cabal. Beyond any doubt, however, there was a whispering campaign within the congress criticizing Washington's leadership of the Continental Army. A faction within congress, led by Thomas Mifflin and Benjamin Rush, both of whom felt they had been treated badly by Washington,* was promoting Horatio Gates, who was a willing accomplice in the scheme, to replace Washington as commander in chief.[17]

There was nothing wholly new about such behind-the-scenes scheming. Generals who lose battles are always subject to second-guessing, and Washington had lost more than his fair share of battles during the first three years of the war. His own adjutant general, Joseph Reed, had launched a covert campaign against Washington in the fall of 1776, citing Washington's "near fatal indecision" on Manhattan. In his private correspondence with General Charles Lee, Reed had suggested that Lee was vastly preferable as commander in chief, feeding gossip mills within the officers' corps that Washington was simply not up to the task. But nothing came of that effort except Reed's eventual resignation. And shortly thereafter, in December 1776, Lee took himself out of the picture by getting captured by a British cavalry patrol while spending a night with an available woman in a New Jersey tavern subsequently named Cupid's Cove.† Prior to Valley Forge, then, while Washington was hardly immune to criticism, most especially for his tactical blunders against Howe, any such criticism remained covert, clandestine, and ineffectual. His stature as the singular embodiment of The Cause rendered any public assault on his reputation almost treasonable.

Washington customarily chose silence as his preferred posture toward all critics, but several friends persuaded him that the gossip about Gates required a response. He concurred in a letter to William Gordon, a friend whom he knew would leak it to the Pennsylvania press. It was

---

* Mifflin believed that Washington had unfairly accused him of disobeying orders during the nighttime escape across the East River in late August 1776. Rush blamed Washington for not supporting him in his efforts to reform the hospital system at Valley Forge.

† Lee's eccentricities were legion. The most experienced senior officer in the Continental Army, Lee also spoke seven languages, carried a copy of Thucydides in his breast coat, and had a pack of dogs at his heels when going into battle. His dress and physical appearance were conspicuously slovenly, and his flair for eloquent profanities conveyed the impression of calculated irreverence.

His Excellency daring his detractors to question his integrity: "I did not solicit this command, but accepted it after much entreaty. Whenever the public becomes dissatisfied with my services, or a person is found better qualified to answer her expectations, I shall quit the helm with as much satisfaction, and retire to private life with an much content, as ever the wearied pilgrim felt upon his safe arrival in the Holy Land."[18]

Perhaps it was purely coincidental, or perhaps Washington's staff had a hand in it, but about the same time gossip mills in the army began to churn out reports from soldiers who fought at Saratoga that Gates had remained at headquarters throughout the conflict, and it was the leadership of Benedict Arnold, with an able assist from the Virginia riflemen under Daniel Morgan, that turned the tide of the battle. Gates was, so the gossip claimed, a hollow hero. The very idea of "Granny Gates" as a replacement for the godlike Washington was preposterous.[19]

Troops in the huts at Valley Forge began to huddle around fires to sing an old ditty from the early days at the Boston Siege entitled "War and Washington." A recently arrived French officer named Lafayette, soon to become one of Washington's closest confidants, urged his commander to ignore the ignorant flutterings about nonentities like Gates: "I wish you could know as well as myself," Lafayette wrote, "what difference there is between you and any other man upon the Continent. If you were lost for America, there is no Body who could keep the army and the Revolution for Six months."[20]

But Lafayette's flattering picture of Washington's status as the singular figure, the one and only indispensable man, was becoming a liability as much as an asset. He had become too godlike. Henry Laurens reported that some anonymous soul calling himself "A Freeman" had placed a list of forty-five charges against Washington on the steps of congress at York. One of them described him as a self-appointed second coming of Christ himself. "The people of America have been guilty of idolatry, by making a man their god. . . . No good may be expected from the standing army, until Baal and his worshippers are bandished from the camp."[21]

Someone equally anonymous was also circulating documents purporting to show—this was literally incredible—that Washington had always opposed American independence and was considering bribes from British agents to switch sides. Henry Laurens assured Washington that delegates in congress, at least most of them, recognized the documents as British forgeries; though there was one faction, which Laurens overruled, that called for a thorough investigation of the charges. Washington apprised Laurens that he did not object to an investigation, in part because he had nothing to hide, but also because the forged documents contained some accurate information that only a few fellow Virginians could know—he suspected a loyalist member of the Randolph family—and he would like the culprit exposed.[22]

The debates in congress inadvertently exposed Thomas Mifflin as the leader of the anti-Washington faction. The multiple conversations behind the scenes, for obvious reasons, never found their way into the historic record. But within the misty cloud of machinations, Mifflin emerged as the central player in a plot to force Washington's resignation and have him replaced by Gates.

The plot envisioned seizing control of the Board of War and Ordnance, increasing its size with pro-Gates members, to include Gates himself, and expanding its authority over the regulations governing the Continental Army. A new office of inspector general would then be created to implement this shift in authority. The person chosen to occupy the office, at the rank of major general, was an Irishman with extensive experience in the French army known to harbor a critical opinion of Washington's military qualifications. His name was Thomas Conway. The fact that Washington and the senior officers of the Continental Army loathed Conway made him the ideal choice.

Washington's reaction to Conway's appointment was incredulity coupled with outrage: "If there is any truth to a report which had been handed to me that Congress hath appointed Conway a Major General in the army," he wrote Richard Henry Lee, "it will be as unfortunate a measure as ever was adopted," adding that "Conway's merit, and his importance to this Army, exists more in his imagination than in reality."[23]

Even prior to his promotion, Conway had earned the reputation as a supercilious snob who pranced about camp with a bloated sense of his significance, like many of the French officers who showed up brandishing inflated credentials, presuming that their previous experience in the European theater qualified them to outrank an inferior collection of American amateurs. At Valley Forge there was some talk among the officers that Conway was a coward as well as a prig, that he had ordered a precipitous retreat of his troops at Germantown. He soon found himself ostracized, issuing orders that everyone ignored, threatening to resign, then sulking in isolated quarters two miles from camp when no one asked him to reconsider. As the handpicked instrument of the Mifflin-Gates conspiracy, Conway proved the worst possible choice, whose only asset was his negative opinion of Washington.[24]

Throughout it all, Washington maintained a preternatural pose of studied indifference. As he explained to William Livingston, the governor of New Jersey, "To persevere in one's duty, and be silent, is the best answer to calumny." Delphic oracles did not speak. In Washington's case, he knew that others were speaking for him. He pretended not to notice when all the brigadiers at Valley Forge signed a joint letter to the Continental Congress, protesting Conway's unwelcomed presence in camp and requesting his immediate removal.[25]

Washington enjoyed two more distant testimonials to his singular status. A German-language almanac published in Lancaster that February described him, for the first time, as "father of the country." Meanwhile, up in New York, Gates approached Daniel Morgan, his friend and Virginia neighbor, whose leadership during the battle at Saratoga had played a crucial role in winning such a lopsided victory.* Gates shared his opinion, confidentially, that many officers, himself included, had reached the conclusion that the commander in chief was obviously inadequate to the task and must be replaced. Morgan listened, nodding that he understood the implication of Gates's words. Then he astounded Gates: "I have but one favor to ask, which is never to mention that detestable subject ever again. For under no other man than Washington would I ever serve." Morgan spoke for the vast majority of senior officers in the Continental Army.[26]

In fact, once the covert scheme that more accurately might (to preserve the alliteration) be called the Mifflin Maneuver became public knowledge, the co-conspirators fell all over themselves insisting they knew nothing about it: "Matters have and will turn out very different to what the party expected," Washington confidently predicted. "G[ates] has involved himself in his letters to me in the most absurd convictions. M[ifflin] has brought himself into a scrape he does not know how to get out of. C[onway] is sent upon an expedition [to Canada] which all the world knew, as the event has proved, was not practicable. In a word, I have a good deal of reason to believe that Machinations of this Junto will recoil upon their own heads." The chief lesson to learn from the little episode, whatever we choose to call it, was that anyone who went up against His Excellency was risking professional suicide, a lesson that held true for the remainder of the war.[27]

---

* Morgan's elite group of Virginia riflemen was feared by British troops, especially officers, more than any other unit in the Continental Army. They were equipped with so-called Kentucky rifles, which had an effective range three times greater than regular muskets because of the longer rifled barrels. (In order to join Morgan's team, you needed to demonstrate the ability to hit an orange at three hundred yards.) At Saratoga Morgan had ordered one of his best marksmen up a tree to shoot a mounted British officer who turned out to be General Simon Fraser. Morgan expressed his regrets upon news of Fraser's death. The only combat commander with credentials comparable to Morgan's was Benedict Arnold, the other real hero at Saratoga.

❦

BY THE WINTER OF 1777–78 the war had become fertile ground for second-guessers of several stripes, for the simple reason that it had gone on much longer than anyone on either side had expected. Since neither side had been able to achieve the expected triumph, it was probably inevitable that both Washington and William Howe, now Sir William for his early victories in New York, would become targets. Washington survived the criticism, in fact emerging stronger than ever before, while Howe did not. The obvious question is why.

At least on the face of it, Howe's sudden vulnerability seems strange. He had bested Washington in every battle in which they were both engaged, most recently at Brandywine and Germantown. Lord George Germain had selected him based on Howe's reputation as the most gifted infantry commander in the British army, and Howe's performance had more than justified that reputation. He had captured America's capital, where the British army was now comfortably quartered, while Washington's troops were starving twenty-three miles away at Valley Forge, in part because Howe had seen fit to send out foraging teams to pick the country clean before Washington could do the same. What's more, Howe's troops loved him, mostly because he displayed a conspicuous concern for their welfare, would never waste them in frontal assaults in the Bunker Hill mode, and his midbattle tactical adjustments could always be trusted to win the day.[28]

The missing word in this otherwise accurate assessment is Saratoga, which proved to be the most consequential battle of the war, not just because the British lost an entire army, but also because it enhanced the horrific prospect of French entry into the war. Lord Germain had granted Howe the discretion to make tactical decisions based on his proximity to the battlefield, and Howe had used that discretion to attack Philadelphia rather than move up the Hudson corridor to join Burgoyne's army coming down from Lake Champlain. Howe also chose a bafflingly roundabout maneuver to reach Philadelphia, sailing south to the mouth of the Chesapeake Bay, then marching north through Delaware. (The maneuver mystified everyone, including John Adams. "We might as well imagine them gone around Cape Horn into the south Seas to land at California," Adams confided to Abigail.) Howe was therefore on his solo mission, beyond the reach of reports that Burgoyne's army was surrounded by a vastly superior American force of Continental troops under Gates and swarming militia from western New England.[29]

The surrender of an entire British army was an unexpected catastrophe. (The verb "to Burgoyne" entered the American lexicon, to mean isolating and capturing a large British force.) Someone had to be held responsible. And Howe rather than Burgoyne became the preferable scapegoat.

Unlike the behind-the-scenes criticism of Washington, Howe's detractors fired away in both houses of Parliament and the London press. *The London Chronicle* speculated that Howe had deliberately disobeyed his orders and taken his army on a mysterious cruise in order to leave poor Burgoyne, whom he purportedly despised, marooned in rebel country. The press had a field day revisiting Howe's openly scandalous relationship with Elizabeth Loring. A little ditty to the tune of "Yankee Doodle" made Loring the reason that Howe seemed unwilling to contemplate an attack on Washington's starving and vulnerable army at Valley Forge:

Awake, arouse, Sir Billy!
There's forage on the plain!
Ah, leave your little filly,
And open the campaign.[30]

Both William Pitt in Lords and Edmund Burke in Commons rose to protest Howe's vilification, claiming that Howe was being made the scapegoat for British policy toward the colonies that had always been fatally flawed. The reputable Sir William had been sent on a fool's errand, and now that he had failed to win the unwinnable war, the British ministry preferred to blame him rather than face their own prevailing incompetence. Pitt and Burke were characteristically eloquent, and history proved them right, but their proposal for a thorough review of British policy was rejected in both houses by overwhelming majorities.

As rumors of his growing disfavor within the British government floated across the Atlantic, Howe chose to pursue the honorable course and submit his resignation. "I am led to hope that I may be Relieved from this painful service," he wrote to Germain, "wherein I have not the good fortune to enjoy the confidence and support of my superiors." Submitting one's resignation was the customary procedure for a British officer when criticized, thereby forcing his superiors to reject the resignation and provide a vote of confidence.[31]

In Howe's case, there is reason to believe he meant it. He and his brother had both believed the official British line that support for the rebellion was skin-deep, that the vast majority of Americans would rally to the British banner once they realized their mistake. Sir William had regarded each battle as an act of political persuasion designed to force his American cousins to see the light. Yet even after the required blows had been delivered at Long Island, Manhattan, White Plains, Brandywine, and Germantown, The Cause had not cracked. One of the reasons Howe had decided to take such a roundabout path to Philadelphia was his hope, based on intelligence reports, that residents of Delaware and Southern Pennsylvania would greet his troops as liberators. He was disappointed to discover periodic ambushes and destroyed bridges rather than cheering crowds.

More than any officer in the British army, then, Howe had reason to realize that, if there were such a thing as "a deluded multitude," it inhabited the halls of Parliament and the corridors of Whitehall. We can never know for sure, but Howe's offer of resignation was quite possibly a shrewd decision to hand the baton to some poor soul—it turned out to be Henry Clinton—who would become the ultimate scapegoat when Great Britain eventually realized that there was no way to win the war. By sheer coincidence, Howe's letters of resignation arrived in London alongside reports that America's premier diplomat, Benjamin Franklin, was working his magic with the French court to bring France into the war. If that happened, Howe had gotten out just in time.

As a result, throughout the Valley Forge winter both sides were living under the shadow cast by the unforeseen consequences of a protracted war. For the British, the shadow took the form of a lame-duck commander in chief and a hovering French presence that upended all previous presumptions about the war's outcome. For the Americans, it assumed the shape of a Continental Army on the verge of dissolution and a war-weary population either unable or unwilling to sustain previous levels of patriotism. Both sides had several ways to lose, and no clear way to win the war.

WASHINGTON HAD REQUESTED a strategic assessment from all his general officers just as the huts were going up at Valley Forge. (Such requests were rare in the British army, where the common practice was for the commander to dictate the strategy, and ask for advice only about how to implement it.) Greene produced a forty-two page memorandum that made three troubling points: first, that the officers' corps was deeply disaffected, ten to twenty officers were resigning every week, and unless something were done to bolster their morale, it would be difficult to mount a spring campaign; second, that outside New England, where patriotism continued to flourish, the citizenry had grown weary of the war, and over time would probably grow even more indifferent; third, he feared that time was on the British side. "It is almost an established maxim in European Politics," Greene wrote, that "the longest purse will remain masters of the field in a long contest, for money is the sinews of war." In effect, the well-oiled British war machine was likely to outlast an American army running on a dwindling supply of patriotism.[32]

None of the other generals were as concerned with long-range forecasts or what constituted "the sinews of war." (The term came from Cicero.) They focused on what was needed to survive the winter and then be ready to launch a spring campaign. There was nearly unanimous consensus that Greene was right about the officers' corps; that the only way to assure the enlisted ranks would fill up by the spring was to impose some kind of draft; that the war had reached a new stage in which sheer resilience must become the highest priority; and that Washington's continued leadership was utterly indispensable. Washington appointed his precocious new aide-de-camp, Alexander Hamilton, to synthesize the recommendations into a comprehensive report for a "New Establishment" to the Camp Committee, which would then forward their recommendations to the Continental Congress.[33]

There was nothing new about the New Establishment. Washington had been pleading for a larger, more professional force modeled on the British army ever since the Boston Siege. And every winter, when the one-year enlistments expired, he had repeated his request for a draft that provided troops obliged to serve "for the duration," warning that at some point in time not enough enlistees would show up, and the Continental Army would cease to exist.

The Camp Report was an updated version of the long-standing Washington refrain to transform the Continental Army from an ad hoc improvisation into a stable institution. The only major addition was the request for a pension plan that provided officers with half-pay for life, the accepted norm in most European armies. Minor additions included specific reforms in designated areas like the quartermaster and hospital departments that had proven inadequate, plus enhanced support for recently created engineering and cavalry units.* The chief difference from previous requests was the context provided by Valley Forge. This

---

* The Camp Report was also distinctive for its overall cogency and what might be called its commanding style. Anyone on the lookout for early signs of Alexander Hamilton's conspicuous intelligence and verbal prowess could find it there.

time, as the Camp Committee would surely confirm, the Continental Army was on the verge of dissolving. If their requests were not approved by the congress, the delegates were voting to lose the war. Depending on your perspective, the Continental Congress was being either warned or blackmailed.[34]

How had it come to this? Washington wanted the Camp Committee and the Continental Congress to know that this existential moment had always been lurking for The Cause, and the fact that it arrived at Valley Forge was not surprising. In an argument echoing Greene's claim that money outlasted patriotism, Washington repeated his abiding conviction that any institution built on the presumption of self-sacrifice had a limited duration. In modern terms, the Continental Army was like an appliance with an expiration date:

> A small knowledge of human nature will convince us that, with far the greatest part of mankind, interest is the governing principle; and that almost every man is more or less under its influence. Motives of public virtue may for a time, or in particular instances, actuate men to a conduct purely disinterested; but they are not of themselves sufficient to produce a preserving conformity to the refined dictates and obligations of social duty. No institutions not built on the presumptive truth of these maxims can succeed.[35]

This message defied the central assumption on which the entire military version of The Cause had rested until now; namely, the belief in a volunteer army hallowed by its association with the patriotic values that The Cause claimed to embody. Washington was suggesting, or perhaps insisting, that the dependence on patriotic volunteers had always been a sentimental illusion, now exposed as such by the long war. If the delegates in congress wanted to win the war, they needed to face this fact; if they did not, American defeat was assured. And defeat would render all virtuous principles irrelevant. If past experience was any guide, the reception to Washington's brutally realistic message was likely to be some combination of incredulity and stunned silence.

The delegates were having trouble raising a quorum at their new quarters in York, and when they finally did, they had greater trouble with Washington's recommendations. The half-pay for life pension for officers met with almost universal disapproval, in part because of the threatening manner it was being proposed. Two months later, after hearing that his report had been sent to a committee, Washington vented his frustration to Henry Laurens: "In a word, at no period since commencement of the War have I felt more painful sensations on account of delay than at present." Hamilton speculated that the source of the problem was the declining quality of the men willing to serve in the Continental Congress. "The present falling off is very alarming and dangerous," he wrote to George Clinton, the governor of New York. "What is the cause? The great men who composed our first council, are they dead, have they deserted the cause, or what has become of them?" The short answer was that many of them preferred to serve in the state legislature, where the real power now resided.[36]

ONE SNOWY AFTERNOON in late February, while the report of the Camp Committee was languishing in committee, unexpected assistance for the Continental Army arrived on a huge sleigh adorned with twenty-four jingle bells, drawn by a pair of black Percheron horses with a prancing gait. The occupant wore a silk robe trimmed in fur and brandished two huge horse pistols as well as a chest full of medals. He carried a letter of recommendation from Benjamin Franklin, describing him as a former general in the Prussian army who had served for two decades as aide-de-camp to Frederick the Great, and had turned down several lucrative posts in Prussia and France in order to offer his services to Washington. His name was Baron Friedrich Wilhelm Ludolf Gerhard Augustin von Steuben.[37]

Although Steuben was a fraud, he proved a lovable fraud. Hamilton, Lafayette, and John Laurens, Washington's trio of young aides and acolytes, immediately found him beguiling. Because they were all fluent in French and Steuben spoke little English, they enjoyed translating his colorful profanities from German to French to English. Although his purported relationship with Frederick the Great at the rank of general was a concoction, Steuben had served as a captain in the Prussian army through the Seven Years' War in Europe, was twice wounded, and could claim more combat experience than any officer in the Continental Army. He also understood instinctively that, when it came to the nettlesome question of rank, the quickest way to Washington's heart was to dismiss the matter with a nonchalant wave of the hand. Steuben's arrival conveniently coincided with Conway's departure, so Steuben was made the acting inspector general. All the senior officers who had castigated Conway immediately embraced Steuben as a highly competent officer with a special knack for drilling soldiers on the parade ground.

Soon after his arrival, Steuben could be seen barking commands in his imperfect English, studded with German profanities, moving troops from column to line with increasing precision, shouting orders to platoons, then companies, then entire regiments. Within weeks his appearance on the parade ground became the major attraction for all visitors to the camp, and Steuben became the acknowledged maestro of military orchestrations.[38]

The daily performance was more than a show. To be sure, modern soldiers justifiably regard marching and drilling exercises as tiresome routines designed to occupy time with no direct connection to their combat effectiveness. But all such apparently meaningless maneuvers are vestiges of disciplined skills that played a crucial role on the eighteenth-century battlefield. The tactical deployment from column to line, or vice versa, proved essential when adjusting to flanking assaults or increasing firepower at the point of attack. Troops needed to learn "the common step" of twenty-eight inches at twenty-five paces per minute to maintain unit cohesion during a strategic retreat. With daily practice, soldiers could double their firepower by loading and firing their muskets four times a minute instead of two. With more practice, retreating troops could reload every hundred yards, turning to fire by squad in unison, thereby sustaining volleys into advancing enemy lines.

Prior to Steuben's arrival, there had been no uniform standard of march and maneuver in the Continental Army. Different units had their own tactical rules, just as they had their own uniforms. To sound a retreat meant to run away, as fast as possible, every man for himself. One of Washington's major deficiencies was the failure to make tactical adjustments in the midst of a battle. In truth, he was severely handicapped, because his troops could not make disciplined maneuvers on the fly, a failure that probably cost him a victory at Germantown.

Steuben proved a genius at teaching the very skills the Continental Army needed to learn if it ever hoped to match the prowess of the British army on a conventional battlefield. One distinctive feature of his pedagogy, unique within the Prussian army, was the insistence that officers must drill their own troops, not delegate the task to sergeants. Unit cohesion required officers to live and train alongside their men. Steuben also recognized that soldiers in the Continental Army harbored American and not Prussian values. "The genius of this nation is not to be compared with that of the Prussians, Austrians, or French," he noted with emphasis to a Prussian colleague. "You say to your soldier 'Do this,' and he does it. But I am obliged to say 'This is the reason you ought to do that,' and *then* he does it."[39]

Just as Greene had been Washington's answer to the supply problem, Steuben became his answer to the discipline problem. No equivalently simple, one-man solution existed for the turnstile problem, the transitory, ever-shifting character of the Continental Army, now rendered more acute by a protracted war that had outlived its glory phase. The only person who could solve that problem was a magician who could wave his magic wand and re-create in the congress and the population at large the patriotic ethos already being referred to nostalgically as "the spirit of '76." No one of that description showed up at Valley Forge, so Washington was left to wait for the snow to melt, wonder why Howe did not attack his vulnerable army, count the number of weekly resignations and desertions, and hope that enough new enlistees would show up to mount a spring campaign. His sole consolation was Martha's arrival in early February. Over the course of the war, she seldom missed a winter.[*40]

THE SOCIAL STRUCTURE of the Valley Forge encampment was a perfect pyramid built out of the classic Aristotelian categories: the one, the few, and the many. The one, of course, was Washington, whose lodgings at the Isaac Potts farmhouse served as operational headquarters, more commodious and comfortable than the ubiquitous huts, but crowded with aides, Martha's personal staff, and periodic visitors. Washington rode out each day to inspect the troops in much the manner he had inspected the slaves and fields of his Mount Vernon plantation.

The many were the enlisted men, between ten and twelve thousand of them living in the twelve-man huts, arranged by regiment around the parade ground. Few were yeoman farmers, who preferred to serve in the local militia. Most were working-class Americans—blacksmiths, carpenters, artisans, wagon masters, itinerant laborers. Many were recently arrived immigrants from Ireland and Scotland, indentured servants, or ex-slaves. As a group, they were closer to the bottom rung of the social ladder than the top. Few owned property, which meant that, unless they lived in Pennsylvania, they could not vote.

Valley Forge was the first winter encampment when slightly more

---

* The most prominent woman at Valley Forge was Catharine Greene, profiled at the end of this chapter.

than half the "soldiery," as Washington called them, were serving for three years or "for the duration," making them the kind of experienced veterans that Washington hoped to become the norm for the entire Continental Army. They were all volunteers who had joined for patriotic reasons, or because they had no better options. Their distinguishing characteristic at Valley Forge was resilience, the ability to suffer in silence, even to joke about it. One trooper from the Connecticut line spread the rumor that headquarters was hoarding a full supply of shoes, but refused to issue them in order to assure the men would not all desert.* They regarded themselves as the core of the corps, and they were. If Valley Forge was the testing time, they were the center that must hold.[41]

The few were the officers, whose demeanor as reflected in the official records comes across as almost inexplicably strange. While the enlisted men shivered stoically, their officers seemed fixated on petty arguments about their relative status in the military hierarchy, at times resembling, as Adams put it, "apes scrambling for nuts." Minor arguments around the campfires often escalated to major matters of honor (e.g., Whose horse should be allowed to feed first? What did you mean by calling me a "competent" officer? Why do you squint when you speak to me?). Because states used different criteria to establish rank, there was incessant bickering about seniority, and threats to resign rather than serve under an officer considered junior. The smallest gesture of disrespect often escalated into an argument about honor, a lengthy exchange of correspondence about whose fragile ego had been most offended, then mutual agreement to meet for an "interview," the euphemism for a duel. Even though dueling was illegal in the Continental Army, it became commonplace at Valley Forge: "The rage for dueling has reached an incredible and scandalous point," one French visitor observed. "This license is regarded as an appendage of liberty."[42]

---

* The standard punishment for desertion was death by hanging. Washington chose not to enforce that standard during the worst months at Valley Forge, replacing it with one hundred lashes.

More accurately, dueling represented an effort by the officers to convince themselves that they were a separate order of men, the chosen few who had remained true to the original meaning of The Cause as it was dying in the population at large. While the enlisted men were suffering silently, their officers seemed obsessed with announcing their distinctive status as an American elite that embodied the core values of the American resistance in its purest form. One might argue that the men in those huts who had signed up for the duration had an equal claim to special status. But honor was an aristocratic value, not expected or suitable for the rank and file, whose virtue took the form of group solidarity. The troops could, and did, fight among themselves. They did not duel.

In the British army, one was an officer because one was an aristocrat, a status derived from bloodlines and inherited wealth. In the American army, one was an aristocrat because one was an officer, a status that was earned by some combination of demonstrable competence and conspicuous acts of courage. Once unmoored from its British and European standards and forced to invent its own guidelines, honor became a constant process of proving oneself, especially on the field of battle. The Marquis de Lafayette was the epitome of the French aristocrat, but he had to earn that status in the Continental Army, as he did at Brandywine by leading his troops against a larger unit of British grenadiers, losing his horse and suffering a leg wound in the process. "The Marquis," observed Greene, "is determined to be in the way of danger." Honor was the centerpiece of an officer's character, not only who you were, but what others already in the fraternity thought you were.[43]

At Valley Forge the officer class, at least those who refused to resign, began to regard itself as a breed apart, the visible saints who sustained the patriotic equivalent of grace while the rest of the American congregation lost the faith. Charles Royster, one of the most prominent historians of the Continental Army, put the point metaphorically: "The spirit of 1775 had continued to fall apart, and the officers rubbed Congress's face in the pieces." If Greene was right and money was "the sinews of war," the officers at Valley Forge were claiming they offset that British advantage with a display of patriotic energy that money could not buy. They would continue to man the last bastion of national unity as The Cause crumbled into state and local fragments all around them.[44]

As a result, the seeds of a national vision were planted in the officers' corps during the winter of 1777–78. It is no accident that George Washington, Alexander Hamilton, and John Marshall would become the leading advocates for the view that a fully empowered national government was a fulfillment, not a betrayal, of the American Revolution, for they were all channeling the lessons of Valley Forge.

THE SINGULAR EXAMPLE of the honor-driven officer—that abstract ideal brought to life in fullest form—was John Laurens. He was the son of Henry Laurens, current president of the Continental Congress, who also happened to be one of the wealthiest members of the planter class in South Carolina. John therefore came by his aristocratic status the old-fashioned way—he inherited it. His father had spared no expense in preparing him for a distinguished career: private tutors as a lad; a classical education at a private school in Geneva, where he picked up French; legal training at the Middle Temple in London. In August 1777, Laurens decided to cut short his reading in the law and leave his new wife and their newborn daughter—he would never see them again—to join the Continental Army.[45]

Washington spotted him immediately. Always on the lookout for talented young men with educational credentials that he himself lacked, Washington offered Laurens a post as aide-de-camp, eventually at the rank of lieutenant colonel. (Not only was Laurens impeccably educated and passionately committed to The Cause, he afforded Washington direct access to his civilian superior in congress.) In October 1777 he joined Washington's inner circle, what Washington called "my family," comprised of Lafayette, Hamilton, and now Laurens. All of them were in their early twenties, young enough to be the sons Washington never had. They were afforded privileged access to the intimate thoughts of a man otherwise disposed to draw a curtain around himself through which only Martha could pass.

Prior to the Valley Forge encampment, Laurens amplified his impressive résumé with conspicuous demonstrations of personal courage at both Brandywine and Germantown—especially at Germantown, where he was wounded in the shoulder leading an assault on Chew House, a heavily defended stone mansion that Washington should have bypassed. His willingness to risk himself verged on the suicidal. "It was not his fault that he was not killed or badly wounded," Lafayette observed. "He did everything necessarily to procure one or t'other."[46]

When word reached Henry Laurens of his son's death-defying exploits, he urged John to control his heroic instincts. The son replied that honor did not afford room for caution or compromise: "You ask me, my dear Father, what bounds I have set to my desire of serving my country in the Military Line. I answer, glorious Death, or the Triumph of the Cause in which I am engaged." It was not merely, as his father implied, a matter of youthful exuberance. It was the principled commitment to a cause larger than oneself that, by definition, rendered any self-interested calculation as dishonorable. Within the secular religion of the officer class, Laurens was an evangelical.[47]

Laurens also carried in his head and heart equally principled and nonnegotiable political convictions. During his London years, while defending the legitimacy of the American commitment to independence against British and loyalist critics, he found himself unable to reconcile the purity of The Cause with the coexistence of slavery: "I think we Americans," he wrote a friend, "at least in the Southern Colonies, cannot contend with a good Grace for Liberty until we have enfranchised our Slaves. How can we reconcile our spirited Assertions of the Rights of Mankind with the galling abject Slavery of our Negroes?"[48]

From our modern perspective, Laurens was being admirably consistent, calling out the hypocrisy of any rationale for American independence based on liberty and equality that conveniently ignored the flagrant and wholly institutionalized exception to those core principles. But given his background as the privileged son of South Carolina, the state where slavery was most embedded, most economically essential, most unquestioned; given that his own father had made his fortune in both the slave trade as well as the exploitation of slave labor, Laurens's conviction that American independence must lead to emancipation was remarkable.

One can deploy Freudian explanations for his dramatic rejection of everything his father represented, but Laurens also shared his most passionate hatred of slavery in correspondence *with* his father: "I have long deplored the wretched state of these men," he wrote from his quarters at Valley Forge, "and consider in their history the bloody wars excited in Africa to furnish America with Slaves, the Groans of despairing multitudes toiling for the Luxuries of Merciless Tyrants." Instead of vilifying his father, young Laurens sought his approval for a more expansive definition of The Cause that would place them both on the right side of history. Henry Laurens did not recoil at his son's antislavery pronouncements; instead he described them as noble ideals worthy of approval in the Continental Congress, but beyond the imagination of anyone that mattered in South Carolina.[49]

This was the kind of argument that John Laurens could not hear any more than he could hear that his behavior in battle verged on the reckless. His sense of honor was all-consuming. It did not tolerate any rational calculation of risk in war or any pragmatic compromise of principle in politics. He processed all information through a finely spun code of honor that filtered out evidence incompatible with its ideals. At some instinctive level, Henry Laurens understood all this, and knew he could not ask his son to be someone else. He worried less about John's unbridled opposition to slavery than his willingness to court death on the battlefield, which might take him away before he could fulfill his obvious destiny as a prominent leader in postwar America.*

Almost as soon as Laurens joined Washington's staff, he and Hamilton recognized each other as kindred spirits. Though they came from different ends of the social spectrum—Hamilton from impoverished origins in the Caribbean, Laurens from the top tier of the planter class in South Carolina—they quickly discovered they had much in common: both were in their early twenties; both were well educated and well read; both aspired to glory on the battlefield; and both saw themselves as members of a highly selective fraternity of officers bound together by an elite standard of personal honor wholly incomprehensible to those outside the veil.

At Valley Forge they became soul mates, working together as translators for Baron Steuben on the parade ground, meeting as members of Washington's staff before the fireplace at headquarters. It was there they discovered they had one more conviction in common. They both believed that slavery was incompatible with the values they were fighting for. Hamilton was just as insistent as Laurens that the taboo topic must be faced. A request from General James Varnum in Rhode Island provided the occasion for a full discussion.[50]

Varnum was requesting Washington's permission to raise a Black regiment comprised of slaves, who would be freed if they served for the duration of the war. Their owners would be compensated from public funds and Rhode Island would thereby meet its enlistment quota for the Continental Army without demanding service from the reluctant white citizenry. Washington endorsed the request in logistical terms, as a response to the manpower problem facing the Continental Army, but it was clearly

---

* At the end of John's letters to his father were often postscripts asking for new books, spurs, a sash, even a horse, all the accoutrements a privileged South Carolina aristocrat took for granted. Henry kept urging his son to write to his wife and daughter in London, but John seldom did. The downside of John's all-consuming commitment to The Cause was that it left no room for his responsibilities as a husband and father.

more than that, and Washington knew it. Apparently, there was a wide-ranging discussion within the staff about the precedent being set. Laurens wrote his father that in those deliberations, "His Excellency became convinced that the numerous tribes of blacks in the Southern parts of the continent offer a resource to us that should not be neglected."[51]

How Washington "became convinced" did not need to be mentioned. Laurens and Hamilton, probably with strong support from Lafayette, were all on record for recruiting enslaved blacks as a way to increase the size of the Continental Army to the desired level, and thereby take a first step toward gradual emancipation.[52]

It would be too much to claim that Washington shared the vision of his precious young aides. He was focused on the immediate advantages of enlarging the troop strength of the army. But his thinking about the anomaly of slavery had moved beyond its previous posture of studied indifference. A few months later he wrote to his manager at Mount Vernon, Lund Washington, saying that all decisions about the slave population there should be made with the knowledge that "every day I aim more and more to get clear of them." At this stage, however, "get clear" meant sell, not free them. But his mind began to move in that direction at Valley Forge after listening to Laurens and Hamilton point the way forward with such passion.[53]

IN THE EIGHTEENTH CENTURY distance still made a big difference. What we call news was deferred for weeks or months at a time, so most news was not really new by the time it arrived. In April 1778 rumors arrived at Valley Forge about events that had purportedly occurred in London and Paris several months earlier: from London, that the British ministry was having second thoughts about continuing the war; from Paris, that the French were poised to recognize American independence and enter the war on the American side. If true, the entire strategic framework for conducting the war was changing dramatically.

The rumors from London were partially true, wholly so if one equated Lord North with the British ministry. Apparently, the shock waves generated by the Saratoga catastrophe had shaken North to the core. He confided to friends that he had never wanted war with the Americans, nor foreseen how costly and apparently endless it would be. It was rumored that the prime minister no longer believed the war was winnable, or at the least worth the cost, and that his highest priority was to extricate Great Britain from a quagmire into which he misguidedly had led them.[54]

Lord North was prepared to make the Americans an offer they could not refuse, for he would grant them everything the Continental Congress had asked for in 1775–76: complete autonomy over their domestic affairs, including taxation; the right to appoint their own governors, judges, and customs officers; as an added bonus, recognition of the Continental Congress as a legitimate body. Just as the colonists had requested, the clock would be turned back to 1763. He intended to appoint a three-man peace commission, eventually chaired by the Earl of Carlisle, to carry these terms to Philadelphia, armed with the discretion to make additional concessions if necessary, though American independence was not one of them.

The rumors from Paris were completely true, though the details of a prospective Franco-American alliance were yet to be worked out. Benjamin Franklin had negotiated the basic framework of a French alliance on February 6. In an act of diplomatic agility seldom if ever duplicated in American history, Franklin persuaded the French foreign minister, Count Vergennes, that the window was closing on the French opportunity to gain revenge for the defeat inflicted by Great Britain in the Seven Years' War. Franklin actually used Lord North's peace initiative as leverage to claim that the Americans might decide to accept North's generous terms, thereby ending the war before France could enter the fray. The tactic worked. When Vergennes asked whether Howe's occupation of the American capital was cause for concern, Franklin rose to the occasion: "No," he responded. "Howe has not taken Philadelphia. Philadelphia has taken Howe." The details needed refinement, but the French were coming.[55]

Reports that Lord North was sending over a peace commission chaired by the Earl of Carlisle, a long-standing opponent of British policy, prompted an immediate reaction within the officers' corps at Valley Forge and the Continental Congress at York.* Washington warned Henry Laurens that the peace initiative was "founded on principles of the most wicked and diabolical baseness, meant to poison the minds of the people. It must be exposed in the most striking manner, for the injustice, delusion, and fraud it contains."[56]

Such extreme language reflected Washington's more sober-minded fear that North's effort at conciliation, if its terms were as generous as described, struck at an ever-widening crack in American popular opinion. "The people of America are pretty generally weary of the present war," he observed, "and therefore vulnerable to the kind of accommodations on the Grounds held out rather than persevere in a contest for independence." In other words, the British ploy might work, even though the offer itself was strong evidence that the British were desperate.[57]

At any rate, now was not the time to conduct a popular referendum, since the outcome might very well be less than desired. Laurens surely knew that the army stood firmly against the alluring offer of reconciliation. The congress needed to do the same. The reasons were clear: "The injuries we have received from the British Nation were so unprovoked, have been so great and so many, that they can never be forgotten. Nothing short of independence can do."[58]

Laurens assured Washington that the delegates in congress were

---

* Lafayette apprised Henry Laurens that he knew Frederick Howard, the 5th Earl of Carlisle, personally: "He is a fine gentleman, very well powdered and a man of *bon joist*. He began by ruining his own fortune, and wanted to get the reputation of a man belov'd by the ladies. While I was in England he was much in love with a fair duchess and pretty ill treated by her." His judgment was not to be trusted, "however he is a good poet."

well aware that the British peace initiative was a ploy to divide the war-weary American people; it was, in fact, a tacit acknowledgment by Lord North that British policy had failed. "They have come to realize that the country cannot be subjugated," Laurens concluded, "and now wish to extricate themselves." Instead of conducting a state-by-state poll, congress issued a declaration that "any man or body of men who make a separate peace with the commissioners might be considered and treated as open and avowed enemies of these United States."

In addition to this declaration, Laurens included an oath of allegiance requiring all officers in the Continental Army to pledge their loyalty to the "free independent and sovereign United States, and renounce, refuse, and abjure any allegiance or obedience to the king of Great Britain." Only officers who signed the pledge would be eligible to receive the pension of half-pay for seven years that the congress had recently, and grudgingly, approved. Washington quickly apprised the senior Laurens that the officers under his command were reluctant to sign such a pledge, regarding it as an insult to their honor and the trust they had earned suffering together for The Cause at Valley Forge, which carried more weight than any mere oath. Laurens surrendered the point by granting Washington sole discretion in enforcing the oath.[59]

ON MAY 4 the Continental Congress unanimously ratified treaties of alliance with France and immediately sent couriers to Valley Forge with the splendid news. In his general orders the next day, Washington announced that the French alliance was no longer a rumor and urged all the troops to join him in "giving thanks to the almighty ruler of the Universe for raising up a powerful friend among the princes of the earth, to establish our liberty and independence upon a lasting foundation." The following morning, May 6, the entire encampment was summoned to the parade ground by booming cannon to hear the treaties read aloud; more than ten thousand lined up in neat rows, only a few still shoeless, muskets oiled and polished; after several days of rehearsal under the sharp eye of Steuben, they were poised to stage a "grand review." The official occasion was the French alliance. The unofficial occasion was the survival of the Continental Army.[60]

At Steuben's command, "running fire" went up one line, then down another, over a thousand men firing in rapid sequence. Thirteen field pieces then repeated the orchestrated discharge, filling the air with smoke. All ten thousand men then shouted "Long live the King of France" in unison, after which they grounded their muskets, re-formed by regiment, and proceeded to demonstrate crisp marching maneuvers at Steuben's command, looking for all the world like an army of disciplined veterans. When the troops were dismissed, Washington ordered a gill of rum poured into each man's canteen. The officers assembled at a huge table in the middle of the parade field for a feast of "fat meat, strong wine, and other liquors." Steuben was toasted for his maestro performance, as well as his now official appointment as inspector general at the rank of major general.

The ceremonials dutifully observed, Washington resumed his private role as warrior in chief. He expressed concern that prospects of the French arrival would generate a false sense of confidence and greater complacency. "I fear," he wrote, "we shall relapse into a state of supineness and perfect security." Rumors, in fact, were circulating in camp that the British might declare a truce and the war never resume. John Laurens worried about that possibility in a letter to his father, fearing that it would end his plans for glory. "It gives me concern," he conferred, "that there is no immediate prospect of closing the war with brilliancy." His father assured him that such worries were unfounded. "It is my opinion that we are not to roll down a green bank and toy away the summer. There is still blood, much blood in our prospect." Lafayette walked around camp crying, though not with joy. He had just learned that his infant daughter had died in France of pneumonia. Hamilton left no record of his thoughts. He was apparently reviewing

Henry Clinton's military career, concluding, somewhat unfairly, that it was undistinguished.[61]

Writing to Gouverneur Morris at York, Washington thought it entirely possible that the British "might relinquish all pretentions to conquest in America." But he was only speculating. "What she will choose, I cannot say. What she ought to do is evident. But how far obstinacy, revenge, and villiany may induce them to persevere, I shall not undertake to determine." His mood was wait and see.[62]

Down in Philadelphia the mood was deeply divided. An overwhelming sense of desperation and despair seized the substantial population of loyalists once it became known that the British army intended to evacuate the city. The Pennsylvania legislature, which was meeting in Lancaster, had issued a proclamation declaring that all residents of Philadelphia who had cooperated with the British occupation would be treated as traitors guilty of treason. The drawing of a hangman's noose appeared at the bottom of the announcement. Mass hysteria swept through nearly a quarter of the city's population, who knew they were about to lose everything they owned, but did not know where they were going, or how they would get there.

For the officers and soldiers of the British army, the mood was defiantly, even exuberantly, celebratory. In honor of General Howe's departure, the officers put up £4000 to stage an elaborate pageant they called a Mischianza, a term derived from two Italian words meaning "mix" or "mingle." The gala event, from midday on May 17 to dawn of the next morning, was planned by Captain John André, a dashing young officer, amateur artist, thespian, and poet whose debonair good looks reputedly won many hearts among Philadelphia's eligible ladies. Tickets to the extravaganza showed a setting sun and a Latin inscription that translated as "I shine as I set, I shall rise up again in increased splendor." Although Sir William was being recalled for his failure to win the war, his men wanted his departure to resemble a glorious triumph.

The entertainment began at Knight's Wharf in north Philadelphia, where a huge flotilla of flatboats, each carrying a regimental band, followed by six barges, three galleys, and two British men-of-war, sailed down the Delaware to the tune of "God Save the King." Both Howe brothers, their staffs, three hundred officers, lady friends, and local dignitaries—all loyalists—smiled and hummed along as they waved to the crowd on the passing shore. After docking at Market Wharf, the passengers were joined by some four hundred guests who passed beneath two Doric arches, one for Sir William, the other for Lord Richard Howe. On the far side they entered a large lawn transformed into an amphitheater, encircled by pavilions and rows of benches, already occupied by another five hundred guests. Ten trumpeters announced the main event, a medieval competition between two teams of junior officers dressed as knights. Seven daughters of the local elite, each wearing Turkish turbans and period costumes, were seated in the front row playing the role of ladies-fair for whose honor the knights would joust with lances.

After the competition, the knights, their ladies, and the assembled crowd moved into a giant ballroom decorated with eighty-five mirrors, a facsimile of the Hall of Mirrors at Versailles. After an hour of dancing there was a spectacular fireworks display that concluded with an illumination of the arch to Sir William. At midnight the doors were thrown open to a dining room set for a thousand guests served by twenty-four Black slaves in oriental dress. Afterward the party resumed on the dance floor, at the bar, and the faro tables, where the participants engaged in, as one observer put it, "acts of elegant dissipation." It was the last public occasion when Sir William and Mrs. Loring were seen together.[63]

It was the largest and most ornate social event of its kind ever staged on the North American continent. In truth, no event of its kind is imaginable: the sentimental celebration of a chivalric code long since dead; a triumphant conceit by an army preparing to abandon its most recent conquest; a heroic tribute for a commander leaving under a cloud: a military version of fantasyland. *Gentlemen's Magazine* called it "Dancing at a funeral." If some deeper message was buried under the layers of romanticized nostalgia, it was an implied statement that the British army would not allow itself, or its departing commander, to be stigmatized for failing to win an unwinnable war. It was the British version of "the few," gathered one last time in a self-consciously fictional world to reassure themselves that failure was not their fault.

PROFILE

CATHARINE LITTLEFIELD GREENE

She was walking among the huts at Valley Forge, dressed as if she was going to an elegant dinner party. While her husband, Nathanael Greene, was out on foraging patrols, Caty Greene was comforting the disabled troops confined to quarters, singing with soldiers gathered by the campfires, listening as lonely young men shared their stories. As an aide to Baron von Steuben later recalled, "the lady of General Greene is a handsome, elegant, and accomplished young woman who gave a bright side to our distress." She radiated warmth against the cold and made herself the feminine face of The Cause.

Not so incidentally, Caty happened to be disarmingly social and stunningly attractive. She was described as "light and agile, with flossy black hair, brilliant violet eyes, clean-cut features." Fluent in French, she enjoyed translating Steuben's profanities on the drill field for the visiting tourists, often adding colorful profanities of her own. She was the lovable sister among the band of brothers, one of those women who obviously enjoyed the company of men.

Caty never missed a winter encampment. A year after Valley Forge, she set the gossip mills spinning by dancing for over an hour with His Excellency himself, who visibly enjoyed his partner. Martha deflected the gossip by declaring for all to hear that she and George both regarded Caty Greene as a daughter. For the other officers, she was the one woman admitted to the male fraternity of "the few."

After the war, when Nathanael Greene died suddenly of sunstroke in 1786, Caty inherited a small plantation on Cumberland Island off the Georgia coast. It had been awarded to her husband for his service in the southern theater. A parade of former officers came to visit, most to pay their respects, a few to propose marriage. She made herself unavailable when Aaron Burr attempted to call on her shortly after killing Alexander Hamilton in a duel.

Earlier she had hired a recent graduate of Yale to tutor her brood of children. His name was Eli Whitney, and he invented the cotton gin at Mulberry Grove in between tutorial sessions. She later helped to promote the invention, but never benefited financially from her efforts as Whitney's business partner.

Caty Greene died of malaria at the age of fifty-nine in 1814, on the same day the British burned the capital city named after her old dancing partner. Penniless but proud to the end, the surviving veterans of Valley Forge remembered her as a lovely angel of mercy and affection during the most trying moment in the war.

Catharine Littlefield Greene with Eli Whitney, date unknown.

PART III

Triumphs and Tragedies, 1780–1783

CHAPTER FIVE

The Protraction

How will it sound in history that the United States could
not, or rather would not, make an exertion, when the means
were amply in their power, which might at once rid them
of their enemies, and put them in possession of that liberty
and safety, for which we have been so long contending?
—Captain Samuel Shaw, July 12, 1780

In the early summer of 1778 one all-important question was hanging
in the air on both sides of the Atlantic: Was the war over? From our
perspective the question seems strange, knowing as we do that the culminating battle at Yorktown was more than over three years away, and
the Treaty of Paris officially ending the war would not be signed until
1783. But for those living in the moment, who were denied our retrospective omniscience, there were sound reasons to believe that recent
events might have forced the British government to face the fact that
the American war was no longer worth the cost. But even William Pitt
found it difficult to acknowledge defeat. In April 1778, he rose in the
House of Lords to urge his colleagues to find a compromise solution
that would keep the Americans in the British Empire, giving emphasis
to his message by collapsing and dying among his lordly peers.[1]

Less dramatically but more strategically, Saratoga and the Franco-
American alliance were like two devastating explosions at the base of a

building already standing on a fault line. And that fault line was now fully exposed. The central flaw in British strategy had always been the conviction that the American rebellion was more an egg than a nut; that it could be quickly cracked, the war ended in one campaign; that a majority of loyalists would fly to the British side when confronted with the overwhelming might of His Majesty's army and navy.

William Howe was sailing home to apprise his superiors at Whitehall that the central British assumption, which he and his brother had once shared, had proven an illusion. The British army could win every battle, as Howe had nearly done, and still be no closer to winning the war. General Burgoyne, his defeated colleague, was already back in London delivering the same dispiriting message. In officers' clubs throughout the city, junior officers back from the war were spreading the word that the American theater was a graveyard for anyone interested in pursuing a military career. Admiral Samuel Graves preferred a naval metaphor: the movement of the British army through the American landscape was "like the passage of a ship through the sea, whose track is soon lost to the waves."[2]

The imminent arrival of the French moved British prospects in the war from highly problematic to virtually hopeless. It would no longer be possible for Lord Germain to devote over half of British ground and naval resources to the North American theater, since they would be needed to protect British possessions elsewhere in the empire. From the beginning, George III had argued that the American rebellion must be crushed, because the loss of the American colonies would set off a chain reaction (i.e., falling dominoes) that put Canada, the valuable sugar islands in the Caribbean, and even India at risk. Now, the entry of Great Britain's most formidable foe into the war threatened to make George III's nightmare into a palpable horror. If he sustained his unequivocal commitment to suppressing the American rebellion, he would leave the rest of the British Empire vulnerable to the very fate he had made the chief rationale for adamantly opposing American independence; but if he shifted British resources to meet the global threat posed by France, soon to be joined by Spain, the prospects for suppressing the American rebellion became remote in the extreme. If the American war had proven unwinnable at full strength, how could it possibly be won with less?[3]

That question dominated the deliberations of the British ministry in the early spring of 1778. The chief players during several strategy sessions were Lord North, Lord Germain, First Lord of the Admiralty Lord Sandwich, Lord Jeffrey Amherst (called out of retirement for his knowledge of the American theater), and His Majesty George III. Germain conveyed the new strategic consensus in a dispatch to General Henry Clinton on March 21: "The object of the war being now changed, and the conflict in America being a secondary consideration, our principal object must be distressing France and defending His Majesty's possessions elsewhere." Clinton was ordered to evacuate Philadelphia as soon as possible, move his army to New York, and assume a defensive posture there. He should conduct no offensive operations inland that placed his army beyond the protection of the British fleet.[4]

The American theater was not being abandoned, but it was being relegated to the periphery of a global war in which France was the chief opponent; the British navy, not the army, was made the proverbial point of the spear; and the epicenter of the conflict moved from North America to the Caribbean. (British imports from the West Indies were valued at £3 million, twice the value of imports from the American colonies.) Clinton could be excused for complaining—as he proceeded to do for the next three years—that he was being consigned to the strategic version of oblivion, condemned to become the last man standing on a forgotten front.[5]

In the deliberations within the ministry, Lord North was alone in arguing that the time had come to abandon the American war altogether, which was the principal reason he kept trying to resign as prime minister. Lord Sandwich, previously a hard-liner, disagreed with

Germain after 1778 about the disposition of the British fleet, arguing in each dispute that the American theater had become primarily
a staging ground for the naval campaign in the Caribbean. Even Lord
Amherst seemed to tilt in the same "cut our losses" direction, insisting
that no less than fifty thousand troops would be necessary to sustain a
defensive presence along the Atlantic coastline, a number that no one
believed possible. Given these dissenting opinions, then add the considered judgment of Generals Gage, Howe, and Burgoyne that the American war could not be won, and the obvious question becomes: Why did
the British decide to protract the war?[6]

THE SHORT ANSWER is that both George III and Germain insisted
on it. To recognize American independence remained unthinkable
from their perspective, for to do so was to acknowledge that they had
led Great Britain into an unnecessary and unwinnable war, the most
serious blunder any statesman could make. Both of their reputations
would be ruined. George III let it be known that he intended to abdicate the throne if he lost his American colonies, that it was "his principle, it was his resolution, to part with his life, rather than suffer his
dominions to be dismembered."[7]

The slightly longer answer is that they could. Great Britain had created a machine for making war over the course of the eighteenth century, what historian John Brewer has called "the fiscal military state."
It featured an administrative network designed to raise, harness, and
deploy resources for military goals, and to maintain borrowing levels through the Bank of England on an unprecedented scale. It was a
machine designed to outspend and outlast any European opponent in
war, which it had proceeded to do in three wars earlier in the century.[8]

In addition to Britain's nearly limitless economic resources, George
III enjoyed political control over both houses of Parliament based on
royal patronage that put a sizable minority of members in his pocket.

(He was allocated £800,000 annually as a slush fund to reward his supporters, thereby controlling more than 150 seats in Lords and Commons.) The comfortable majorities he enjoyed in support of his aggressive policies toward the American resistance from 1774 to 1778 were made possible by supporters who could not find Virginia or Massachusetts on a map, but who owed their income, their title, and their very seats to His Majesty.[9]

The most compelling answer, which became Germain's fondest hope, was that a sustained British presence might, over time, cause the American rebellion to collapse on its own. This represented a change in British strategy, based on reports Germain received from members of the Carlisle commission upon their return to London, claiming that support for the war throughout the American population was dying. (The peace commission had evolved into a fact-finding agency.) The original expectation that a majority of Americans would actively oppose The Cause remained misguided, but an increasing majority were tired of the war and were refusing to rally to the American banner either. The Continental Army was on life support because the state legislatures refused to provide money or men. The American economy was bankrupt, the debt increasing exponentially, inflation out of control. And the so-called government under the Articles of Confederation was an inherently dysfunctional body, a mere platform for state and local rivalries. Everything the British war machine did so well, the Americans could not do at all. In sum, the British did not need to win the war—they merely had to wait, remain resilient, and allow the Continental Army to dissolve and the American rebellion to self-destruct.[10]

The bitter truth, at least from the American perspective, was that Germain's rationale for protracting the war was an accurate description of the political and economic paralysis afflicting any robust commitment to The Cause. There is no barometer to measure patriotism, but the heady days of 1775–76 were clearly over. "How will it sound in history," wrote Samuel Shaw, a young aide to General Henry Knox, "that the United States could not, or rather would not, make an exertion, when the means were amply in their power, which might at once rid them of their enemies, and put them in possession of that liberty and safety, for which we have been so long in contending?"[11]

That was a dispiriting question that haunted Washington, day and night, from 1778 to the end of the war. If the protracted conflict was forcing Germain to rethink British strategy, it was also forcing Washington to rethink the heretofore unseen but deeper meaning of The Cause. To be sure, it meant American independence. But to reach that goal it needed to expand that meaning to something larger, broader, and deeper, something he had glimpsed, but never fully grasped until now. The word "continental" was a clue. The word he was still groping for, a word that did not yet come naturally to most Americans, was "nation." The Cause must come to mean American nationhood. For without a fully empowered national government capable of drawing out the full resources of the American population, the war was lost. As it turned out, it almost was.

IN EARLY JUNE 1778 Washington had more pressing matters on his mind than his evolving revolutionary vocabulary. He had no way of knowing about Germain's recent orders to Clinton, nor the deliberations of the British ministry. He was still sifting through the rumors that French entry into the war had persuaded the British to cut its losses in North America. His spies reported that a flotilla of British ships had docked in Philadelphia's several harbors, obviously preparing for the evacuation of Clinton's army. If the ships headed out into the Atlantic, they were sailing back to England or the West Indies. If so, that meant the war was over. Instead, Clinton's army of ten thousand troops, along with three thousand loyalists, marched northeast in a column twelve miles long, heading across New Jersey to New York. That meant the war would continue.

Washington waited a week before convening a council of war—later regretting the delay—then presented his general staff with three options: do nothing about Clinton's army, but instead reclaim possession of Philadelphia; harass Clinton's column, but avoid a general action; or attempt to "Burgoyne" Clinton's column while it was vulnerable inland, beyond the reach of the British fleet. Although he did not say so, Washington clearly preferred the last option, which offered the opportunity to end the war outright by isolating and capturing the flower of the British army and, not so incidentally, besting Horatio Gates's triumph at Saratoga.[12]

In the ensuing discussion, the recently returned Charles Lee played a major role, arguing that the army's proper posture should be defensive, while waiting for the French, and Lee's eloquence won the day. (Lee had spent over a year as a British prisoner, but upon return in exchange for a high-ranking British officer was again regarded as second in command to Washington.) Both Hamilton and Laurens strongly disagreed with the conclusion, Hamilton claiming that the deliberations of the general staff "would have done honor to a society of midwives."[13]

Nathanael Greene also disagreed, and not only did Washington trust his judgment more than any other senior officer, but Greene also enjoyed the advantage of telling him what he wanted to hear. "If we suffer the enemy to pass through the Jersey's without attempting anything upon them," Greene argued, "I think we shall ever regret it." Greene proposed an aggressive harassment of Clinton's column, poised to draw the redcoats into a full-scale battle. If successful, it might well be the last battle of the war.[14]

A version of Greene's scenario happened at Monmouth Court House on June 28 in what proved the longest battle of the war on the most hellishly hot day. After much back-and forth with Lee, who was on record as opposing the attack but in the end insisted on leading it as the senior officer, Washington gave him command of the vanguard brigade of five thousand troops. Shortly after the first shots were fired,

Washington came upon Lee leading a headlong retreat in total disarray after encountering an apparently smaller British force under General Charles Cornwallis. Clearly outraged, Washington relieved Lee on the spot, some witnesses claiming that his language contained profanities never before heard from His Excellency.[15]

While sitting calmly astride his horse, fully exposed to a blistering British artillery barrage, Washington halted the retreat and moved the confused troops to more favorable terrain, what Lee and his defenders later claimed he was attempting to do before Washington intervened. In the ensuing battle the continentals displayed their newfound discipline acquired under Steuben's eye at Valley Forge, most especially in strategic retreats that featured sustained firepower while moving backward, a trademark tactic of the Prussian army.

After halting the British advance, the continentals moved forward with conspicuous confidence to drive the stunned British regulars from the field, inflicting much heavier casualties than they suffered. (Both sides falsified the official casualty reports, as was the custom throughout the war.) That night, as Washington and Lafayette slept on the ground under the same blanket, Clinton kept his campfires burning while stealing away in the dark. Two days later, Clinton's column staggered into Sandy Hook on the Jersey shore, where British transport ships awaited to carry them to safety in New York.[*16]

Washington wrote a friend that it was as if both armies had traded places. "It is not a little pleasing nor less wonderful to contemplate, that after two years of maneuvering and undergoing the strangest vicissitudes that perhaps ever attended any one conflict since the creation, that both Armies are brought back to the very point they set out from." Only now it was the British trapped in New York, "reduced to the use of the spade and pick axe for defense." (He might have added that Clin-

---

* Approximately one thousand British soldiers deserted after the battle, over half of them Hessians, who had apparently formed relationships with German-speaking families in and around Philadelphia.

ton now played the role of Washington as the master of escape.) And now, based on his army's performance at Monmouth, he no longer commanded an improvised collection of amateurs, but rather a force with a hard core of veterans capable of matching British regulars on a conventional battlefield.[17]

The one loose end after Monmouth was Charles Lee. He remained his irreverent self, demanding a court-martial to clear his name and writing vitriolic letters claiming that Washington had stolen the victory he was in the process of winning before being removed in such an undignified fashion. The court-martial found him guilty of disobeying orders and disrespecting the commander in chief.[18]

Lee's subsequent diatribes against Washington eventually led John Laurens to challenge Lee to a duel. With Hamilton serving as his second, Laurens wounded Lee in the side. (Legend has it that, while lying on the ground, Lee congratulated Laurens on his marksmanship.) Lee's truly fatal wound was self-inflicted, attempting to duel with Washington. He retired from the army in disgrace, dying in Philadelphia a year before the war officially ended, in 1782. Eccentric to the end, he left instructions to be buried with his beloved dogs, as far from any Presbyterian church as possible. Many years later, British sources revealed that Lee had provided valuable intelligence to his British captors when imprisoned—in effect, he had committed treason.[19]

MONMOUTH COURT HOUSE was the last major battle Washington would fight until Yorktown. For the next three years, between 1778 and 1781, he kept coming back to the same mental picture: the French fleet was blocking New York Harbor as the Continental Army laid siege to the city; after its capture he was leading the victory parade, thereby redeeming his own honor in the very place where it had been most seriously stained. New York became Washington's all-consuming obsession, "the first and capital object upon which every other is dependent."[20]

This made strategic sense. New York was the great British enclave in North America, the nest from which ships and troops radiated British power, what one historian has called "Redcoat Central." It was also the ultimate haven for all loyalists in the region, to include most of the refugees from Philadelphia. If you believed, as Washington had come to believe, that Great Britain would never abandon its North American empire without suffering another devastating defeat, New York seemed the preordained place where providence had designed destiny to happen.[21]

Unfortunately, Washington's dream kept colliding with two stubborn realities. The first was the competing agenda of the French fleet. From the French perspective, the Caribbean was a higher priority, more specifically the islands lost to Great Britain in the Seven Years' War. The French also had their own dreams, the most alluring an invasion of England, which required a threatening presence in the English Channel. (In 1779, rumor had it that a French army of fifty thousand troops was advancing on London. In truth, a huge French and Spanish armada, poised for invasion in the English Channel, had returned to Brest because of bad weather and miscommunication.) A campaign against New York never made it to the top of France's list of naval priorities.[*22]

The second stubborn reality was the small size of the Continental Army. If and when the French fleet became available, a successful siege of New York would require at least thirty thousand troops, more than twice the size of the Continental Army at any given time. In fact, the Continental Army remained too small to conduct any major offensive operations at all between 1778 and 1781. The refusal of the states to provide men and money for the Continental Army was, of course, a

---

* There was one exception. A small French fleet did appear off Sandy Hook in July 1778, but proved incapable of crossing the sand bars into New York Harbor. The French admiral, Count d'Estaing, then sailed up to Newport to attack the British garrison there. But a combination of gale-force winds and the incompetence of the American commander, General John Sullivan, transformed the amphibious operation to capture Newport into a muddled failure.

long-standing problem. But it grew worse after the French alliance, as the state governments became even more reluctant to support a war that appeared less important than state and local priorities, now that the outcome seemed assured.

In a steady flow of correspondence with the Continental Congress and in Circular Letters to the States, Washington was at pains to explain that the outcome was not assured, that the only way to reach that glorious goal was to deliver a decisive blow—here the New York dream became a routinized refrain—and that the only way to deliver a decisive blow was to provide the resources necessary for a properly sized Continental Army. Failure to do so would protract the war, thereby expanding its cost, and place the ultimate outcome in doubt.[23]

In one sense, the message Washington delivered hit the same chord he had been sounding since the early days of the Boston Siege, in a song entitled "Give Me an Army." Now, however, there was a new sense of urgency to the message, a more desperate tone driven by his growing fear that, just when victory was within America's grasp, his civilian superiors in congress and the state legislatures would not allow him to grab it. If so, it would not be his fault. "If we fail for want of proper exertions in any of the Governments," he warned, "I trust the responsibility will fall where it ought and that I shall stand justified to Congress, to my Country, and to the World."[24]

While his strategic vision remained locked on New York, Washington's correspondence reveals a mind searching for explanations of what he called "an epidemical disease which is infinitely more dreaded than the whole force of Great Britain." In letters to his Virginia friends, he tended to focus on the decline of leadership within its delegation to the Continental Congress: "Our Affairs are in a more distressed, ruinous, and deplorable condition than they have been since the commencement of the war. Where is [George] Mason, [George] Wythe, Jefferson, [Wilson Cary] Nicholas, [Edmund] Pendleton, [Thomas] Nelson and another [i.e., Benjamin Harrison, the recipient of the letter] I could name?"

Virginia was not unusual. The shift in power from the federal to the state level was occurring everywhere, a development that Washington bemoaned as a viral strain in the "epidemical disease" that was killing The Cause, though at this stage he kept thinking that getting the "best men" to serve provided a cure. "Little does it avail for the States respectively to be framing laws and regulating their own internal police by the abilities of the first statesmen," he complained, "while the great political machine which is the support and must give energy to the whole is defective."[25]

After playing somewhat clumsily with the metaphor of the wheels of a clock, he made his point more straightforwardly: "In a word, our measures are not under the influence and direction of one Council, but thirteen, each of which is actuated by local views and politics. We have become a many-headed Monster, a heterogeneous Mass that never will nor can steer to the same point." The clock metaphor became more applicable at this stage of his thinking. Not only was he waiting for the French fleet to arrive; he was also waiting for thirteen clocks to chime simultaneously.[26]

IN THE INTERIM, Washington was forced to make do with what he had, which came naturally after three years of practice. Valley Forge was not just a forgotten brush with catastrophe, but the new normal. Troop strength declined each winter when enlistments expired, averaging between 3000 to 5000 fit for duty. It expanded in the spring to between 12,000 and 15,000. He deployed the army in a great arc that extended from Philadelphia through New Jersey into the Hudson Highlands near West Point, then down into the hill country of western Connecticut. This deployment served three strategic purposes: it allowed the army to remain poised for the attack on New York; it protected the Hudson corridor from any British campaign to isolate New England, the original Germain plan; and it established a military presence in America's most populated and prosperous agrarian region, thereby denying food and forage to the British army, and assuring a measure of political control over the civilian population. A new term entered the strategic vocabulary, "cover the country."[27]

The term had originated with Nathanael Greene, who coined it to describe foraging expeditions during the Valley Forge winter. In the huge, crescent-shaped region surrounding New York, the term referred to foraging patrols by both sides that led to skirmishes between the two armies fighting for control over the allegiance of the civilian population, what modern-day military historians would call "a fluid zone of irregular warfare." While there were no full-scale battles, there were countless encounters and many massacres of civilian families who were trapped in the killing zone, where allegiance to one side assured retribution when foraging patrols from the other side passed through. The result was a dirty little war that kept grinding away for three years, leaving few traces in the historical record; it all amounted to perhaps a thousand civilian deaths not counted in the official casualty lists, masked only by family burial grounds soon to be reclaimed by nature.[28]

In this invisible war the British pursued a more brutal policy toward the civilian population than the Americans did. The Queen's Rangers under Colonel John Simcoe, an Oxford man, was the elite British foraging unit, comprised primarily of loyalists. It was infamous for taking no prisoners in skirmishes with continental patrols. It presumed that most families living in the contested region were patriots, whose crops and livestock must be seized or destroyed. In his memoir Simcoe took pride in conducting a savage campaign designed to terrorize the civilian population by executing adult males and raping women of all ages before burning their homes and barns to the ground. Simcoe made a point of always being preoccupied while his troops were committing the atrocities.[29]

Washington, on the other hand, gave strict orders to commanders of foraging patrols to avoid unnecessary violence: "I would recommend in the strongest manner," he instructed General Anthony Wayne, "the preservation of the persons and properties of the inhabitants from wanton or unnecessary violation. They have, from their situation, borne much of the burden of the War, and have never failed to relieve the distress of the Army when properly called upon." Even when "properly called upon" meant confiscating all their crops and livestock, farmers should receive certificates of purchase, which were in truth worthless, but symbolically important. Whenever possible, families should be left with enough food to get them through the winter. Soldiers who stole food or family possessions for their own use should be disciplined, usually with a hundred lashes. In the battle for control of the hearts and minds, Washington wanted the civilian population to regard the Continental Army as their protector. And by and large, they did.[30]

Given his limited resources, Washington was extremely reluctant to deploy his forces outside the arc around New York. In 1779, when the persistent belief that Canada was predestined to become the fourteenth state bubbled to the surface again in Congress, he adamantly opposed another Canadian campaign. On this occasion the Canadian dream enjoyed the enthusiastic support of Lafayette, who envisioned another campaign to capture Quebec, this time with the assistance of the French fleet coming down the St. Lawrence River. Lafayette was Washington's fondest aide, almost an adopted son, but the Marquis received a paternal lecture on the way the world really worked.

"Men are very apt to run into extremes," Washington observed, "and hatred of England may carry some into excessive confidence in France, especially when motives of gratitude are thrown into the scale." If and when French troops occupied Quebec, he warned, they would never leave. "Attached as they are by ties of blood, habits, manners, religion and former convictions of government," he explained, "I fear this would be too great a temptation to be resisted by any power actuated by the common maxim of national belief." It was the earliest expression of Washington's fervent conviction that nations must never be trusted to behave in any way other than self-interest, a core belief later enshrined in his 1796 Farewell Address, the definitive statement of the realistic tradition in American foreign policy. Lafayette, the ultimate idealist, reluctantly accepted Washington's judgment. (He really had no other choice.) There would be no Canadian campaign.[31]

The singular exception to Washington's New York fixation was the western frontier, primarily because tribes of the Iroquois Confederacy, or Six Nations, were raiding American settlements in the Mohawk Valley in upstate New York and the Wyoming Valley in western Pennsylvania, threatening to annihilate the entire white population. All the tribes except the Oneida had chosen to side with the British, who paid the raiding parties on a per-scalp basis, even providing the tribes with steel-bladed scalping knives shipped in from London. In the absence of an American military presence in the region, the massacres were occurring with impunity.*

In the spring of 1779, Washington ordered a substantial detachment of five thousand troops under General John Sullivan to retaliate against the Six Nations with equivalently annihilistic intentions. Sullivan was ordered "to carry the war into the Country of the Six nations, to cut off their settlements, destroy their next year's crops, and do them every mischief which time and circumstances will permit." The Oneida was the only tribe to be spared, since they had sided with the Americans and already paid a heavy price for doing so. During the late summer and early fall of 1779, Sullivan conducted a scorched-earth campaign that destroyed nearly twenty Iroquois towns and villages. Casualties on both sides were low, primarily because most tribes chose to flee to British protection in Canada at the approach of Sullivan's overwhelming force. The Iroquois Confederacy never fully recovered from this devastating blow. Though wartime conditions gave it a rationale and special

---

* See the profile of Joseph Brant at the end of this chapter.

coloration, the Sullivan campaign proved to be the first picture of what Indian removal would look like over the next century.[32]

By 1779 the war had become a stalemate. Both sides had adopted a defensive posture, the British focusing their fullest energies in the Caribbean theater, the Americans barely maintaining the Continental Army as a military force. How this strategic standoff looked and felt on the ground depended on where you were standing. If you were a New Jersey farmer trapped in the foraging war, it was a permanent night-mare of routinized terror. If you were a Native American in western New York, it was the beginning of the end of the world as you knew it. If you were an American prisoner of war aboard one of the ghost ships in the East River, it was a losing struggle against malnutrition and disease in a British death camp. If you were a British soldier on the way to St. Lucia, it was a one-way ticket to an unmarked grave in a malaria-infested jungle. Despite the absence of any major battles, lives were still being swept up in the crisscrossing currents of the protracted conflict, being carried to horrible fates and early ends that never regis-tered on the official records of the war or had any discernible impact on its future direction.[33]

For Washington it was the nadir, what he would look back upon as the most frustrating phase of his life. There were over 100,000 men of military age available for service. All he needed was 30,000 troops, ready to capture New York once the French fleet sailed up from the West Indies. Instead, the states refused to pay their allocated taxes or fill their troop levies. His men were starving, most of them were "half naked," none had been paid for over a year, and whenever the paymas-ter did arrive the currency was worthless, because the government, if it could be called a government, was bankrupt. Even worse, no one seemed to care. "I find that our prospects are infinitely worse than they have been at any period of the war," he apprised congress, "and that unless some capital change can be instantly adopted, a dissolution of the army for want of subsistence is unavoidable." There was only one way for America to lose the war, and his civilian superiors seemed intent on pursuing it.[34]

Washington was singing a familiar song, and his audience in the Continental Congress and the state legislatures might be forgiven for dismissing his lamentation as a boring refrain. But now there was a new note, one that he would keep sounding for the remainder of the war. The new term was "capital change." He no longer believed that "a few good men" were sufficient to rescue The Cause from self-destruction. The problem was embedded in the structure of the political framework endorsed by the congress in 1777, the Articles of Confederation, still awaiting ratification by the states. If the British had created a central-ized state designed to project its power, the Americans had created its mirror opposite: a confederation of sovereign states designed to block any projection of power whatsoever—indeed, to regard any robust exer-cise of concentrated political power as a betrayal of republican princi-ples. It was the ultimate irony: a doctrinaire insistence on a principled commitment to the core values of The Cause rendered the triumph of The Cause itself problematic.

Washington was no political philosopher, but his agenda as com-mander in chief made him acutely sensitive to the political absurdity of losing American independence in the name of American principles. "Certain I am," he wrote one Virginia delegate in the congress, "that unless congress speaks in a more decisive tone; unless they are vested with powers by the several states competent to the great purposes of War, or assume them as a matter of right, our Cause is lost. We can no longer drudge on in the old way. If congress fails to expand its mandate and dictate rather than recommend, it will be madness in us to think of prosecuting the war."[35]

One recently arrived member of congress, John Jay, got Washing-ton's message loud and clear. Appointed president almost immediately upon arrival in the summer of 1779—this kept happening to Jay—he issued a Circular Letter to the States in September demanding that they do their duty, claiming that the moral authority of his demand resided in nothing less than the language of the Declaration of Independence.

He reminded all the state legislatures that in July 1776 the former colonies "did mutually pledge their LIVES, their FORTUNES, and their SACRED HONOR" to the achievement of American independence. "Was there ever a union more formal, more solemn, or more explicit?" he asked rhetorically. Until the war was won, every request from congress should be regarded as a command for all the states "to honor their pledge to the Common Cause and to posterity." Indeed, they were honor bound to do so. Jay was attempting to shame all the states by reminding them of the sacred vow they had taken in the summer of 1776. The ineffectiveness of Jay's forceful reminder was rendered distressingly clear the following year, when the budget figures for 1780 arrived in congress; it had requested $3 million from the states, and received $39,138. The French government was paying more to support the Continental Army, by far, than all the states put together.[36]

Much in the manner that militia could not be trusted in battle, it was equally clear that virtue could not be trusted when it came to paying taxes. In response to that demonstrable fact, and to the skyrocketing inflation that accompanied the printing of money without revenue to back it up, several New England states met in Boston, then Hartford, in August and November 1780. The two conventions called for a united front to address the current crisis.

If Jay harked back to the summer of 1776, the New England delegates harked back to the Common Cause of 1774, when all the states rallied to the defense of Massachusetts in the wake of the Coercive Acts. The delegates urged all state legislatures to rally in a similar fashion by granting the Continental Congress "powers competent for the government and direction of national affairs." If any state failed to fill its quota of money and men for the Continental Army, "Congress should direct the Commander-in-Chief, without delay, to march the Army into such State, and by Military Force, compel it to furnish its deficiency." In effect, Washington should be granted emergency powers as dictator to rescue the economy and avert the imminent collapse of the Continental Army.[37]

The efforts by Jay and the New Englanders to remember the all-consuming patriotism of 1774 and 1776 were nostalgic gestures that deliberately ignored "the spirit of '77," the year the Articles of Confederation were adopted by congress. In that document, all references in the earlier Dickinson Draft to the prospective powers of any central government were dropped; and any doubt where sovereignty resided was clarified in an amendment by Thomas Burke of South Carolina: "Each state retains its sovereignty, freedom, and independence, and every power, jurisdiction, and right, that is not by this Confederation expressly delegated to the United States, in Congress assembled."[38]

The Articles were distinctive in declaring what the new Confederation Congress could *not* do. In the cogent summary of one historian, "it could not pass effective laws or enforce its order; it could ask for money, but not compel payments; it could enter into treaties, but not enforce their stipulations; it could provide for the raising of armies; but not fill the ranks or provide for repayment; it could advise and recommend, but not command." It was designed to be weak, because weakness was what the vast majority of Americans wanted at the federal level, lest they create a domestic vision of Parliament, which they were rebelling against. From the perspective of ordinary Americans, who lived and died locally, the Confederation Congress was a foreign government; its inadequacy was reassuring.[39]

It was anything but reassuring to the author of *The Continentalist*, a series of essays that began to appear in the *New York Packet* in the spring of 1781. Quite the opposite, the Articles of Confederation were a recipe for small-minded provincials, who were locked into merely local perspectives and prejudices; it was the ideal framework for failure:

"A number of petty states, with the appearance only of union, jealous and perverse, without any determined direction, fluctuating and unhappy at home, weak and insignificant in the eyes of other nations." By what magical reasoning, asked "The Continentalist," did weakness at the center become a political strength? "It is to this source," in fact, "that we are to trace many of the fatal mistakes, which have so deeply endangered the common cause, particularly A WANT OF POWER IN CONGRESS."[40]

"The Continentalist" was Alexander Hamilton, home on furlough outside of Albany, enjoying a delayed honeymoon with his new bride, Elizabeth (Betsy) Schuyler. In five essays, Hamilton displayed his formidable prowess as the most gifted polemicist of an age not lacking for worthy rivals. (Anyone looking for a preview of his performance as "Publius" in *The Federalist Papers* could find it—both in style and substance—in "The Continentalist.") More immediately, he was giving words to an idea that Washington had been groping toward since Valley Forge but lacked Hamilton's verbal talent at articulating with equivalent cogency. The idea was simple but profound: The Cause had initially meant American independence, nothing less and nothing more; but the experience of the war had forced an expansion of its meaning to include American nationhood, without which The Cause would die, and with it any hope for American independence.

Hamilton described the early years of the war as a learning experience, when "our notions of government were vague and provincial," primarily because "we possessed ideas adapted to the narrow colonial sphere in which they had been accustomed to move." Provincial presumptions reigned supreme, as did local perspectives, all of which were perfectly understandable and excusable. "But now," Hamilton observed, "we have had sufficient time for reflection and experience to rectify our errors."[41]

It was clear for all to see, according to Hamilton, that the confederation framework, where sovereignty resided in the states, was inherently incapable of drawing out the resources of the American population, providing the focus necessary to sustain the army, manage the economy, and carry the patriotic energies of the citizenry forward as a single people. That could happen only with a fully empowered central authority "of that enlarged kind suited to the government of an INDEPENDENT NATION." Americans needed to think nationally, and that could happen only within the framework of a truly national government. Otherwise the war would drag on inconclusively, the army dissolve from neglect, and the infant republic disintegrate into a series of regional confederacies.[42]

As Hamilton was drafting these warnings, the delegates in congress were engaging in a bitter and ultimately unresolvable debate that seemed almost designed to make his point. Massachusetts, New Hampshire, and New York were blocking the proposed admission of Vermont as the fourteenth state based on claims to the land between the Hudson and Connecticut Rivers, referred to as the New Hampshire Grants. Pierce Butler of South Carolina joined the opposition, claiming that Vermont's petition for statehood was a power play by New England, which he described as the "Northern Interest" contrary to the "Southern Interest," a plot "by which the sectional balance in the congress will be quite destroyed." Frustrated by the gridlocked debate, Ethan Allen was organizing support within the aspiring state to secede from the union and join Canada. An analogous argument was occurring within the Virginia delegation, which insisted that its extravagant claims to land beyond the Alleghenies must be resolved to its satisfaction prior to ceding control over its so-called domain to congress. Almost simultaneously, a mutiny broke out in the New Jersey line, which threatened to march on Philadelphia to protest their lack of food and back pay. Congress was unable to consider their claims because it lacked a quorum.[43]

Hamilton was fully aware of the almost comical cacophony within the congress, which only underlined the urgency of his argument for political reform that transformed the confederation into a reliable federal government. But it also exposed the reasons that such a transformation was highly unlikely: the confederation model was designed to permit the coexistence of different regional, state, and local agendas under one banner. In that sense, the very reasons Hamilton was insisting that a fully empowered national government was necessary were also the reasons it could not happen. For there was no national ethos. He was arguing, in his disarmingly precocious fashion, that the tail needed to wag the dog; in effect, that the only way to achieve national unity was to establish a national government that thereby fostered political unity around The Cause as the foundation for an American nation-state.

While there is nothing so powerful as an idea whose time has come, there is nothing so powerless as an idea ahead of its time. Hamilton's critical analysis of the Articles in *The Continentalist* proved prophetic six years later at the Constitutional Convention, where half of the fifty-five delegates were former officers in the Continental Army, and over half of those veterans of Valley Forge. They were the originators of a national vision, Hamilton their most eloquent spokesman, because their experience as victims of political disarray under the Articles made them appreciate the downside of a purposefully weak central government. But as the protracted war dragged on, no one was listening to them; and for many delegates in the Continental Congress, not listening was a patriotic act.[44]

IN MARCH 1779, Washington sent another plaintive request to congress, again warning the delegates to resist the seductive belief that the war was over. It would not end, he predicted, "without another desperate effort on the part of the enemy," and that effort was likely to occur somewhere south of the Potomac. "The operations of the enemy in the Southern States do not resemble a transient incursion," he warned, "but a serious conquest." Support for the Continental Army must remain a priority since "the contest is not so near an end as we could wish."[45]

He was right, of course, and he was also right about the shift in the strategic focus of the war. Between 1775 and 1778, all the major battles occurred in Canada, New England, New York, New Jersey, and Pennsylvania. After 1778, they occurred in Georgia, the Carolinas, and Virginia. Historians have adopted the term "southern strategy" to describe British military policy during the last three years of the war. The term is simultaneously accurate yet misleading, in that it suggests a deliberative thought process by the British ministry to shift the full energies of its army and navy from the northern to the southern sides of the American theater. What actually happened was more improvisational.

The British never abandoned their strategic decision to relegate the war in North America to the sidelines after French entry into the conflict. They diverted their ground and naval resources to defend the British mainland, the Mediterranean, the Caribbean, even their far-flung garrisons in India. Washington's accurate perception of increased British naval activity off the Carolina and Georgia coasts was not the first sign of a southern campaign, but rather an exploratory effort to establish safe harbors for the British fleet during the hurricane season in the West Indies. Charleston and Savannah were being eyed as platforms for the British campaign in the Floridas and the Caribbean.[46]

An early version of "mission creep" began in January 1780. A small force of three thousand British troops under Lieutenant Colonel Archibald Campbell was ordered to take Savannah, which he proceeded to do against only token resistance. Campbell then, on his own, advanced inland and captured Augusta, where he was greeted as a conquering hero by the bulk of the population, who regarded him as a protector against recent raids by the Creek Indians. Campbell announced that Georgia was once again a British colony: "I have taken a stripe and star from the Rebel flag of America," he announced. And, at least for several months, Georgia was the only state to return to British control under a royal governor.[47]

For obvious reasons, the unexpected Georgia triumph did not escape Germain's attention. Here, at last, the original Germain doctrine actually worked. American resistance crumbled upon the arrival of British troops. Latent loyalism burst out into the open. Loyalist voices in London, Joseph Galloway in the lead again, offered the intriguing suggestion that perhaps the initial British invasion of America should have been launched in the southern colonies. Perhaps the proper British strategy all along should have been a southern strategy.

Charleston made strategic sense as the next target, since it provided both an excellent harbor for the British fleet and a central location for launching a major effort into the Carolina interior to test the viability of a more robust southern strategy. Washington's spies in New York kept him abreast of British plans as they evolved. "My own opinion of the matter," he wrote, "is that they will keep a respectable force at New York and push their operations vigorously to the Southward, where we are most vulnerable and least able to afford assistance." Given his overriding fixation on New York, Washington's first instinct was to regard the prospective southern campaign by the British as an opportunity to attack New York when Clinton reduced the garrison there in order to move on Charleston. Washington had no means of transporting troops southward anyway, so the American army in Charleston, under the command of General Benjamin Lincoln, would have to fend for itself.[48]

One way to bolster the defense of Charleston was to enlist the support of the enslaved population of South Carolina, the only state with a majority of African Americans. In the spring of 1779, Washington granted the request of John Laurens to return to his home state with a proposal to create and lead an all-Black regiment of one thousand slaves, who would be offered freedom in return for service. Laurens presented his proposal to the South Carolina legislature, along with his visionary

conviction that the current crisis represented an opportunity to initiate a policy of gradual emancipation throughout the southern states,
thereby eliminating the central contradiction staining The Cause.[49]

As Henry Laurens had warned his son, the proposal was greeted
with some combination of incredulity, silent contempt, and widespread
belief that the younger Laurens had lost his mind. Rather than free
their slaves, the South Carolina legislature declared that it was prepared to surrender Charleston to the British army. Governor John
Rutledge drafted terms of surrender whereby South Carolina would
accept the British occupation of Charleston and become a neutral state
for the remainder of the war, thereby "deferring the question whether
it belonged to Great Britain or the United States to be waived until
the conclusion of it [the war], and when that should happen, accepting
whatever was granted to the other states." If forced to choose between
slavery and independence, South Carolina chose slavery.[50]

The following spring, when Henry Clinton's invasion force of
8700 British troops appeared in Charleston Harbor, Clinton refused
to accept South Carolina's terms of surrender because they required the
release of Lincoln's entire army. The ensuing siege and bombardment
left the city in ruins. Lincoln, a competent but cautious commander,
hesitated when the last opportunity to evacuate the garrison came and
went. The white flag went up on May 12, 1780. It was the most costly
American defeat in the war, with 5500 regular troops and militia taken
prisoner, including a wounded Laurens. "I have the Strongest Reasons
to believe," Clinton wrote to Germain, "that the general Disposition of
the People to be not only friendly to Government, but look forward to
take up Arms in its Support." The southern strategy seemed to be working even more splendidly than expected. In June, Clinton sailed back to
New York, leaving command of the southern army in the capable hands
of Charles Cornwallis, who was poised to expand the crack in the rebellion throughout the Carolinas.[51]

❧

A PROTÉGÉ OF William Howe, Cornwallis had served alongside him in all the campaigns from Long Island to Germantown. He also shared Howe's strategic assessment that the war was a mistake and, in all likelihood, unwinnable, especially after French entry. Clinton's seniority blocked his advancement, even though Howe let it be known that he regarded Cornwallis as his heir apparent. He owned a handsome estate in Suffolk, where his famously beautiful wife, Jemima, longed for his return and his retirement by her side; and that apparently was Cornwallis's intention as well, or so it seemed when he requested a return to England late in 1778. When granted a five-hour private audience with George III, he had the temerity to apprise the king that the subjugation of America was probably a hopeless cause, not a view calculated to court royal favor or further his career.[52]

But his wife died shortly thereafter, a loss from which Cornwallis never fully recovered. (He never remarried.) Despite his outspoken reservations about British prospects in the war, Cornwallis was regarded, after Howe, as the most gifted infantry commander in the British army. Germain offered him a promotion to serve under Clinton and inherit his command upon Clinton's departure. Cornwallis did not believe in the war, but he did believe in himself. What Howe could not do in the north perhaps he could do in the southern theater. His only family now was the British army, and he rejoined it during the siege of Charleston in February 1780.

When Clinton returned to New York after the capture of Charleston that June, he took 4500 troops with him, leaving Cornwallis with only 4000 British regulars to pacify a southern theater larger than France. The only way that could possibly happen was if a large loyalist population were lurking beneath the surface of southern society, waiting for Cornwallis to call them forward to the British flag. In July, Cornwallis moved his army inland to confront a large detachment of continentals under Horatio Gates, the hero of Saratoga, who had been dispatched by congress to counter the British occupation of Charleston.* While defeating Gates was important, the engagement would also allow Cornwallis to test the larger prospects of Great Britain's southern strategy.

When the two armies faced off at Camden on August 16, Gates enjoyed a nearly two-to-one advantage (7500 to 4000), but over half his troops were militia. Cornwallis exploited the confusion among militia units on the left flank of the American line to conduct a classically Howe-like flanking maneuver that permitted his cavalry under the command of Colonel Banastre Tarleton to charge through the breach and wreak havoc. The continentals who stood their ground were massacred. Gates and his staff were among the few who escaped the slaughter, riding over 180 miles before stopping. In an instant, Gates went from the hero of Saratoga to the coward of Camden. Tarleton secured his emerging reputation as the most feared and ruthless officer in Cornwallis's army, as the term "Tarleton's quarter" came to mean killing all prisoners.[53]

Despite their overwhelming victory—and partially because of it—Camden created a backlash against any potent British military presence. Lord Francis Rawdon, second in command to Cornwallis, claimed that the reaction to the Camden triumph "unveiled to us a level of disaffection in this province of which we could have formed no idea." Instead of rallying to their side, "the majority are in arms against us." Adjutant General Charles O'Hara voiced the same dispiriting conclusion: "How impossible must it be to conquer a country where success cannot ensure permanent advantages, but acts like Electrical Fire by rousing every men upon this vast continent to persevere." Cornwallis was understandably stunned that his clear win at Camden had somehow proved a recruitment bonanza for the rebels, attributing it to the fact that "any person daring to speak of it being threatened with instant death."[54]

---

* Washington did not support the choice of Gates to lead the southern campaign, but given the bad blood between them, he did not actively oppose the appointment for fear it would appear partisan.

If winning battles somehow proved counterproductive, losing was worse, especially when the losing British force was comprised primarily of recently recruited loyalists. This was the fate of a loyalist regiment of 1125 troops on October 7 at Kings Mountain, a mile from the North Carolina border, commanded by Major Patrick Ferguson. A twenty-year veteran of the British army, Ferguson was a charismatic but ruthless leader in the Tarleton mode. His regiment of mostly local volunteers regarded looting and rape as justifiable rewards for service. Once ensconced on Kings Mountain, he issued a warning to the local populace that men should expect to be executed, their wives and daughters abused by marauding loyalists if they refused to pledge themselves to the British side. "If you choose to be pissed upon forever and ever ruled by a set of mongrels," he declared, "say so at once, and let your women turn their backs upon you."[55]

Unknown to Ferguson, approximately 1800 backwoodsmen, calling themselves the Over-a-Mountain Men, were assembling at the base of Kings Mountain. They had come from across the Blue Ridge, seeking revenge for their friends and families, who had been savaged by Ferguson's regiment. Their motives were less political than deeply personal. The result was a massacre. More than 300 loyalists were killed, including Ferguson, whose body was riddled with bullets, and the rest were taken prisoner. The dead bodies were piled up to serve as a reminder of the fate awaiting all aspiring loyalists. It would be atrocity for atrocity. All hope for recruiting loyalists in the Carolina backcountry ended, and Cornwallis was forced to fall back to his secure garrison at Camden. He reported to Clinton that "tortures and inhuman action are every day committed by the enemy," not mentioning that his own officers, especially Tarleton and Lord Rawdon, were equivalently ruthless.* "With-

---

* Cornwallis gave explicit orders to treat civilians gently, but he could not control his subordinate officers. He was especially critical of Hessian units, who were accustomed to regarding pillage and rape as presumptive prizes of war. But the loyalist units under Tarleton and Rawdon were actually the worst offenders.

out restraints," Cornwallis warned, "the war in this quarter will become truly savage." It already was.[56]

BY THE FALL OF 1780, both sides could correctly conclude they were losing the war. For the British, it had become depressingly clear that The Cause could speak with a southern accent. Even though the British press was hailing Cornwallis as the second coming of Hannibal after his victories at Charleston and Camden, the more enduring comparison was the second coming of William Howe. Like Howe, Cornwallis was tactically brilliant but also fated to discover that, once the British army went inland in the Carolinas, victories in battles were like brief bursts of light in a prevailing darkness.

Meanwhile, up in New York, Washington's dire predictions about the imminent collapse of the Continental Army were inching closer to fulfillment. Troop strength fluctuated between three and ten thousand men, but those troubling numbers were deceptive, since the percentage of sick, starved, and shoeless cut the effective force by half. "There is a greater disproportion between the total number and the men fit for duty," Washington observed, "than in any army in the world." The army remained a forever fluctuating force, "constantly sliding from under us as a pedestal of Ice would do from a Statue in a Summer's Day." And the ice kept melting. One more campaign season and it would be gone. Based on his revised estimate that forty thousand troops would be necessary to conduct a successful siege of New York, Washington commanded a force that would never be able to win the war.[57]

The French, of course, could change that dispiriting strategic equation. An advance contingent of French troops had landed at Newport under General Jean-Baptiste Donatien de Viemeur, Count Rochambeau that summer. On September 22, 1780, Washington and Rochambeau met at Hartford to confer about strategy. Both sides expressed instant disappointment to confidants, Washington in the small size

of the French force (five thousand troops), Rochambeau at the shabby
condition of the continentals accompanying Washington. (Slightly over
a year later, Rochambeau would correct his first impression, describing
the fighting prowess of these apparent ruffians as remarkable.) They
agreed on three major goals: New York was the preferred target; naval
superiority was essential for success, and only the large French fleet
currently deployed in the Caribbean was sufficient for the task; the
size of the French army needed to be increased to at least fifteen thousand troops.[58]

Rochambeau insisted on adding one codicil to the plan: if for
whatever reason the logistical resources to capture New York proved
insufficient, the French fleet should go to the Chesapeake and the main
military effort should be aimed at Virginia. What Rochambeau did not
tell Washington was that the French fleet was never coming as far north
as New York, because that would take Admiral de Grasse, the commander of the French fleet, too far from his main theater of operations
in the West Indies. Rochambeau recognized that Washington's fixation
on New York could not be opposed without risking an eruption that
could be felt as far away as Paris. It would also be undiplomatic to confront His Excellency with the unvarnished truth that France regarded
the American theater as a mere sideshow, only to be visited by the major
French fleet during hurricane season in the Caribbean. Rochambeau did
feel free to apprise Washington that the French army was under orders
to remain in Newport until word arrived that the French fleet was on
the way. There was no way of knowing when that would happen.[59]

Washington was brooding over this disappointing exchange with
Rochambeau on the way back to camp when more bad news arrived,
this time from a wholly unexpected direction. "Transactions of the most
interesting nature and such as will astonish you—have just been discovered," he dashed off to Greene. Benedict Arnold, generally regarded as
the most courageous and preternaturally gifted combat commander in
the Continental Army, had gone over to the British. Apparently, Arnold

had been negotiating for weeks to deliver the American garrison at West Point into British hands in return for a substantial bribe. The plot was exposed at the last moment when Arnold's British contact, Major John André, was stopped and searched by local militia, who found the entire scheme spelled out in papers that André had hidden in his boots. Arnold himself got word of his exposure just in time to escape down the Hudson on a British warship, appropriately named *Vulture,* and was greeted warmly by General Henry Clinton, who welcomed him into the British army.[60]

André was tried and convicted as a spy. Despite pleas from several of his aides, including Hamilton, that André be executed by a firing squad as befits a soldier, Washington ordered him hanged as a spy. André's heroic demeanor on the gallows was widely reported in the British press. It was the only heroic act in his brief military career, but made André the designated British martyr in the war. Arnold became the most famous traitor in American history.[*]

Washington attempted to put the best face on the troubling episode, declaring in his general orders that "the providential train of circumstances which led to it affords the most convincing proof that the Liberties of America are the object of Divine Protection." The whole affair, he claimed, was really a sign of British desperation. It was "remarkable that this is the first instance of such a major defection."[61]

The exact opposite was true, and Washington knew it, because Arnold was not just "a major defection." He was the best of the best, the singular embodiment of the honor code proudly brandished

---

[*] Arnold's motives have been scrutinized by several generations of biographers, historians, and novelists. Briefly, he had cause to believe that his exploits on the battlefield merited promotion to higher rank. Instead, he was accused of profiteering during his command of the American garrison in Philadelphia, which somewhat unfairly put his reputation under a cloud, a fate he deeply resented. Peggy Shippen, his new wife, was a closet Tory during the British occupation of Philadelphia, and she had flirted with André. Shippen encouraged Arnold's resentments and shabby treatment from his inferior military superiors and encouraged the contact with André. Her tearful performance when interviewed by Washington after the plot was exposed suggests she would have enjoyed a brilliant career as an actress.

by the favored few in the officers' corps of the Continental Army. If Arnold could betray The Cause . . . well, one did not wish to finish that thought. Arnold's defection was an ominous crack in The Cause, a clear sign that the sacrifices being endured by the army had reached the breaking point. Two months later, when the New Jersey line threatened to march on Trenton to demand their back pay and protest the lack of shoes and food, the mutineers saw fit to shout "We are not Arnolds." In one sense, that refrain was uplifting, but Washington, taking no chances, ordered the two ringleaders of the mutiny shot by their own followers. The crack could not be allowed to widen.[62]

UNTIL THE FALL OF 1780, Washington had paid little attention to the southern theater. The capture of Charleston and the humiliation of Gates at Camden were major misfortunes, to be sure, but irrelevant to the outcome of the war, which he was virtually certain would be decided at New York. All requests for military assistance from southern governors received a diplomatic brush-off, some version of the claim that he was thinking "on a larger scale" and could not afford to divert troops from his northern army. Moreover, sending a small detachment south to the vast Carolina and Georgia backcountry would be like firing a cannonball into outer space.

Washington was forced to revise his thinking shortly after receiving a request from congress to replace the disgraced Gates as commander of what remained of the southern army. In early October he received reports that Cornwallis had decided to ignore orders from Clinton and, instead of retiring to the garrison at Charleston, was marching inland with his little army, now down to three thousand troops. Washington no longer regarded every British initiative as a challenge to duel, but Cornwallis's apparent belief that he could move through the Carolinas with impunity caught his attention. Recent rumors from across the Atlantic also cast a new light on the southern theater.

Though not verified for several months, spies in London and allies in Paris reported the vague outlines of a European initiative to negotiate a diplomatic armistice to end the war. In several European capitals—Paris, Madrid, Vienna, St. Petersburg—plans for an intervention were under consideration to end the fighting on the grounds that it had proven too costly for all concerned, and was disrupting all the European economies. (It was characteristic of the Eurocentric mentality to presume that its own interests were hegemonic.) If and when the armistice went into effect, the doctrine of *uti possidetis*, roughly translated as "keep what you own," would freeze the contested regions of North America based on military control at the time fighting ceased. This in turn meant that, if Cornwallis were allowed to roam about the southern theater unopposed, Great Britain could claim possession of all the land south of Virginia.[63]

No matter how far-fetched this scheme seemed—and it proved a pipe dream—Washington could no longer afford to retain his casual posture toward the southern theater. A small but elite force needed to be dispatched southward to counter Cornwallis without delay. No extensive deliberations about who should command the effort were necessary. "Amidst the complicated dangers with which you will be surrounded," Washington wrote to Nathanael Greene, "a confidence in your abilities is my only consolation."[64]

Greene's response showed that he instinctively understood the strategic parameters of his assignment: "My first object will be to equip a flying army to consist of about eight hundred horses and one thousand infantry. I see little prospect of getting a force to contend with the enemy on equal grounds, and therefore must make the most of a kind of partisan war." His chief goal was not to win battles but rather to "cover the country," so that no British claim to control the interior regions of the Carolinas or Georgia could become credible.[65]

All tactical considerations followed naturally from that core strategic assumption. Greene knew he needed a small, fast-moving force with a large complement of cavalry. Virginia was famous for its fast horses, which Greene acquired on his way south. The river-riddled terrain of the Carolina backcountry demanded a large supply of portable boats and rafts for swift crossings at otherwise impassable fords. Greene had them built before he entered North Carolina. His supply line for food and equipment required an experienced logistical wizard to remain in Virginia and keep the supplies flowing. Greene requested and received Baron von Steuben for the task.

Finally, Greene needed a co-commander he could trust, with proven skill at handling local militia. Washington provided Daniel Morgan and his elite corps of Virginia riflemen without even being asked. Everyone knew, in part because the "Old Wagoner" (as Morgan was known) kept telling them, that bad things happened to the British army whenever he and his "boys" showed up. Even before the fighting began, then, Greene's preparations foreshadowed what military historians consider the most brilliant performance by any American field commander in the war. Washington was sending his most trusted lieutenant and the most battle-tested warrior in the Continental Army to seize and sustain control of the southern interior. Cornwallis had no way of knowing what he was about to encounter.[66]

The first major engagement occurred at Cowpens, formerly a grazing field for cattle located close to the North Carolina border in western South Carolina. Greene had deliberately violated a cardinal principle of conventional strategy by dividing his army in the face of a superior British force, thereby compelling Cornwallis to follow suit. While Cornwallis went after Greene to the east, the redcoat commander sent Tarleton's legion after Morgan to the west. He caught him at Cowpens on January 17, 1781.

The night before the battle, Morgan moved from tent to tent, reassuring his militia, drawing in the dirt their prescribed location in two lines two hundred yards apart at the front edge of the battlefield. The first line should wait until the British regulars were fifty yards away,

The Southern Theater, 1780–1781

fire two volleys, then retreat to the second line, where the combined militia units would fire two more volleys, then retreat to the main body of continentals, two hundred yards to the rear. "Remember boys," he reminded them "you are *supposed* to retreat." Morgan's plan was designed to transform the chief liability of militia, its tendency to run away, into a tactical asset.

The always impetuous Tarleton took the bait. Believing that the retreating militia signaled the start of a rout, he charged into the trap with his whole force, which was greeted by a sustained stream of high-velocity lead from Morgan's veteran marksmen. Tarleton was one of the few British officers to survive. Shouts of "Tarleton's quarter" were heard as whole British units tried to surrender, but summary executions were rare, as the high number of prisoners revealed. In all, Tarleton lost over 800 of his 1100 troops killed or captured; Morgan suffered only 72 casualties. Neither Tarleton's reputation nor Cornwallis's southern army ever fully recovered. Morgan secured his status as heir apparent to Benedict Arnold as America's most legendary warrior.[67]

For the next two months the southern campaign became a series of races to river fords, highlighted by Greene's successful "race to the Dan" a few hours ahead of Cornwallis's increasingly beleaguered and shrinking army. By any realistic estimate, Cornwallis should have moved the surviving elements of his army to the Carolina coast and a protective enclave at either Wilmington or Charleston. But he refused to do that. His fixation, as potent as Washington's obsession with New York, was the destruction of Greene's army. In order to match Greene's speed on the march, Cornwallis ordered his troops to discard everything but their muskets and horses. "In this situation," wrote his aide Charles O'Hara, "without baggage or provisions of any sort, in this most barren, inhospitable, unhealthy part of North America, opposed by the most savage, inveterate cruel enemy, with zeal and bayonets only, it was resolved to follow Greene's army to the end of the world."[68]

Guilford Courthouse was not the end of the world, but a small village surrounded by wooded pastureland in north central North Carolina. Cornwallis did not catch Greene's army there on March 15. Greene decided to make a stand, inviting an attack, in part because he had been reinforced by 2000 Virginia and North Carolina militia. His total force of almost 4000 men outnumbered Cornwallis's army two to one. Morgan, however, was missing. A debilitating case of sciatica forced the Old Wagoner, much against his will, to head home to Virginia. At his suggestion, Greene adopted his three-lined Cowpens plan for the larger battlefield at Guilford.[*]

It worked again, though not nearly as well. Without Morgan's on-the-field leadership, the militia units did not just appear to run away, they actually fled the battlefield. In addition, Cornwallis was not Tarleton. Instead of rushing into the trap impetuously, he delayed the assault on the final line of continentals, even ordering his artillery to fire on his own troops when they first engaged with Greene's last line of defense at the courthouse. After three hours of savage fighting, Greene decided that he had made his point, and abandoned the field, thereby allowing Cornwallis to claim victory.[69]

But it was a ruinous victory. Guilford courthouse was a southern version of Bunker Hill. Cornwallis suffered more than 500 dead and wounded, including some of his most experienced officers, over twice the casualties suffered by Greene's army. The Cornwallis victory came at a huge cost, nothing less than the abiding relevance of the British army in the Carolinas. Greene's report the day after the battle captured the confidence he carried away from Guilford: "Our army retired in good order. We are now in the most perfect readiness to give the Enemy Action again." Or, as he later put it, "we fight, get beat, rise and fight again." Greene was fully prepared to lose his way to victory in the south.[70]

At least initially, the British ministry misinterpreted the results of

---

* This is the battle depicted, albeit in highly fictionalized form, in the popular film *The Patriot*.

Guilford. Desperate for good news, Germain spread the word that the new British Hannibal had won a great victory, which now put the Carolinas and Georgia under British control. The exact opposite was true. Greene's little army was moving with impunity into the interior, now accompanied by two soon-to-be legendary guerrilla leaders, Francis Marion (the Swamp Fox) and Thomas Sumter (the Carolina Gamecock), both of whom bore personal grudges against British and loyalist atrocities, which they were fully prepared to punish with atrocities of their own making. (Sumter recruited over a thousand men into his legion, promising to provide each man with a slave and as much plunder as he could carry away from each engagement.) By the spring of 1781, the British occupied the coastal cities of Wilmington, Charleston, and Savannah, plus an outpost in South Carolina called Ninety-Six. Otherwise, political and military control rested in rebel hands, though roving bands of loyalist militia continued to terrorize the countryside for well over a year, making "control" a misleading word throughout the Carolinas.

IF SUPPORT FOR the Continental Army was an accurate measure of patriotism, The Cause was dying. Writing in code to John Laurens, whose fluency in French had prompted Washington to dispatch him on a fundraising mission to Paris, His Excellency sounded an ominous note: "It is equally certain that the troops are fast approaching to nakedness, and that we have nothing to clothe them with; that the hospitals are without medicines, and our sick without nutriment except such as well men eat; that all our public works are at a stand. . . . But why need I run into detail, when it may be declared in a word that we are at the end of our tether."[71]

For obvious reasons, Washington regarded the Continental Army as the institutional embodiment of The Cause. And from that perspective his lamentations made perfect sense. But the campaign in the south revealed that there was a bottom-up version of patriotism that remained alive and well, indeed flared into full bloom whenever British troops or loyalist units appeared in the vicinity. This was the local, on-the-ground version of The Cause. It could not be appeased by British gestures at leniency or killed by the more prevalent British brutality, which in fact only amplified its passionate intensity. Like Walt Whitman, The Cause contained multitudes.

Even in moments of relative calm, it never went away. The same farmers, artisans, and tavern owners who resented paying taxes to support the Continental Army continued to serve in the local militia as a roving police force. Along with their wives and mothers, they continued to enforce oaths of allegiance by Committees of Safety and of Inspection. All the governments at the town, county, and state levels remained in the hands of the resistance. These local embodiments of The Cause were invisible to the British ministry in faraway London, but they were the underlying reason that interior regions throughout the American theater remained a no-man's-land for the British army. They were also, however, the underlying reason any national version of The Cause would encounter powerful headwinds, because local allegiances were confined to face-to-face relationships that did not translate to a larger, national arena.

While the British could draw on their impressive fiscal and military resources to sustain their army and navy in North America almost indefinitely, this bottom-up version of The Cause provided a strategic trust fund, more valuable than money, to sustain the American resistance no matter how long the war continued.* It was a recipe for prolonged stalemate. Only an unforeseeable turn of events could break the deadlock. As it turned out, the outcome depended on the weather in the Caribbean.

---

* There is no way to construct a computer program that plays out the scenario if the Continental Army had ceased to exist in the spring or summer of 1781, which at the time was a realistic possibility. But the bottom-up version of The Cause provided a permanent safety net that defied subjugation. Even if the British maintained a ground force of fifty thousand troops in country for several decades, a logistical impossibility, the American resistance would have persisted until the British realized that the game was not worth the cost.

PROFILE

JOSEPH BRANT

Joseph Brant was the Mohawk chief primarily responsible for leading the warriors of the Six Nations on a devastating campaign in 1778 designed to eliminate white American settlements in Iroquois country. His tactics were both bold and ruthless, leaving Washington wholly frustrated. "To defend an extensive frontier against the incursion of Indians under Brant," he lamented, "is next to impossible." If the war for independence generated opportunities for leadership among the former American colonists, the same selection process occurred among the Native American tribes. And Joseph Brant became the George Washington of the vaunted Iroquois Confederacy.

The stunning portrait by George Romney captures Brant during his visit to London in 1775, where he was introduced to British society as "Colonel Joseph Brant, King of the Mohawks." He was already being groomed as an invaluable British ally, the "noble savage" who could consolidate the military prowess of the Six Nations against the emerging American rebellion. This made eminent sense to Brant, who regarded the British presence as the principal protection against the budding American invasion to the east. He welcomed British patronage, but his highest priority was preservation of Native American sovereignty.

Brant was spotted as a prospective prodigy at a young age
by Sir William Johnson, the
highly respected British superintendent for Indian affairs in the
northern colonies, who just happened to be married to Brant's
older sister, Molly. Johnson saw
to it that Brant was sent to Elea-
zar Wheelock's School for Native
Americans, which eventually
became Dartmouth College.
There he converted to Christian-
ity, became fluent in English, and

Thayendanegea (Joseph Brant) by George
Romney, 1776.

studied Latin and Greek classics. He could dress like an English gentleman but always carried a tomahawk.

Brant's Iroquois warriors were invincible against local militia opposition in western New York and northeastern Pennsylvania during the
1778 campaign. But they were no match for the overwhelming force of
Continental troops Washington dispatched under General John Sullivan in 1779. Despite the price on his head, Brant escaped with the
surviving core of his small army and took refuge in the British garrison
across the Canadian border at Niagara.

He spent the rest of his life in Canada, attempting to create a
western version of the Iroquois Confederacy in what is now southern
Ontario. In 1785 he returned to London in order to protest the terms
of the Treaty of Paris, which he described as the total abandonment of
Native American rights to the new American government. The inherent
weakness of that government gave him hope, since its likely collapse
would afford the opportunity to recover some portion of the Iroquois
empire. Another portrait, done by Gilbert Stuart during this second

London visit, depicts a visibly aging man still proud, but no longer the picture of supreme confidence.

Brant died in 1807, thoroughly disillusioned with the prospects for the Native American population in the United States and frustrated with the British support for his people in Canada. In 1850 his body was exhumed and reburied in the town named after him. Eventually a statue was unveiled in his honor that still stands in Victoria Park, Brantford, Ontario. Over twenty thousand loyalist descendants attended the ceremony. In the United States his name remains synonymous with savagery. In Canada he is remembered as a national hero for his loyalty to the British Empire and his ardent advocacy for Native American rights.

CHAPTER SIX

The Chesapeake

It was a most wonderful and very observable
coincidence of favorable circumstances.
—Jonathan Trumbull, Yorktown, September 28, 1781

Early in 1781, George Germain discovered Chesapeake Bay. It had
always been there, of course, always in this case meaning thirty-
five million years. About that time a meteor struck the Atlantic coast
near present-day Cape Charles, creating a crater a mile deep and fifty
miles wide. As the glacier covering North America melted, the water
pouring down the east side of the Appalachian range formed more than
150 rivers and streams that flowed into the crater, in the process carving
out geological indentations that produced a remarkable 3600 miles of
interior coastline.[1]

If an admiral instead of a general had shaped British strategy at
the start of the war, the Chesapeake would surely have caught his eye.
For here was a giant collection of natural harbors sitting squarely in the
middle of the American theater with multiple avenues of entry for inva-
sions of Virginia, Maryland, Delaware, and Pennsylvania. Thirty-five
years later, during the war of 1812, the Chesapeake became the naval

platform for the British invasion force that burned much of Washington City.

In December 1780 the Chesapeake captured General Clinton's attention as the gateway to Virginia, which had become the chief source of supplies for Greene's army in the Carolinas. Although it was the largest and most populous state, the Old Dominion had somewhat strangely escaped the ravages of war. That all ended when Clinton dispatched the recently appointed General Benedict Arnold with 1600 mostly Hessian troops to seize the harbor at Portsmouth, then conduct raiding parties inland to disrupt Greene's supply line. Arnold expanded his mandate by attacking the new Virginia capital at Richmond, burning it to the ground, then marching through the Tidewater region in a scorched-earth campaign that many of his subordinate officers found excessively vengeful. Arnold clearly believed that he had something to prove.[2]

He was also aware there was a price on his head as the most hated man in America. (Arnold kept two small pistols in his pockets to ensure that he would never be taken alive.) The fact that the ultimate traitor was roaming freely through the largest state, wreaking havoc, essentially unopposed, forced Washington to send Lafayette with 1200 troops to contest the British presence in Virginia. All of a sudden, both sides were breaking out their maps of the Chesapeake.[3]

Germain joined the list of map readers in part because he and George III were harboring the illusion that Cornwallis had established British control over the Carolinas and should now carry the momentum of his southern campaign into Virginia. "I am commanded by His Majesty," Germain apprised Clinton, "to acquaint you that the recent recovery of the Southern Provinces should lead to the Prosecution of the war by pushing our Conquests from *South* to *North*," which meant that "Virginia is to be considered as the Chief principal object for the Employment of all the Forces under your Command."[4]

Cornwallis, of course, was fully aware that his campaign in the Carolinas had failed but for that very reason was eager to end his futile marches hither and yon in quest of a decisive battle that never came. Anything to escape the malarial swamps and impossibly fractured social and political networks of the Deep South. Germain's Virginia strategy therefore struck Cornwallis as a brilliant idea, which he immediately embraced. "If we mean an offensive war in America," he explained, "we must bring our whole force into Virginia, for we might then have a stake to fight for, and a successful battle may then give us America."[5]

More realistically, it might give the British Virginia, the most valuable piece on the American chessboard if and when the doctrine of "keep what you control" became the guiding principle in a negotiated settlement. "I cannot help expressing my wishes that the Chesapeake may become the Seat of the War," Cornwallis informed Clinton, "even at the expense of abandoning New York." On April 25, even before Clinton endorsed the decision, Cornwallis moved his army into Virginia, where he hoped to meet his destiny as the one man with the daring and vision—Clinton presumably would be relegated to the sidelines—to rescue the British Empire from the frustrations of a protracted war.[6]

UP IN HIS HEADQUARTERS at New Windsor, ten miles north of West Point, Washington remained convinced that his own destiny, and America's, still lay a day's ride south at New York. In May he requested a meeting with Rochambeau in Wethersfield, Connecticut, where it was decided that Rochambeau should move his 5000 troops from Newport to a location near New York. There he and Washington could reconnoiter the British defenses on Long Island and Manhattan. In what could be considered either an act of duplicity or diplomacy, Rochambeau once again did not let Washington know they were both wasting their time, because the major French fleet in the Caribbean commanded by Admiral de Grasse was never sailing as far north as New York, only as far as the Chesapeake, and only after the hurricane season in the Caribbean began in August. Rochambeau did manage to extract a promise from Washington that, if the New York option proved unattainable, the alternative target should be Virginia. That conclusion was actually foreordained, but Rochambeau realized that Washington needed to reach it in his own time and way.[7]

That, at any rate, is essentially what happened. Despite the existence of a newly named Confederation Congress, all requests for support went unanswered, in part because the congress was having trouble raising a quorum. Without another 10,000 troops, New York remained impregnable.

Moreover, now that it was clear that Cornwallis was moving into Virginia, there was no way that Lafayette, with only 1200 troops, could contain the damage. And any successful British occupation of Virginia had ominous implications. "From the most recent European intelligence," Washington wrote to Governor Thomas Jefferson, "the British are endeavoring to make as large seeming conquests [in Virginia] that then may enlarge the plea of *uti possitetis* [sic] in the proposed mediation." Without Virginia, an independent America made little geographic or political sense.[*][8]

In his diary entry for July 30, Washington confessed his concern about "my obstinacy in urging a measure to which his [Rochambeau's] own judgment was opposed"—that is, insisting upon New York as the target. Three days later he wrote Robert Morris, the recently appointed superintendent of finance, requesting the funds to cover the cost of thirty transport ships in Philadelphia as soon as possible, explaining that New York had been "laid aside" and that "Virginia seems to be the next object."[9]

Washington and Rochambeau were now on the same page, but at this stage neither man knew where Cornwallis would place his army.

---

* Keep in mind that Virginia at the time included the subsequent states of West Virginia and Kentucky.

Having assumed command of the British troops stationed in Virginia, Cornwallis now led a formidable force of 7000 men trailed by a caravan of nearly 4000 former slaves, marching inland as far as Petersburg in quest of Lafayette's token force. "The boy," Cornwallis boasted, "cannot escape me."[10]

Johann Ewald, a Hessian officer serving with Cornwallis, described the army on the march as "a wandering Arabian or Tartar horde" that descended "like locusts" on every acre of farmland it passed: "Every officer had four to six horses and three or four Negroes, as well as one or two Negresses for cook and maid. Every soldier had his Negro, who carried his provisions and bundles." By carrying the war into Virginia, the British had provided an opportunity for slaves in the largest slave-owning state to flee for freedom wherever the British army appeared. The entourage with Cornwallis included seventeen slaves from Mount Vernon and twenty-three slaves from Monticello. Ewald was mystified by the multicolored caravan, as well as by Cornwallis's intensity, which seemed unrestrained. No one knew where this bizarre collection of soldiers and servants was going, except to glory.[11]

In June Rochambeau wrote to de Grasse, confirming the Chesapeake destination, but also preparing the admiral for an unpleasant surprise. "I must not conceal from you, Monsieur, that the Americans are at the end of their resources, that Washington will not have half the troops he has reckoned to have. It is therefore of the greatest consequences that you take on board as many troops as possible, that 4000 or 5000 men will not be too many. These, Monsieur, are the actual and sad pictures of the affairs of this country." Wherever the battle occurred, it would have to be a French show.[12]

As Washington began to make preparations for the five-hundred-mile trek to the lower Chesapeake, it would soon become clear that "a French show" also meant covering the costs of the entire campaign. Robert Morris informed Washington that his first act as superintendent of finance was to check the account books of the congress. He learned that the total debt of the United States was $30 million and growing by $5 million annually. The printed continental dollars had depreciated further, now being traded for specie at 500 to 1. When Morris reported these unattractive facts to the congressional delegates, many of them appeared to be shocked, apparently unaware the government was bankrupt. The reason was simple: the states refused to pay their annual tax levies. The war effort was almost entirely dependent on French loans.[13]

Morris eventually sent a Circular Letter to the Governors, lecturing them on their patriotic duty: "While we do nothing for ourselves, we cannot expect the assistance of others. It is high time to relieve ourselves from the Infamy we have already sustained. This can only be done by solid revenue. We may be happy or miserable as we please." When he received complaints from several governors that their constituents adamantly refused to pay taxes, Morris was unmoved: "The complaint is nothing new to me, nor to anybody. The Complaint is quite as old as Taxation itself and will last as long."[14]

In the meantime, funds were needed to transport 7000 continentals, five hundred horses, and several tons of heavy cannons to Virginia. Morris stepped into the breach by making himself acting quartermaster, then drafting personal checks against his own credit to pay for all supplies and food. He knew that eventually the French would compensate him because a shipment of silver from Paris was due in Boston within weeks. Not for nothing was Morris called The Financier.

While Morris worried about money, Washington worried about secrecy. How could he get 12,000 French and American troops, marching in a column nearly three miles long, past New York without being detected? The answer was to take the entire column fifty miles north of New York before crossing the Hudson, then heading south across western New Jersey to Philadelphia. It worked, considerably assisted by the fact that Clinton had intercepted two of Washington's letters of May, urging New York as the optimum target. Clinton was expecting an attack on Staten Island and did not realize Virginia was the new target until Washington and Rochambeau were parading through Philadel-phia on September 2, too late to catch them.[15]

Three days earlier, on August 30, Admiral de Grasse had appeared at the mouth of the Chesapeake with twenty-eight ships of the line. That splendid news prompted Washington to write Lafayette: "If you get anything new from any quarter, send it I pray on the *Spur of Speed,* for I am almost all impatience and anxiety at the same time." The next missive from Lafayette confirmed his earlier report that Cornwallis had inexplicably decided to move his entire army to the bluffs at the end of the Yorktown peninsula. He had placed himself in a trap, and de Grasse has just sealed it on the ocean side.[16]

This strange decision was based on a direct order Cornwallis had received from Clinton, an order written when Clinton still believed that Washington and Rochambeau intended to attack New York, and there-fore ordered Cornwallis to transport half his army up the coast from the harbor at Yorktown. Once Clinton realized that New York was not the target, he sent several confusing and contradictory orders to Cornwal-lis, but all of them left no doubt that Cornwallis should stay put until told otherwise. By disposition an aggressive tactician, defending an entrenched position was not in Cornwallis's repertoire, nor was hesita-tion, especially when he was fully aware that a trap was closing around him; nor was any respect for Clinton, whom he loathed, and whose orders he had routinely ignored throughout the Carolina campaign. Yorktown proved the fatal exception to all his long-standing tendencies. By mid-September the opportunity for a breakout had come and gone. The only hope was a rescue mission by a naval squadron that Clinton was sending down from New York.[17]

Unfortunately for Cornwallis, the commander of the British fleet sailing south to save him was Thomas Graves, the most undistinguished admiral in the British navy, a man famous for his extreme caution and flair for indecision. The obvious choice to lead the British navy in the most significant and consequential naval battle in the war was Admiral George Rodney, the gruff, domineering, but also most dominating British combat commander on the high seas. But Rodney had come down with a serious prostate illness and was on his way back to London for treatment. And so Thomas (Safe Harbor) Graves led nineteen ships of the line south to engage twenty-five warships commanded by de Grasse in what became the Battle of the Chesapeake, the largest naval engagement of the war in the Atlantic theater.

As Gates approached the Yorktown peninsula, he was stunned at the size of de Grasse's force, since he had been informed that de Grasse would leave a portion of his fleet in the Caribbean to protect French interests there. (Before sailing for London, Rodney had recommended that course in his customary tone of certainty.). But de Grasse had brought all the major ships of the line in the French navy with him, and was also expecting additional support when Admiral de Barras brought his smaller fleet down from Newport. The French were all in, with their top fighting admiral in command. The British had underestimated the level of the French commitment, were significantly outnumbered, and led by an elderly mediocrity.

Given all these disadvantages, the five-day Battle of the Chesapeake (September 5–9) was a closely contested affair, a murderous exchange of broadsides at close range in which both sides suffered heavy casualties. The British ships enjoyed a tactical advantage because they were all "coppered," meaning equipped with copper bottoms that made them faster and more maneuverable. But on September 9, when the French fleet was bolstered by the arrival of the Count de Barras's squadron from Newport, Graves called a council of war, which supported his decision to withdraw rather than risk total destruction of the heavily damaged British fleet. The following day the British flotilla set sail for New York, where Graves hoped to have his damaged ships repaired, then return at full force to rescue Cornwallis and his army, which would have to hold out until then.[18]

On September 14, Washington and Rochambeau arrived in Wil-

liamsburg, barely in time to view the British sails on the horizon, limp-
ing back to New York. "What may be in the Womb of Fate is very
uncertain," Washington wrote upon his arrival at Yorktown, "but we
anticipate the reduction of Lord Cornwallis with his entire army." Fate,
in fact, had already spoken, since the last opportunity for Cornwallis's
extraction was now gone with the proverbial wind.[19]

By early October Cornwallis's situation had become hopeless.
His 7200 troops and 2000 former slaves—the latter down from 4000
because of smallpox—were surrounded by nearly 40,000 French and
American soldiers and sailors. It also happened that Rochambeau
was a proven master of siege warfare, and his military engineers were
renowned as the best in Europe. Once they started digging their angled
trenches, then moved their heavy artillery into point-blank range, death
would rain down on the helpless British defenders all day and night.
Cornwallis moved his headquarters into a cave.

Washington was given the honor of firing the first cannon shot,
which by sheer luck happened to score a direct hit on Cornwallis's staff
having lunch. (The luck was equally divided at Yorktown: the British
got all the bad; the Americans and French all the good.) After his ceremonial performance, Washington had little to do but observe, though
Joseph Plumb Martin did recall him crawling in the trenches one night,
checking on Martin's unit of sappers and miners, who were doing the
digging. Martin's recollection of the scene in his memoirs made it legendary in subsequent histories, helpfully obscuring the fact that the climactic battle of the American war for independence was almost entirely
a French operation.*[20]

One symbolically significant exception occurred on the night of

---

* It took the United States over a century to repay the debt it owed the French. In 1917, upon
arriving in Paris with the American Expeditionary Army, Colonel Charles Stanton, recalling the
debt, declared, "Lafayette, we are here."

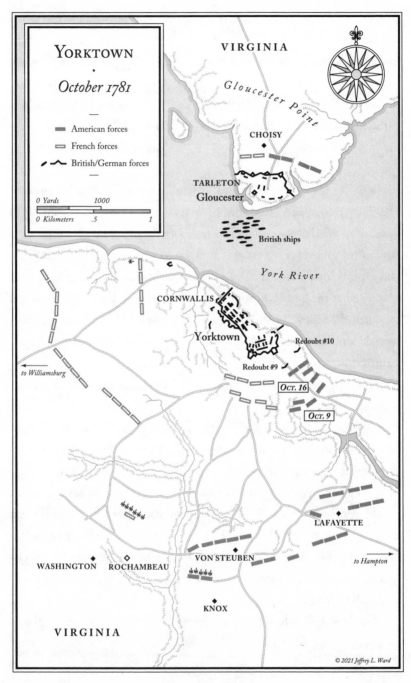

Yorktown, October 1781

October 15. A heavily defended redoubt on the British perimeter needed to be taken in order to complete the last row of siege trenches. Washington had chosen Lafayette to lead an elite company of African American troops from the mostly Black Rhode Island regiment to conduct the assault. Hamilton persuaded His Excellency to let him lead the charge, which was the combat assignment Hamilton had been craving for years. Hamilton then recruited his best friend, John Laurens, to join him.

For about fifteen minutes, Hamilton and Laurens lived their honor-driven dream of glory, charging across the pockmarked no-man's-land, airbursts from British mortars their only source of light, risking their lives together at the head of Black troops whose cause they had both championed. Hamilton vaulted into the redoubt on the back of a Black sergeant while Laurens circled to the rear in order to block the escape of fleeing British troops. After brisk hand-to-hand fighting inside the redoubt, the surviving British defenders surrendered and Hamilton shouted an order that they all be spared. The Stars and Stripes then went up to signal victory. It was the purest version of The Cause imaginable for officers like Hamilton and Laurens, the triumph of "the few." It was also the only major American-led attack at Yorktown.[21]

The incessant artillery barrage generated thirty to forty British casualties a day. The freed slaves with Cornwallis's army were dying at a faster rate, some from bullets and shrapnel, more from the raging smallpox epidemic. The roughly four hundred horses could not be fed or protected, so Cornwallis ordered them all destroyed, their carcasses thrown into the York River. But the tide carried them back to shore, where their decaying bodies produced the smell of death throughout the British encampment. On October 16 Cornwallis decided that the remnant of his army had suffered enough, was in no condition to oppose the inevitable assault, and that Clinton's promised rescue was not coming in time. He sent an officer carrying a white flag across the lines with a note requesting the terms of surrender.[22]

Washington's response was short but not sweet: "The same Honors will be granted to the Surrendering Army as were granted to the Garrison at Charles Town." This was an allusion to the severe terms imposed by General Clinton on Benjamin Lincoln's 5000 troops at Charleston in 1780, who were denied the customary "honors of war." The British would not be treated with the mutual respect customarily reserved for defeated but honorable fellow soldiers. They would not be allowed to fly their regimental colors. After the ceremony, all the soldiers and officers except generals would be marched to prison camps.[23]

Cornwallis had no alternative but to accept these terms, but he did request one personal favor. He wanted the sloop *Bonetta* to sail out of Yorktown "without examination," officially to carry news of his capitulation to Clinton, unofficially to allow about 250 loyalists and former slaves serving with the British army to escape retaliation. Washington concurred with a silent nod.

The surrender ceremony occurred on October 19, four years to the day after Burgoyne's surrender at Saratoga. A Trumbull painting shows Washington seated on Nelson, his favorite mount, with his faithful servant, Billy Lee, seated beside him.* The British troops, wearing fresh uniforms, marched out between two rows of troops stretching for over a mile, the French resplendent in official dress, the Americans in hunting shirts, tattered pants, some without shoes. Several eyewitnesses remembered that the British troops cast only insolent glances at the Americans, preferring to recognize the French as victors. Legend has it that the British band played a popular tune entitled "The World Turned Upside Down." Nobody really knows, but the legend captures the British sense of incredulity at losing the battle, perhaps the war, to a motley gang of American provincials.[24]

Cornwallis pleaded illness to avoid the humiliating ceremony, passing the duty to General Charles O'Hara, the talkative Irishman

---

* See the profile of Billy Lee at the end of this chapter.

who had served with him throughout the Carolina campaign. O'Hara attempted to surrender his sword to Rochambeau, who declined and pointed him toward Washington, who declined to accept the sword of a subordinate officer and pointed O'Hara to Benjamin Lincoln, who accepted it, then led the British column to an adjoining field to stack their arms. Many British soldiers were cursing, others crying.[25]

The most consequential battle in American history had just ended. And its outcome had depended upon a series of unpredictable events that needed to occur in the proper sequence: the hurricane season needed to arrive in the Caribbean just when Cornwallis moved his army onto the Yorktown peninsula; Clinton needed to believe that the approaching French and American army was intending to attack New York rather than head south to Virginia; Robert Morris needed to use his personal credit to subsidize the movement of the Continental Army to Yorktown; de Grasse needed to take his entire fleet to the Chesapeake, not leave a significant force in the Caribbean as the British presumed he would; Cornwallis needed to act with uncharacteristic hesitancy by not attempting a breakout before the full French and American force arrived to seal the trap; and late in the game, when Cornwallis ordered a partial evacuation of British troops by rowboat to Gloucester, on the opposite shore of the York River, a sudden and violent storm came up to block even that last desperate effort.

Such a stunning series of coincidences was almost enough to convince Washington that, in addition to the French, The Cause enjoyed supernatural allies. He began to use terms like "providential" and "standing miracle" to describe the looming American triumph. Writing to Greene in 1783, he predicted that historians would have a difficult time telling the true story of the war, because "it is more than probable that Posterity will bestow on their labors the epithet and marks of fiction." In fact, no novelistic rendering of Yorktown as it really happened would have been deemed credible.[26]

IT TOOK FIVE WEEKS for the shock waves from Yorktown to cross the Atlantic. On November 25 Germain gathered himself, walked to Lord North's residence, and delivered the bad news; North received it "as he would have taken a ball in the breast." It was common knowledge that the prime minister had been searching for a way out of the war ever since Saratoga, and had tendered his resignation to the king so frequently that cartoons in the London press described it as a ministerial minuet. Now, the loss of another British army, commanded by no less than Great Britain's designated Hannibal, rendered all diplomatic dancing irrelevant. Germain described Lord North pacing across his study swinging his arms wildly, repeating, "Oh, God. Oh, God. It is all over."[27]

Strictly speaking, Lord North was right; at least militarily, Yorktown was the last major engagement in the North American theater. Politically, however, it would take several months for the reverberations to rumble through the corridors of Whitehall and Westminster. The comfortable majority the king had enjoyed for the past decade, much of it due to royal patronage that kept about 160 members in his pocket, began to decline precipitously. The forever rumpled, always eloquent, and reliably irreverent Charles James Fox, the self-appointed Whig spokesman, rose routinely to demand the resignation of North, Germain, and Sandwich, whom he characterized as war criminals.

Fox was joined by the newest and youngest member of Commons, twenty-two-year-old William Pitt, son of the late Lord Chatham, who picked up where his father left off: "I am persuaded, and I will affirm, that it is a most accursed, wicked, barbarous, cruel, unnatural, unjust and most diabolic war," Pitt thundered. "The expense of it has been enormous, yet what has the British nation received in return?" Pitt had the numbers on his fingertips: the national debt had doubled since 1775, from £127 million to £250 million; the total cost of the war was approaching £116 million. Reliable casualty figures were not yet available to Pitt, but approximately fifty thousand British, Hessian, and loyalist soldiers and sailors had perished; all that to retain three besieged coastal garrisons in New York, Charleston, and Savannah. His father's most horrific predictions had all come true. Edmund Burke observed that Pitt the Younger was not just a chip off the old block, but the block itself.[28]

At least initially, George III apparently believed that denial was his highest duty. In his first address to Parliament after Yorktown, he barely mentioned the catastrophe, then only to describe it as a minor detour on the road to British triumph. Any mention of American independence in cabinet meetings was not permitted. Rather than accept the unacceptable, he reiterated his threat to abdicate and even ordered his staff to have the royal yacht always ready for a one-way voyage to Hanover, where he would occupy his other throne. He would never surrender.[*]

But as his majority in Commons withered, even George III was forced to face the fact that his threats to stand alone were merely melodramatic postures. If he were Louis XVI of France or Catherine the Great of Russia, who were divine-right monarchs claiming to derive their authority from God, his threats would have carried greater credibility. But he was a British king, who, since the Glorious Revolution, derived his authority from Parliament. Indeed, George III had based his entire imperial initiative to impose greater control over the American colonies on the principle of Parliament's sovereignty. By casting himself in the role as chief defender of that principle, George III had managed to expand the range of his royal authority, making himself the face of the British Empire.

But all these accumulated powers depended upon retention of

---

[*] Several British historians, including the estimable Piers Mackesy, have compared George III's uncompromising posture to Winston Churchill's defiant role in 1940 during the London blitz and looming Nazi invasion. Among several difficulties, one stands out: Churchill knew that, if Britain could hold out, the Americans would come to the rescue.

comfortable majorities in Parliament, which were now dissolving in the wake of Yorktown. It did not help that, upon his return to England as a paroled prisoner of war in January 1782, General Cornwallis himself declared to assembled reporters that "the conquest of America by fire and sword is not to be accomplished, let your numbers be what they may." If there were a British version of The Cause, it was a top-down version, and Cornwallis had just delivered its eulogy.[29]

Germain remained the chief defender of the government's American policy in the House of Commons, declaring during debate on December 12, 1781, that he would "never put his hand to an instrument conceding the independence of the colonies." Both Fox and Pitt responded with sarcastic references to Germain as "the coward of Minden" and the chief architect of British humiliation at both Saratoga and Yorktown. During the debate Lord North stood up and left the government bench in the front row and moved to the back behind Germain, who was left alone to defend what had become the indefensible within the Commons. Germain told friends that he intended to resign, but before he could do so North apprised him that the king, with great reluctance, had requested his resignation. "You say I must go," Germain jauntily remarked to North, "very well, but pray, why is your Lordship to stay?"[30]

Germain's question was not merely rhetorical. On March 27, 1782, North himself rose in the House to announce his resignation. For three years, ever since French entry into the war, North had been a voice within the cabinet for acknowledging the failure of British policy, gradually withdrawing British troops from America, and seeking the best diplomatic resolution possible. But he did not wish to defy His Majesty publicly and performed his duty as chief manager of the dwindling support for the war in Parliament. Now, however, such support no longer existed, and his final effort to resign could not be refused, because the sovereign source of political authority in the realm had effectively declared his ministry over by delivering a de facto vote of no confidence in any plan to continue the war. His Majesty must now prepare to form a new government and face the fact that it would be—indeed must be—a government committed to the recognition of American independence. The obvious person to lead such a government was Lord Rockingham, who led the antiwar faction in the House of Lords.

Not that George III had become irrelevant, or a mere figurehead. But for him to stand alone against the clear consensus of Parliament was politically impossible. Several critics of the war in Parliament, chiefly Edmund Burke and William Pitt the Younger, accused George III of overstepping his authority during the war, placing his finger too heavily on the scale of an aggressive and even punitive policy toward the American colonists, and claiming to act on behalf of Parliament while using his patronage to purchase the loyalty of its members in what amounted to a rigged majority. One of Rockingham's conditions for accepting the office of prime minister—the other was recognition of American independence—was a dramatic reduction of the annual budget provided for royal patronage, which had seriously compromised both the independence and sovereignty of Parliament.[31]

Moreover, ever since French entry into the war, George III's domino theory had come under serious scrutiny. The Earl of Sandwich, as Lord of the Admiralty, had become the chief voice in the cabinet for making the Caribbean theater the main military priority and, if necessary, abandoning the American war altogether. In fact, both George III and Germain had it exactly backward; the dominoes fell in the opposite direction. The major possessions of the British Empire would be placed at greater risk if military resources were devoted to sustaining the commitment to the American theater, which was probably a lost cause anyway.[32]

This line of argument received unexpected support in April 1782, when Admiral Rodney, recovered from his prostate problem, soundly defeated and nearly destroyed the French fleet of Admiral de Grasse near a necklace of small islands in the Caribbean called Les Saintes.

Rodney's spectacular victory confirmed the conviction within the admiralty that, if he had commanded the British fleet in the Chesapeake, Yorktown would never have happened, a conclusion that Rodney himself endorsed with his customary bravado.[33]

The Battle of Les Saintes recovered what the British regarded as the natural order on the high seas by reestablishing British domination in the Caribbean, most especially the retention of Jamaica, its crown jewel. It also created a new hero ("The Saint of the Saintes") to replace the tarnished Cornwallis and seemed almost designed to focus British attention on a triumph that offset Yorktown. It marked the moment when Great Britain could more comfortably decide to cut its losses in North America and get on with the larger task of dominating the rest of the world. Germain, North, and eventually Sandwich (somewhat unfairly) would play the essential role of scapegoats. The unspoken goal was to move forward without looking back.

WASHINGTON WAS ALSO focused on the future, and what he saw was one more year of war. "My greatest fear," he confided to Greene, "is that Congress may think our work nearly closed, and fall into a state of languor and relaxations." During a three-day visit with the delegates in Philadelphia in November 1781, he made the case for sustaining the Continental Army at its current strength for one year. His goal, as he explained, was "to wage one more vigorous campaign to end the war by driving all British troops from America." When an armistice was declared and diplomatic negotiations began, he wanted to have eliminated all British claims south of Canada and north of the Floridas, thereby rendering the doctrine of *uti possidetis* moot.[34]

Congress did not need to be convinced. The delegates endorsed Washington's request for $8 million to fund the army for one final campaign. They even dispatched representatives to all the state legislatures to make the case for one last contribution to The Cause. This time, however, the state legislatures had a new reason to resist the request. As far as they were concerned, the war was over. Within their own borders, they saw no necessity for one last campaign. In the end, congress received pledges for $5500, barely enough to fund the army for one day. Washington described the response as yet another chapter in a running joke:

> The army, as usual, are without Pay—and a great part of the Soldiery without Shirts—and tho' the patience of them is equally threadbear, the States seem perfectly indifferent to their cries. In a word, if one was to hazard for them an opinion, upon this subject, it would be, that the Army had contracted such a habit of encountering distress & difficulties—and, of living without money, that it would be impolitic & injurious to introduce other customs in it![35]

Washington's sarcasm was an attempt to ridicule the calculated negligence that had barely sustained the Continental Army since Valley Forge. What was new after Yorktown, however, was the prevailing belief that there was no longer any need for an army at all. Washington deeply disagreed, seeing himself as the designated American sentinel, determined to remain on duty at his post until the last vestige of British military occupation was driven from the United States. "It would be an incredible blot to the reputation of this country," he explained to Greene, "not to mount one final campaign to expel them from the Continent."[36]

Moreover, there was no way of knowing with the necessary confidence that the British were genuinely committed to a peace settlement. "My opinion of the matter," he wrote to James McHenry, a member of his general staff, "is that the British Ministry will obtain supplies for the current year, prepare vigorously for another Campaign, and then prosecute the War or Treaty of Peace as circumstance and fortuitous events may justify." He, and of course his army, needed to be ready to meet all possible eventualities. A letter from John Adams, currently negotiating with Dutch bankers in Amsterdam, fortified Washington's worst fears that "the British intend to gain time by lulling us into security and then resume the war." Franklin chimed in from Paris, observing that "the British are unable to carry on the war, and too proud to make peace." He added with a wink that he had recently sent a letter to his old friend Edward Gibbon, along with notes for a book entitled *The Decline and Fall of the British Empire*.[37]

By spring of 1782, however, any hope for a final campaign had fallen victim to the British victory in the Battle of Les Saintes, which destroyed the entire French fleet in the Caribbean. No assault of New York or Charleston was thinkable without French naval support, which no longer existed. Greene's little army was still grinding away in the Carolinas, mostly fighting a guerrilla war against roving bands of loyalists still conducting terrorist raids in the backcountry.* But up in Newburgh, New York, Washington's main army of ten thousand troops had nothing to do but train. Indeed, Washington believed his troops were more combat-ready than at any time earlier in the war, just when the last battle had already been fought.

Eventually the gossip mill began to float stories that Washington intended to declare himself the American Caesar. Why else, so the stories went, would he maintain his army at full strength, when it was clear to all informed observers that the war was over? Why would he appoint himself sentinel in chief and detect looming threats that no one else could see? An old friend from Boston, Thomas Gordon, who was already at work on a history of the war, described a rumor that conjured up comparisons with Julius Caesar and Oliver Cromwell, who had used the Roman legions and the New Model Army, respectively, to establish military dictatorships. And since these two republican experiments

---

* "Bloody Bill" Cunningham, a British colonel of Irish descent, and his outlaw band were waging a war of revenge against patriot families. Their trademark tactic was to make wives and children watch as the father was tortured, then hanged, their home plundered, then burned to the ground.

were the only significant efforts of their kind in recorded history, the pattern had ominous implications.[38]

Nor did it help matters when Alexander Hamilton, probably in his cups, let it be known that The Cause would be best served if Washington marched the army to Philadelphia and ordered the congress to disperse. In May 1782, Lewis Nicola, a junior officer at the Newburgh encampment, put in writing what many officers were whispering behind the scenes: "The congress's erratic conduct of the war had exposed the weakness of all republics; and that certain disaster would befall postwar America unless Washington declared himself king." (If the royal title caused problems because of its offensive association with George III, Nicola expressed confidence that "His Excellency" would work just as well.) Washington delivered a stern lecture to Nicola, urging him "to banish these thoughts from your Mind," denouncing the scheme as "big with the greatest mischief that can befall my Country." But critics described his warning as just the kind of hollow promise that always preceded a military coup.[39]

Nothing came of these whisperings. As in the so-called Conway Cabal, Washington displayed his uncanny flair for silence. And no one stepped forward to risk public assault on Mount Washington. But the episode proved a preview of the postwar political battle between opposing visions of what an independent America should look like. There were, it soon became clear, two irreconcilable versions of The Cause.

On one side stood the confederationists, who dominated the state legislatures and enjoyed the support of their constituents in the towns, villages, and farms, who had served in the local militia but not the Continental Army. They regarded the delegation of authority to the Continental Army and Congress in 1775–76 as a provisional and temporary response to a wartime crisis, which was now over, or at least ending. As the patriotic waters completely receded—they in fact had been receding for years—all political authority should flow back to the thirteen separate mini-republics, where it naturally belonged, and where

American allegiances most comfortably resided. Any effort to resist that downward flow, to prolong or expand the emerging powers of either the Continental Army or the Confederation Congress, was a violation of the original meaning of The Cause—indeed, they would be domestic embodiments of the British leviathan that the victory at Yorktown had presumably banished forever.

On the other side stood the nationalists, a decided minority, though they enjoyed the invaluable support of Washington and the officers' corps of the Continental Army, plus a cluster of current and former members of congress. The common feature of this faction was its exposure during the war to the embedded inadequacies of the confederation framework, which Washington had spent the entire war deploring. While the commander in chief had begun to speak publicly about the need for a federal government after the war that was "competent for general purposes," the most cogent articulation of the nationalist perspective had been Hamilton's series of *Continentalist* essays, published just before Yorktown. After Yorktown, the most prominent advocate for a more expansive version of The Cause, and the most vulnerable target of its opponents, was Robert Morris.

A CENTURY BEFORE the Horatio Alger rags-to-riches story took hold in American mythology, Morris lived that story to perfection. Like Benjamin Franklin's biography, Morris's also has an opening scene in which a teenage boy arrives in Philadelphia with little more than his wits and the clothes on his back, and twenty years later has become the most prominent—in Morris's case, the wealthiest—citizen of the city.

Unlike Franklin—but like Hamilton—Morris was an immigrant, born in Liverpool in 1734. He followed his father, an aspiring tobacco merchant, to the Eastern Shore of Maryland in 1747, and was soon sent as an apprentice to a Philadelphia shipping firm headed by Charles Willing at age thirteen. Eight years later, at the tender age of twenty-one, Morris was made a full partner in Willing, Morris and Company, the largest and most lucrative mercantile house in America's largest port city. Under his canny eye the company tripled the size of its shipping fleet, established agents in all the European capitals, then throughout the Caribbean, and became a de facto bank, with surplus capital always on hand that sent a signal to customers in all its markets that any note Morris signed was as good as gold.[40]

Morris thought economically, and his central idea was "credit," from the Latin *credere*, meaning "to believe." One economist has defined credit as "money of the mind," not the money you actually possess at the time of a transaction, but what customers believe you will later be able to pay. It is the core concept in what will later be called "finance capitalism," and even though the eighteenth century was a pre-capitalistic era, it accurately described Morris's mentality. To the planter class of Virginia, which was deeply in debt to British bankers, it was a form of magical thinking.[41]

Morris was a latecomer to The Cause. Appointed to the Continental Congress in 1775, he sided with the moderate faction led by John Dickinson and only grudgingly embraced the inevitability of American independence. He abstained himself from the vote on July 2, 1776, much like Dickinson warning that the war would prove ruinous for both sides. But then, unlike Dickinson, Morris signed the Declaration on August 2, probably one of the most reluctant signers in the congress.

He then threw his full energies and his matchless list of European and Caribbean contacts into the procurement of arms and equipment for the Continental Army. Before French entry into the war in 1778, he and Franklin worked closely on the Secret Committee, which sustained clandestine transatlantic trade with France that provided munitions, arms, and uniforms for Washington's beleaguered army. As already noted, he used his personal credit to provide supplies and transport for Washington's march toward Yorktown, later claiming with obvious pride that "I can obtain whatever is wanted for the public service by a *stroke* of the pen." Rather awkwardly, the credit of Robert Morris was more credible than that of the American government.[42]

As if Morris did not already know, Franklin felt the urge to warn his old colleague about the hostile response sure to come his way as superintendent of finance:

> You are sure to be censured by malevolent Criticks and Bug Writers, who will abuse you while you are serving them, and wound your Character in nameless Pamphlets, thereby resembling these dirty little stinking Insects, that attack us only in the dark, disturb our Repose, molesting and wounding us while our Sweat and Brood is adding to their subsistence.[43]

Franklin never uttered a more prescient prophecy. For Morris's chief task was to apprise the members of Congress that they were very good at printing money, but very bad at raising taxes, which meant that all that printed money was worthless—in fact, it had been for several years. This in turn explained why the United States was carrying an ever-expanding national debt, currently calculated at $35 million, which then rendered comprehensible the skyrocketing price of bread, corn, and beef and the judgment of European bankers that loaning America money was like tossing it into the ocean.

Within this dismal and dark cloud, Morris, as was his wont, saw a silver lining, which was an answer to the question everyone with a nationalistic persuasion was asking after Yorktown: What will hold the states together once the war officially ended? Morris argued the answer was debt. Whether the states knew it or not, they were now bound together to pay for the cost of The Cause.

A first step was congressional approval of the impost, a 5 percent duty on imports that required unanimous approval by the states because it was, albeit indirectly, a tax, and therefore must be treated as an amendment to the Articles. The money raised by the impost would barely make a dent in the national debt, but Morris strongly endorsed it as a crucial signal to European bankers that the Americans were serious about ending their insolvency. "If the impost is approved, it is possible the public credit will be restored," he explained to the state governors. "But if not, our Enemies will draw from thence strong Arguments that we are unworthy of Confidence, and our Union is a Rope of Sand."[44]

The full Morris program, which took shape in the spring and summer of 1782, envisioned a national bank, called the Bank of the United States, which was modestly capitalized at $40,000; the impost; the federal assumption of state debts; a land tax of one dollar per hundred acres; a poll tax; and an excise tax on liquors. (It was virtually identical to the financial program that Hamilton later proposed as secretary of state in his 1791 *Report on Public Credit*.) Morris was making a precocious effort to create the financial foundation for what he described as "a firm, wise, manly System of federal government," effectively to move the United States from "pluribus" to "unum" nine years before it actually happened.[45]

As he knew full well, his bold effort was guaranteed to generate criticism from ardent enemies. He described them as "those vulgar souls whose narrow Opticks can see but the little Circle of their selfish concerns," adding that "unhappily such Souls are but too common and but too often fill the Seats of Dignity and Authority." All efforts to engage such creatures in a serious argument about the fragile fate of the postwar American republic proved impossible, "like preaching to the Dead."[46]

Morris was not alone. Washington's argument for a more expansive, fully national version of The Cause had become a formalized refrain in his correspondence, especially with fellow officers in the Continental Army who shared his experience of prolonged frustration during the war. "For it is clearly my opinion," he wrote to Hamilton, "that unless Congress have powers competent to all general purposes, that the distresses we have encountered, the expense we have incurred, and the blood we have spilt in the course of an eight years' war, will avail us nothing."[47]

Hamilton, now serving in the New York legislature, needed no prodding. The former aide to Washington now saw himself as a protégé of Morris, most especially as an accomplice in the establishment of an adequate economic foundation for any viable postwar American government. Hamilton's hand was almost certainly behind a proposal entitled Resolution of the New York Legislature Calling for a Convention of the State to Revise and Amend the Articles of Confederation. He was still making the counterintuitive argument that the absence of a national mentality was the very reason a fully empowered federal government was essential to create the political framework in which a national ethos could develop. (Morris's idea to make the national debt the rationale for the postwar vision of The Cause became a strategic insight that Hamilton came to regard as his own invention.) On the presumption that the states were likely to go their separate ways as soon as the war officially ended, Morris began to think that "a continuance of the War is Necessary until our Confederation is more strongly knit, until a common sense of the Obligation to support it shall be more generally diffused among all Ranks of American Citizens." For obvious reasons, he shared the opinion with only a few close friends.[48]

Although the trio of Morris, Washington, and Hamilton was a formidable force, they were vastly outnumbered by ordinary Americans up and down the Atlantic coast who had no interest in political or economic arguments about some putative American nationhood. Those citizens wanted the war to end so they could resume their blissfully ordinary lives undisturbed by outsiders claiming to speak for them, whether they resided in London or Philadelphia. Taken together, they constituted a hegemonic force for enlightened indifference with a potent momentum of its own. Hamilton described that momentum metaphorically. "To borrow a figure from mechanics, the centrifugal is much stronger than the centripetal force in the states—the seeds of discussion much more numbers than those of union." To switch the metaphor, Morris and his supporters were paddling against a powerful current.[49]

The backlash against Morris's financial plan was inevitable, for he was attempting, almost single-handedly, to impose a national economic architecture on a political foundation that vested sovereignty in the states. Even more alarming, he was claiming that a fully empowered American nation-state was the fulfillment of The Cause, not its betrayal.

The first wave of opposition, adopting the title "True Whigs," flowed onto the scene in July 1782 in a campaign to block passage of the impost, which eleven of the thirteen states had already ratified. David Howell, a newly elected member of the Rhode Island delegation in the congress, became the chief voice for the view that the impost was an updated version of the Townshend Acts, and therefore a first step backward "tending towards the establishment of an aristocratical and monarchical government," a direct repudiation of everything The Cause purportedly stood for. If the Confederation Congress passed the impost, Howell argued, it would be announcing that it had become "a foreign government colored in the shade of Parliament."[*50]

Howell was a previously obscure figure, a new voice joining the chorus of more venerable statesmen in Virginia and Massachusetts with impeccable revolutionary credentials. The two most prominent True Whigs were Richard Henry Lee and Samuel Adams, who could both testify to being present at the creation of The Cause, and that Morris's vision of postwar America as a strong nation-state on the British model

---

* Howell was a former mathematics teacher at Rhode Island College (later Brown University) who enjoyed the support of the merchant classes of Providence and Newport. The impost would fall disproportionately on their businesses, and they hired Howell to defend their own economic interests. That said, Howell's convictions as a True Whig were deeply felt political principles that he embraced with theological fervor.

was not what they ever had in mind. If The Cause was a creedal conviction, and the American people were a congregation, the True Whigs were the self-appointed saints now poised to call out Morris as a flagrant sinner who must be cast out of the church.[51]

The strongest and shrillest voice in the True Whig chorus belonged to Richard Henry Lee's younger brother, Arthur Lee, whose political antennae were poised to detect any stirrings in the atmosphere that disrupted the natural order he was divinely ordained to detect. Lee regarded himself as morally obliged to warn his fellow Americans that Robert Morris was the second coming of George III.[*]

In late July 1782 Lee wrote Samuel Adams, whom he considered a kindred spirit, apprising Adams that he was launching a political campaign to expose Morris. "The accumulation of offices in this man, the number of valuable appointments in his gift, the absolute control given him over all Revenue officers, his money and his art," Lee observed, "render him a most dangerous man to the Liberty of this Country." Lee simultaneously began to take aside members of the Virginia delegation in congress, lobbying them to vote against the impost, vilifying Morris as a well-known wartime profiteer. The newest and most up-and-coming member of the Virginia delegation, who still styled himself James Madison Junior, expressed dismay at Lee's relentless assault on Morris's reputation, which struck Madison as a vendetta of paranoid proportions.[52]

---

[*] Lee possessed impressive credentials. Born to the wealthiest and most prominent family in Virginia, he held degrees in medicine from Edinburgh and in law from London's Middle Temple. In the run-up to the war, his dispatches from London, frequently containing reports based on strolls in the woods with William Pitt the Elder, had provided valuable intelligence about Parliament's commitment to an imperial agenda. During his service on the American diplomatic team in Paris, however, he demonstrated a flair for vendettas against fellow diplomats—chiefly Silas Deane, whom he accused of profiteering, and even Benjamin Franklin, whom he accused of harboring pro-French sympathies and being slightly senile. Franklin, in turn, described Lee as more than slightly out of his mind.

☙

THERE HAD ALWAYS BEEN a paranoid edge to American arguments against Parliament and the British ministry, chiefly the claim that the British effort to reform the empire was really a plot to transform loyal subjects into abject slaves. In that sense, Lee's' conspiratorial mentality had a patriotic pedigree, for he was deploying an ideological weapon against Morris that enjoyed honorable origins during the run-up to the war. In Lee's hands, being a True Whig meant bringing the same level of suspicion toward any projection of consolidated power by an American official as had previously been directed at Lord North or George Germain. And The Cause had always encouraged an oppositional way of thinking that needed conspicuous enemies to mobilize its fullest energies. Lee's conspiratorial mentality therefore aligned almost seamlessly with earlier repudiations of British tyranny. It therefore enjoyed semi-sacred status as an essential emotional component of The Cause.[53]

Lee eventually decided that his vilification of Morris could not be confined to private correspondence or backroom lobbying. In order for Lee to be effective, Morris had to be ruined publicly. Under the pseudonym "Lucius," Lee published five essays in the *Freeman's Journal*. Lee's specialty was erudite fulminations, hatchet jobs with a sharp rhetorical edge. He was also adept at assassination by innuendo, in this instance claiming that the absence of evidence for his charges against Morris was the truly clinching evidence of the man's artful duplicity. For example: "In fine, sir, is not the disbursement of eight million annually in contracts, is not the profit and influence arising from this, is not the hourly offerings of incense and adulation from surrounding parasites . . . sufficient to satiate your vanity, pride, and avarice?"[54]

It is impossible to calculate the impact of Lee's campaign against Morris. But it is clear that by the fall of 1782 Morris's hopes for an

expanded version of The Cause had collapsed. The impost, which
Morris regarded as the essential foundation of his program to establish American credit, was rejected in November. The national debt
climbed from $35 million to nearly $40 million. The capital Morris
hoped to assemble in the Bank of the United States had to be spent as
revenue to sustain the Continental Army. Morris announced his intention to resign, declaring, "I am heartily tired of Financiering." In a letter to Washington he tried to swallow the bitter pill of failure with a
smile. "I hope my successor will be more fortunate than I have been,"
he observed, "and that our glorious Revolution may be crowned by
these Acts of Justice without which the greatest human Glory is but the
Shadow of a Shade."[55]

IN RETROSPECT, Morris's program failed because most Americans
were not ready for it. Their experience of the war had occurred within
their local communities, so that, unlike Morris or Washington, their
political horizons did not extend beyond a day's walking distance. If
perchance they had encountered Hamilton's quite brilliant idea that the
absence of a national ethos rendered a more robust federal government
even more essential, it would have struck most of them as incomprehensible. Only later, when the inadequacies of the Articles of Confederation became more obvious, would Hamilton's precocious insight gain
traction. And when it did, Hamilton would make Morris his role model
in framing a national fiscal policy.

Finally, hindsight permits us to see how Arthur Lee and his True
Whig colleagues exposed more fully than ever before the two-sided
character of The Cause. Their insistence that any powerful federal government was a betrayal of the original understanding of The Cause
contained more than a kernel of truth. And their conspiratorial posture
toward any form of consolidated power—indeed, toward government

itself when it originated from afar—had played a crucial role in mobilizing popular opinion against Great Britain's policy of imperial expansion after 1763. As a result, The Cause contained a double-barreled legacy: government was "Them," and government was "Us." The dialogue between those two competing legacies of the founding became, and still remains, the great debate in American political history.

PROFILE

WILLIAM (BILLY) LEE

Billy Lee was the invisible man of the American Revolution. For nearly eight years, 1775 to 1783, Billy was at George Washington's side wherever he went: the Boston Siege, the debacle on Long Island, the escape across the East River, the winter at Valley Forge, all engagements leading up to and including the British surrender at Yorktown. He slept in Washington's tent every night, laid out his uniform, brushed his hair, and tied it with a bow every morning.

Several visitors at Valley Forge described Billy as a recognized celebrity, the personal emissary of His Excellency, greeted on a first-name basis by officers and troops alike. The two visual renderings of Billy in portraits by John Trumbull depict him wearing a turban, perhaps a personal affectation, perhaps his costume as designated leader of the servants kept by other senior officers. He was the most famous African American slave in America.

The relationship between Washington and Billy was always formal and official in public, unknowable in private. Later witnesses at Mount Vernon reported they communicated with silent nods and eye movements requiring no words. We do know that Washington began to struggle with the awkward contradiction of slavery during the war years, and it seems likely that the intimate relationship with Billy was an element in his education.

Billy was the only slave whom Washington freed outright in his will, providing an annual allowance of thirty dollars for the rest of his life. "Thus I give him as a testimony of his sense of attachment to me," Washington wrote, "and for his faithful service during the Revolutionary War." Billy remained at Mount Vernon as a free man, sought out by visitors and reporters for stories about his service alongside the General.

He died in 1810 and is believed to be buried in the enslaved cemetery at Mount Vernon, though he died free.

George Washington and William Lee by John Trumbull, 1780. (Metropolitan Museum of Art)

CHAPTER SEVEN

The Exit

The moderation and virtue of a single character probably
prevented this revolution from being closed, as most others have
been, by a subversion of the liberty it was intended to establish.
—Thomas Jefferson to Joseph Jones, April 16, 1784

By the summer of 1782 it had become clear that nothing was clear. George III had grudgingly appointed Lord Rockingham to succeed North as prime minister and launch a peace process that, for the first time, acknowledged American independence. But Rockingham came down with the flu, then raging in London, and died before assembling a diplomatic team that could initiate serious negotiations. It did not help that no British statesman of stature was interested in the assignment. Franklin's earlier remark remained relevant; the British wanted to end the war, but could not bring themselves to make peace.[1]

Three thousand miles away, outside of Newburgh, New York, Washington kept drilling his ten thousand troops in preparation for a final battle that was never going to happen. Reports from London required three months or more to cross the Atlantic, so news of the ever-shifting factions in the British ministry was neither accurate nor new by the time it reached American shores. The distance problem was making a huge difference for both sides as the war moved from its military to diplomatic phase, prompting Horace Walpole, a longtime opponent of the war and London's most erudite gossip, to regret the existence of the Atlantic Ocean: "It is so inconvenient to have all letters come by way of the ocean," he wrote a prominent lady friend. "People should never go to war above ten miles off, as the Grecian states used to do."[2]

Whenever optimistic reports arrived, Washington was predisposed to doubt them. He kept up a regular correspondence with Greene, who was still tracking down roving gangs of loyalists in the Carolinas and Georgia. "From the former infatuation, duplicity, and perverse system of British Policy," he wrote Greene in August 1782, "I am induced to doubt everything, to suspect everything." A month later he wrote James McHenry, his former aide, upon hearing that the Earl of Shelburne had replaced Rockingham as prime minister. "Our prospect of peace is vanishing," he told McHenry, since Shelburne was known to be a close friend of George III and had once declared "the Sun of Great Britain will set the moment American independency is acknowledged." Shelburne had made that declaration several years earlier and was famous, or infamous, for his perfect blend of duplicity and inscrutability. But Washington interpreted his appointment as a clear sign that the war would continue. In fact, Shelburne's appointment was not a clear sign of anything.[3]

Although there was no way Washington could have known it—the distance problem again—three days before he wrote Greene, a diplomatic meeting had occurred in the royal library at Versailles that established the framework for ending the war. John Jay and the Spanish minister to France, Count Aranda, were hunched over a map of North America. Both men were speaking French, and both men kept pointing at different places on the map.

Jay had just joined the American negotiating team in Paris after spending two frustrating years in Madrid, attempting, without success, to extract a loan from the Spanish government. He was left by himself to begin preliminary discussions, what he called "the skirmishing business," because the other American ministers were preoccupied: Benjamin Franklin was laid up with the gout in his residence at Passy; John Adams was shuffling between Amsterdam and Leyden, attempting to negotiate a loan with reluctant Dutch bankers; and Henry Laurens, recently appointed to replace Thomas Jefferson, who bowed out because of the recent death of his wife, had been captured at sea and thrown into the Tower of London as a prisoner of war.

Prior discussions with a long, ever-changing list of British diplomats had been conducted almost entirely by Franklin, whom the British press described as the "American Prometheus." To most British diplomats, it seemed incongruous, almost unfair, that a country comprised of stammering bumpkins should be represented by the acknowledged diplomatic champion of the world. Even the British press recognized that Franklin's combination of sagacity and savvy defied comparison with anything or anyone the British could bring to the table. Over the months since Yorktown, Franklin had insisted, and British negotiators had reluctantly accepted, that recognition of American independence was nonnegotiable; that is, it was not a bargaining chip in the game, but a precondition without which negotiations could not proceed.[4]

There were compelling reasons why Jay was meeting with Aranda. The American negotiators were under strict orders from the Confederation Congress "to undertake nothing without the knowledge and concurrence of France." And since the French were bound by treaty to consult with Spain, Jay was obligated to meet with the Spanish minister. To put it more crudely, Jay needed to know what Spain expected to extract from the collapse of the British Empire in North America as the price for its quite limited, virtually nonexistent contribution to The Cause. Based on his recent experience in Madrid, Jay recognized from the start that Spain was a declining European power that retained an inflated sense of its abiding significance.*

Looking down at the map, Aranda placed his fingers on what is now Lake Erie, traced a line south through modern-day Ohio, then down to the middle of the current Florida Panhandle. Everything east of that line belonged to the United States, he pronounced, everything west to Spain. Jay did not need to draw a line. He pointed to the Mississippi River as the western border of the United States. Moreover, he declared the claim, like American independence itself, to be nonnegotiable.

Jay then hurried to Franklin's quarters at Passy to report on the meeting with Aranda. Pacing back and forth while puffing on his clay pipe, Jay argued that America's interests would be held hostage to predatory Spanish claims unless they violated their instructions, abandoned the French, and made a separate peace with the British. He tossed his clay pipe into the fireplace for emphasis, then awaited the reaction of America's senior statesman.[5]

With the possible exception of Washington, no one was more aware than Franklin of how much the success of The Cause was indebted to French largesse. But gradually he embraced Jay's recommendation, no doubt wondering how even the most accomplished diplomat of the age could explain the decision to Count Vergennes, the French foreign minister. When Adams came down from Holland a few weeks later, he endorsed the decision to bypass the French as a truly wonderful idea. "It is glorious to have broken such orders," Adams pronounced, with all the gusto of someone whom Vergennes had prohibited from attending the French court for gleefully urging this very course of action.[6]

---

* During his tenure as president of the Continental Congress in 1779, Jay had seen fit to apprise the acting Spanish minister, Don Juan Miralles, that he regarded Spanish claims of control over navigation rights on the Mississippi River as preposterous presumptions, sure to be exposed as such when the demographic wave of American settlements flowed westward over the ensuing decades. Jay therefore arrived at the library in Versailles fully prepared to call Aranda's bluff about Spanish versions of the North American map.

When formal negotiations began in early September, the American diplomatic team had, on its own, decided to violate its orders from the congress not only by abandoning the French but by expanding its mandate to make acquisition of the entire British Empire in North America south of Canada a precondition for any treaty ending the war. When word reached Philadelphia that the American diplomats in Paris had arbitrarily decided to negotiate a separate peace with Great Britain, the delegates in congress were astounded, with several of them proposing that the entire diplomatic team be charged with treason. By then, however, it was too late.

A provisional treaty ending the war had been signed on November 30. Treason charges dissolved as soon as the terms of the treaty were made public.* In addition to the great principle of American independence, the United States had also acquired the great prize, a landmass larger than England, France, and Spain combined. It was, at least in retrospect, the most lopsided triumph in the history of American statecraft. Copies of the treaty were denounced and burned in the London streets. George III again threatened to abdicate rather than live with a treaty that repudiated everything his royal reign had stood for. The Shelburne ministry quickly collapsed, with Shelburne himself cast into permanent political exile, and no obvious choice to succeed him proving immediately available or acceptable to the king.[7]

WHAT HAD JUST HAPPENED? The Americans negotiating team had stacked the deck, dealt themselves all the good cards, and left the Brit-

---

* Once independence and the Mississippi border were recognized as givens, the major outstanding point of contention was reparations for loyalists, which the British insisted upon, threatening to walk if they were denied. Franklin spent the night of November 29 preparing an account of American towns burned to the ground, houses vandalized, to include his own home in Philadelphia, and the documented murders and rapes by British and Hessian troops. The Americans would agree to tabulate their losses, then compare that figure with loyalist losses, and whoever owed the most would pay the difference. The stunned British delegates promptly backed off the loyalist claims.

ish side with a very weak hand. As a result, the meaning of The Cause had just expanded to include the addition of a western domain with all the ingredients of a looming American empire. At the start of the war, no one endorsing independence had argued that it meant the acquisition of Great Britain's entire American empire. Nor did the instructions to the American negotiators provide any guidance that pointed in that westerly direction.

But when Jay so decisively pointed to the Mississippi in that Versailles library, he was not acting quite so boldly as it must have seemed to Aranda. The trans-Appalachian region had been a major factor in the dispute with Great Britain from the very start of the imperial crisis in 1763, when George III issued his proclamation purportedly blocking American migration "over the mountains." Starting with debates over the Dickinson Draft in 1776, then continuing throughout the war in sessions of the Continental Congress—whose very name suggested western horizons—there was a recurring argument over how to resolve state claims to western lands based on their colonial charters. The presumption throughout those debates was that, if and when America won its independence, all or some portion of the western domain would revert to American control. In that sense, The Cause had always contained an unspoken and more expansive meaning.[8]

In fact, three weeks after Jay's dramatic meeting with Aranda but months before words of its occurrence reached American shores, the Confederation Congress at last achieved a quorum that allowed the delegates to vote on a motion by New Jersey's John Witherspoon designed to resolve the land disputes in the unsettled territories. Witherspoon argued that the vast tract of western land the British had acquired in 1763 by winning the French and Indian War should revert in its entirety to the United States upon winning independence, then become a national domain held in trust by the union of states created under the Articles: "This controversy was begun and the war was carried on by the united and joint efforts of the thirteen states. By their joint exertions and not by any one State, the dominion of Great Britain was broken, and consequently the rights claimed and exercised by the Crown devolved on all, and not any individual states."[9]

Witherspoon was directing his words at the Virginia delegation, lecturing them on their responsibility to surrender their territorial claims, arguing that doing so was a condition for membership in the "Perpetual Union" established in the Articles of Confederation. At the time, word had not made it across the Atlantic about the acquisition of the western domain in the provisional Treaty of Paris. But Witherspoon and the other delegates in congress were already assuming that some portion of the land between the Appalachians and the Mississippi was almost certain to be acquired. (The correspondence of some delegates suggests that members were not oblivious to the likely claim that Spain would make during the diplomatic deliberations.) Witherspoon's major contribution was to insist that whatever land was acquired was owned collectively by all the states, not as a nation, but as a union. The term "union" was less controversial than "nation," since it permitted nationalists and confederationists to coexist under the same roof, and both camps to believe the future was on their side. The capitalized term The Union was becoming an acceptable postwar version of The Cause, and would remain so until the Civil War.

KNOWING WHERE history was headed had become a habit of mind for Alexander Hamilton, and he believed that it was moving from the battlefield to the political arena. "The time has come for all aspiring leaders of the emerging American republic," he wrote to John Laurens, "to quit the sword and put on the toga," and he wanted his best friend to join him in the new incarnation of "the few." Laurens was commanding a cavalry squadron outside Savannah at the time. Hamilton urged him to resign his commission and join him in the Confederation Congress as a representative of South Carolina. "We have fought side by side to make America free," he explained, "let us hand in hand struggle to make her happy."[10]

Laurens never got the letter. On August 25, 1782, he led a senseless charge against a British foraging patrol. Riding straight into a salvo of British muskets, he was struck squarely in the heart, dead before he hit the ground. Upon receiving the news, Washington shook his head. A future American leader of boundless promise had gone down in a meaningless scrimmage. Greene received the news more fatalistically. Given his reckless concept of courage, this was the way the Laurens story was meant to end.[11]

Washington still could not see the end of his own war. (All generals have a difficult time accepting defeat. Washington had a difficult time embracing victory.) He had always regarded the Continental Army as a projection of himself, and now he had the opportunity to drill and train it to a level of proficiency that met his own high standards. "Notwithstanding the troops are verging near to perfect," he declared in general orders, "there was always room for improvement." Throughout the war, the regular soldiers had worn their hair long, in different styles designed to declare their own personal independence. Now, however, all soldiers would be required "to wear their hair cut or tied in the same manner throughout the whole corps." Predictably, and true to form, the rank and file resisted the order, which their officers obligingly refused to enforce.[12]

The officer class was focused on more serious concerns than hairstyles. Throughout the fall of 1782 there were multiple meetings, all of them covert and unrecorded, where senior officers shared their mutual frustrations and grievances. They had come to regard themselves as an American elite, the virtuous few who had stayed the course, remained true to The Cause, and now won the war, or at least forced the British to lose it. But they had not been paid in two years, and many had run up debts to sustain their families, so faced the prospect of being thrown in jail as debtors upon returning home. The promised pension of half-pay for life, which had always generated resistance from several states, now appeared a dead letter for the simple fact that the government was bankrupt.

Washington was not oblivious to their maneuverings. "The temper of the Army was soured," he observed to a Virginia friend, "and has become more irritable than at any period since the commencement of the War." He had hoped to take a furlough and spend a few weeks with Martha at Mount Vernon, but decided that now was not the right time to leave the army. The soldiers' grievances were wholly justified, he kept repeating, for "no part of the community has undergone equal hardships, and borne them with the same patience and fortitude that the Army has done." Patience now seemed to be wearing thin, however, and the worrisome gossip was not bubbling up from the troops, but flowing down from the most senior officers in the army.[13]

In late December 1782, thirteen generals signed a petition that General Alexander McDougall and four fellow officers carried to Philadelphia and formally presented to congress: "We have borne all that men can bear," it began. "Our property is exhausted, our private resources are at an end, and our friends are wearied out and disgusted with our incessant application for support." It ended with a not so veiled threat: "The uneasiness of the soldiers for want of pay is great and dangerous; any further experiments on their patience must have fatal effects."[14]

Hamilton, who had recently been elected to the New York delegation in congress, quickly apprised Washington that the officer class was threatening mutiny: "It appears to be a prevailing opinion in the army that the disposition to make recompence for their service will cease with the necessity of them, and that if they once lay down their arms, they will part with the means of obtaining justice." Washington confessed to Hamilton that "the predicament in which I stand as a Citizen and Soldier is as critical and delicate as can well be conceived." His loyalty to the officers of the Continental Army had a powerful emotional edge. He also believed they had justice on their side and that they were correct to conclude that "the prospect for compensation for past Services will terminate with the War." But to threaten mutiny . . . The sentence could not be finished; for Washington the thought was inadmissible.[15]

It took Washington several weeks to realize that two separate plots were being hatched in Newburgh and Philadelphia, and he had become the central figure in both dens of intrigue. The officers in the army were divided into moderate and radical factions. The former, led by Henry Knox, was willing to threaten mutiny but was loyal to Washington and therefore never intended to act on the threat. The latter, led by Horatio Gates, Washington's old nemesis, was fully prepared to do so, refusing to fight if the war resumed, or following Gates over the Appalachians as an army in revolt if the war ended.

Meanwhile Hamilton had met with Robert Morris and Gouverneur Morris (no relation), Hamilton's colleague in the New York delegation. No one knows who uttered the thought first, but all three agreed to use the threat posed by the military as leverage to pressure the congress, and eventually the state legislatures, to reconsider and pass the impost, even to consider seriously New York's year-old resolution to call a convention that revised the Articles of Confederation in order to eliminate its obvious defects. This was a dangerous game, as the trio of conspirators fully recognized, but Hamilton assured his co-conspirators that Washington could be counted on to block any attempt at mutiny before it got out of control. "His virtue, his firmness would never yield to any dishonorable or disloyal plans," Hamilton explained, adding that "he would sooner suffer himself to be cut to pieces."[16]

"There is something very mysterious in this business," Washington wrote to Hamilton once he realized, as he put it, "that some people have been playing a double game." He wanted Hamilton to know that he strongly endorsed the grievances of the army, "which has suffered more than any Army ever did in the defence of the rights and liberties of human nature." If their demands were rejected, and they were sent home without compensation for their sacrifices, "then shall I have realized a tale, which will embitter every moment of my future life."[17]

He also wanted Hamilton to know that "no man in the United States is or can be more deeply impressed with the necessity of reform in the present Confederation than myself. No man has felt the effects of it more sensibly, for the effect thereof, and want of powers in Congress, may justly be ascribed the prolongation of the war. Indeed, all my private letters have teemed with these sentiments."[18]

But all that said, Washington also wanted his former aide to know that both he and Robert Morris—Washington was apparently unaware of Gouverneur Morris's role—had stepped across the line. Their laudatory goals could not be reached by enlisting the army in a conspiracy that defied the core principles of The Cause itself. However well intentioned, their behind-the-scenes plotting was both dishonorable and extremely dangerous, for it ran the risk of releasing political energies beyond their control that possessed the potential to generate a civil war.

Hamilton responded with a confession coupled with a defense of his actions. He acknowledged that he and Morris had decided "to use the threat of the army to generate support for general sources of revenue," and to reach that goal "the necessity and discontents of the army presented themselves as a powerful engine." As for Morris's role, his credentials as a patriot were beyond reproach: "I believe no man in this country but himself could have kept the money-machine going during the period he has been in office." In fact, Morris had been writing personal checks to cover the costs of food for the army, doing so discreetly, for several months. "The men you criticize for abusing the army," Hamilton concluded, "are the most unequivocal *friends of the army*. In a word, they are the men who think continentally."*[19]

---

* Thirteen years later, in 1796, when he was enlisting Hamilton's assistance in drafting his Farewell Address, Washington amplified Hamilton's earlier remark about thinking "continentally": "A century in the ordinary intercourse," he wrote to Hamilton, "would not have accomplished what the Seven Years' association of Arms did in forging loyalty to the Union and destroying state loyalty."

∂∑

A FACTION OF THE 550 officers at Newburgh—how large is unclear—were thinking more narrowly. As they saw it, they were about to be discharged without their back pay, without their previously promised pension, and without the dignity they deserved. All they wanted was justice, and despite Washington's ardent claims to identify with their dilemma, he had refused to lead them down the only path that offered any prospect for a just resolution of their grievances.

Horatio Gates was willing to step into that leadership vacuum, threaten a coup, and act on that threat if it proved necessary. (Gates had been rehearsing for the role of Brutus to Washington's Caesar ever since Saratoga. The optimum opportunity had not yet arrived, ironically because Washington refused to play the role of Caesar.) Moreover, many of the junior officers, who knew Washington only from afar, found him almost preternaturally cold, more monument than man. "His extreme resolve," Hamilton observed, "mixed with an asperity of temper, both of which have increased recently, has contributed to his loss of popularity." A plot was afoot to replace Washington with Gates as a first step toward defying civilian control. The Gates faction called a meeting of all officers to coordinate their strategy and gauge their support. The meeting was scheduled for March 11 in a large auditorium recently built by the troops called the Temple because it was also used for religious services.[20]

Washington issued an order canceling the meeting, calling it "irregular." Instead he rescheduled a meeting four days later, on March 15. (No one appeared to notice, but it was the Ides of March, the day Brutus assassinated Caesar.) Washington requested a summary of the meeting, signaling he did not plan to attend. He immediately began drafting the speech he fully intended to deliver, which was the most important speech of his life.

Gates had just called the meeting to order when an unexpected guest

entered the side door and walked straight toward the lectern. He was
trailed by his entire staff, who proceeded to assume assigned locations
on the sides of the room. The intrusion had obviously been fully orchestrated. All the officers in the room were stunned, most especially Gates.

If his entry was a brilliant flanking maneuver, Washington's speech
was a frontal attack on the plot to stage a military coup as a treasonable
act. He made no effort to appease the plotters, but intended to shame
them as betrayers of The Cause that so many of their close friends had
died to defend. "In the name of our common country and your own
sacred honor," he called them to duty one last time, to join him in
opposing those "who seek to overturn the liberties of our country and
open the flood gates of civil discord." If they stood by him in this final
battle, history would record their abiding commitment to the core values of The Cause. They would become examples of "the last stage of
perfection to which human nature is capable of attaining."[21]

Washington spent much of the speech letting the officers in the
room know that he took their purported plans for mutiny personally.
Here is a sample passage:

> But as I was among the first who embarked in the cause of our
> common Country—As I have never left your side one moment, but
> when called from you, on public duty—As I have been the constant
> companion & witness of your Distresses, and not among the last
> to feel, & acknowledge your Merits—As I have ever considered my
> own Military reputation as inseperably connected with that of the
> Army—As my Heart has ever expanded wth joy, when I have heard
> its praises—and my indignation has arisen, when the Mouth of
> detraction has been opened against it—it can scarcely be supposed,
> at this late stage of the War, that I am indifferent to its interests.[22]

Near the end of his speech, Washington began to read a letter he had
recently received from a Virginia congressman, Joseph Jones, reporting

that there was a movement among several delegates to consider a partial pension, what they called "commutation," which would provide half-pay for five years for all officers. Washington then hesitated and pulled a pair of reading glasses he had recently acquired from his waistcoat pocket. Only his aides had ever seen him use them. "Gentlemen," he said, looking over his glasses, "you will permit me to put on my spectacles, for I have not only grown grey but almost blind in service to my country."[23]

Witnesses reported that a wave of emotion swept through the audience. Several officers wept openly. They had never seen His Excellency expose his human frailty. Whether this exposure was inadvertent or carefully orchestrated can never be known. But it worked. Knox was immediately on his feet to lead the applause as Washington left the stage. After a decent interval, Knox stepped forward to read from a set of resolutions, all previously prepared, to thank Washington for his speech and become their official advocate in subsequent negotiations with congress. A final resolution condemned "some unknown persons" for attempting to promote "a movement totally subversive of discipline and good order." All the resolutions were approved by a voice vote. The Newburgh conspiracy was over.

The most perilous moment in the brief history of the not so United States had just passed. There was only one American who could play the role of Caesar, and he had just refused it. The thought of doing so never occurred to Washington. Hamilton, who knew his man, had put it most succinctly; Washington would rather be "cut to pieces."

The United States was extremely fortunate to enjoy the leadership of this singular figure fully capable of defying the dominant historical pattern. Washington actually reversed the pattern. Previous and subsequent dictators portrayed themselves as synonymous with the revolutionary movement they headed, which would, so they convinced themselves, die without their permanent presence. Washington made himself synonymous with The Cause in order to declare it was incom-

patible with dictatorial power. In the new American republic, all leaders, no matter how indispensable, were disposable.

A full appreciation of Washington's rock-ribbed assurance on that
score requires a recovery of the political context in 1783: the Continental Army, which he truly loved, was about to be summarily cast
into oblivion; the Confederation Congress, which he knew to be fatally
flawed as a postwar government, was currently beyond redemption; the
American economy was floating atop an ever-increasing pool of debt;
all proposals for political and economic reform were castigated by self-
appointed True Whigs as a plot to hijack The Cause from its original intentions. It would not have required much personal ambition for
Washington to conclude that he, and he alone, could rescue America from its toxic combination of ignorance and indifference. But he
remained resolute in his conviction that to do so would have defiled and
eventually destroyed The Cause itself.*

THE COLLAPSE OF THE Newburgh conspiracy ended any threat of
a military coup, but it also ended any hope for reform of the Articles,
and therefore any prospect for rescuing the American economy from
bankruptcy. Trying to sound an upbeat note, Henry Knox proposed an
elegantly simple solution: "As the present constitution [the Articles] is
so obviously defective," he wrote to Gouverneur Morris, "why do not
you great men call the people together and tell them so. That is, have a
convention of the states to form a better constitution." Four years later,
Alexander Hamilton would do precisely that, but in the late spring of
1783 he had reached the conclusion that any expansive understanding

---

* Any conspicuous display of personal ambition was repulsive to Washington. Recall that he
pleaded incompetence when asked to head the Continental Army, explaining to Martha that
he had no choice in the matter. The pattern repeated itself when he was elected president. No
president in American history did not want to be president more than George Washington. Not
seeking political power had become his chief credential as a leader who, for that very reason, could
be trusted to exercise it wisely.

of The Cause was itself a lost cause. "I fear," he lamented to Washington, "that we have been contending for a shadow."[24]

In a long letter to Jay, congratulating him on his diplomatic triumph in Paris, Hamilton spelled out his realistic vision of the forces in play at the end of the war:

> We have now happily concluded the great work of independence, but much remains to be done to reach the fruits of it. Our prospects are not flattering. Every day proves the inefficacy of the present confederation, yet the common danger being removed, we are receding instead of advancing in a disposition to amend its defects. . . . It is to be hoped that when prejudice and folly have run themselves out of breath we may return to reason and correct our errors.

In a much briefer letter to Nathanael Greene, Hamilton made the same point, adding that "there is no motive for a man to lose his time in the public service at present." He was quitting the congress in order "to begin the business of making my fortune."[25]

The awkwardly large loose end was the army. In April the congress had approved a pension of half-pay for five years, but the commitment was really a promissory note of dubious value. Washington was outraged that the most dedicated patriots could be treated so shabbily, "disbanded without a pittance like a set of beggars, needy, distressed, and without prospect." It was a sight that "should drive every man of Honor and Sensibility to the extremist Horrors of Despair." He demanded that all soldiers receive three months pay before they headed home, which he calculated would total $750,000 for the entire army.[26]

One final time, Robert Morris came to the rescue. He agreed with Washington that sending the soldiers home penniless verged on a criminal act that he, in good conscience, could not witness. He spent his last days in office writing six thousand checks, called "Bob notes," to cover the entire cost of the final payment. It was a gracious gesture by

Morris that almost bankrupted him, but was his way of refuting critics like Arthur Lee. Morris was saying, and showing, that he was never in it for the money.[*27]

The troops began to leave in late May. There were no farewell ceremonies or parades. Technically, they were not discharged but placed on furlough, since the official Treaty of Paris had not been signed. (Neither, for that matter, had the provisional treaty, because the congress could not raise a quorum—and the superintendent of foreign policy post remained vacant.) Joseph Plumb Martin remembered the departure as a sad occasion, when a "family of brothers" were turned adrift, "like worn out horses." Officers returning to New England states were greeted with newspaper editorials describing them as "blood-beaked vultures feeding at the public trough," a reference to the pensions, the cost of which New England taxpayers feared would be passed along to them. Rather than march in parades in their honor, veterans of the Continental Army were expected to disappear.[†28]

Prior to their departure the officers met and agreed to establish a fraternal order that would preserve their memories of the most intense collective experience of their lives. They also agreed to create a fund to care for widows of fallen brothers and provide medical assistance for veterans with life-altering wounds. They called their fraternity the Society of the Cincinnati after the Roman general Lucius Quinctius Cincinnatus, famous for retiring at the peak of his power, exchanging his sword for the plow. By acclamation they elected Washington the society's first president.[29]

While its very name announced its intention to avoid meddling in politics, the Society of the Cincinnati was an avowedly elitist enter-

---

* Morris's reputation remained under a cloud for two centuries, in large part because historians, especially disciples of Charles Beard in the Progressive School, depicted him as an early-day robber baron. Only recently, with the publication of Charles Rappleye's biography in 2010, has a fuller and fairer depiction of Morris become available.

† See the profile of Joseph Plumb Martin at the end of this chapter.

prise explicitly designed to memorialize the superior virtue of men who had answered the call, stayed the course, and servèd The Cause until it was won. They were thereby separating themselves from the majority of their generation, who sat out the war or served in the local militia. Now that it was clear that neither congress nor the states intended to recognize and reward their service monetarily, and virtue had proven their only reward, the Society of the Cincinnati was their way of embracing that outcome, advertising its moral supremacy, and declaring themselves the purest embodiment of The Cause. In order to assure its continuation over the years, membership in the society would be passed along to the eldest male descendant in the next generation, a suggestion probably originating with Baron von Steuben. Ironically it excluded Washington, who had no biological heirs.

By making membership in the Society of the Cincinnati inherited through bloodlines, the retiring officers opened the floodgates for waves of antagonism toward the Continental Army that had been building up for several years. As the only surviving remnant of a national embodiment of The Cause, the Continental Army was regarded by all True Whigs as an alien presence. The local mentality that dominated the state legislatures reinforced this prevailing hostility, which had kept the army small, barely on life support throughout the war. Ever since Yorktown, these critics from above and below had been waiting for the Continental Army to die. Now the officers were declaring that the memory of their superior patriotism would never die.

The reaction was both immediate and hysterical. Up in Boston, Samuel Adams smelled a plot to establish a British-style aristocracy poised to undermine the egalitarian values that all New Englanders had fought and died for. The Massachusetts legislature took up the conspiratorial message, citing Lexington, Concord, and Bunker Hill to insist that militia, not the Continental Army, had won the war. One delegate proposed that the Bay State should secede from the union rather than risk infection from an embedded aristocracy. In Connecticut, retired officers who wore armbands with the Cincinnati insignia were visited by Committees of Safety and treated like loyalists who had to disavow the society or leave the state. In South Carolina, Judge Aedanus Burke published a diatribe claiming that returning members of the society intended to establish a hereditary nobility aiming to replace the duly elected state government. Burke endorsed a New England narrative with a southern accent, insisting that everybody knew the war in the south was won by militia.[30]

Conspiratorial arguments against Parliament and the British ministry had served The Cause well in the run-up to the war. The True Whigs were fully prepared to deploy the same quasi-paranoid arguments against both the Confederation Congress and the Continental Army. The Society of the Cincinnati had made itself uniquely vulnerable to such charges by adopting the hereditary principle. Two distinguished voices from abroad, neither of which could be accused of paranoia, joined the list of critics who found this hereditary principle worrisome.

Thomas Jefferson, writing from Paris, warned Washington that his association with the Society of the Cincinnati would place his otherwise glorious legacy at risk: "It [the society] is a cancer planted in the heart of the Republic," Jefferson observed, "and a single fiber left of this institution will provide a hereditary aristocracy which will change our governments from the best to the worst in the world." Benjamin Franklin, also writing from Paris, chose to give his warning with a satire. Franklin joked that the members of the society had gotten it all wrong, in fact exactly backward. The hereditary principle should be reversed, designating ancestors (preferably mothers) as members rather than descendants, since they were most responsible for instilling patriotism in the entire generational line.*[31]

---

* A Marxist model based on class resentment does not work in this case, because most critics of the society were wealthier than the veterans they were accusing, who were claiming to be a natural aristocracy based on superior virtue, not wealth.

Washington was stunned at the negative reaction to the society, which he described as "an innocent institution with immaculate intentions." Greene concurred: "The clamor raised against the Cincinnati was far more extensive than I expected. I had no conception that it was so universal." What both men were witnessing was the release of the latent hostility toward the Continental Army that had been building up throughout the war, and that became more openly critical of the "standing army" after Yorktown.[32]

What they were also witnessing was the opening round of the postwar debate for control of the narrative about the true meaning of The Cause. Most of the histories written in the wake of the war were state based. The star of that story was the militia, which gushed forward at Lexington and Concord, rallied to entrap Burgoyne at Saratoga, and stymied Cornwallis in the Carolina interior. There was more than a kernel of truth in this story line, since the militia had played an essential role as a roving police force that sustained American control over the vast American theater beyond the coastline that the British army could never subjugate. But the emerging narrative might also have been entitled "The Myth of Militia," for it erased the central role of the Continental Army from the picture. Strangely, Washington remained the dominant figure, a one-man army surrounded by a cast of liberty-loving volunteers who came, fought bravely, then went home to their families.

The officers who created the Society of the Cincinnati had unknowingly done something deeply offensive. They had formed an organization designed to preserve the memory of the Continental Army as the institutional embodiment of The Cause, which in fact it was. That version of the war for independence needed to be demonized, stigmatized, better yet forgotten rather than remembered, for it had collective implications with nationalistic overtones. It was an inconvenient truth that needed, like all old soldiers, to fade away.

༄༅

THE POWER OF the Continental, then Confederation Congress had
been fading away ever since the crisis days of 1775–76. By 1783 it had
become a platform for state and regional jealousies, a league of mini-
nations without any pretense of governing. As Arthur Lee, the self-
appointed spokesman for the True Whigs, put it, weakness was what
the vast majority of Americans wanted: "It is better for Congress to
remain a rope of sand, rather than a rod of iron."[33]

Weakness went on public display in early June 1783, when three
hundred recently furloughed soldiers from the Pennsylvania line, dissatisfied with the "Bob notes" and demanding their back pay, marched on
the Pennsylvania State House, where the congress was sitting. Enjoying
the support of local residents, who provided free alcohol to the troops,
for several hours they made menacing faces at the delegates through
windows, shouted obscenities, and aimed their muskets at any delegate
who protested the demonstration. Though rowdy, the troops remained
nonviolent and eventually marched back to their barracks to the cheers
of the assembled crowd.[34]

Hamilton, who was a member of congress, was incensed at being
the target of intimidation. (In his highly refined code of honor, his man-
hood had been challenged.) He wrote a blistering letter to John Dickinson, then serving as president of the Pennsylvania Council, demanding
to know why the Pennsylvania militia had not been called out to
disperse the mutinous troops. Dickinson explained, probably correctly,
that the militia might very well have joined the mutiny. Whereupon
Hamilton drafted a resolution, endorsed by the full congress, that the
obvious inability of the Pennsylvania government to provide security
for the delegates meant that the seat of the fragile American government should move to New Jersey.[35]

Thus, began a long odyssey for the congress, first to Princeton, then

Trenton, then Annapolis, and finally New York. The odyssey quickly became the butt of jokes about wandering minstrels, floating crap games, and itinerant travelers moving from boardinghouse to boardinghouse. When congress could not reach a quorum, pundits explained that delegates were unsure where they were supposed to show up. Hamilton bemoaned his role in creating the appearance of a phantom American government that the European powers were already disposed to regard as a joke.[36]

Washington believed he was watching the infant American republic commit suicide. "The disinclination of the individual States to yield competent powers to Congress will be our downfall as a Nation," he wrote to Virginia governor Benjamin Harrison, adding that "this is as clear to me as A,B,C." Unfortunately, most Americans were working with a different alphabet that did not recognize the existence of an American nation.[37]

In a more resigned mood, Washington thought his fellow citizens would eventually come to their senses. "I believe all things will come out right at last; but like a young heir come a little prematurely to a large inheritance, we shall run riot until we have brought our reputation to the brink of ruin, and only then do what prudence and common policy pointed out in the first instance." Things would have to get worse before they could get better. But for the foreseeable future, as Washington saw it, The Cause would remain a promise unfulfilled. "Certain it is in my opinion," he wrote Knox, "that there is a kind of fatality attending all our public measures. In fact, our federal Government is a name without a Substance. How then can we fail, in a little time, becoming the sport of European politics, and the victims of our own folly?"[38]

When Washington referred to the "large inheritance" his fellow Americans were about to squander, he was not thinking idealistically about the semi-sacred values embodied in The Cause. (Thinking idealistically struck him as an unnatural act.) He was instead referring to the enormous tract of land between the Appalachians and the Mississippi that had been acquired in the provisional Treaty of Paris. In effect, at its birth the infant American republic possessed a huge trust fund larger than any emerging nation in world history had ever enjoyed.

Alone among the most prominent members of the founding generation, Washington had glimpsed the eastern edge of the vast American interior as a young surveyor, then as a militia commander in the French and Indian War. He also owned thirty thousand acres in what is now West Virginia, western Pennsylvania, and eastern Ohio, a reward for his service fighting alongside the British army. So when Washington sat down to draft his last Circular Letter to the States on June 8, 1783, he was writing from personal experience. His prose was uncharacteristically lyrical, nothing less than a visionary version of what the recent American victory actually meant:

> The Citizens of America, placed in the most enviable Conditions, as the sole Lords and Proprietors of a vast Tract of Continent, comprehending all the various soils and climates of the World, and abounding with all the necessaries and conveniences of life, are now by the late satisfactory pacification, acknowledged to be possessed of absolute freedom and Independency. They are, from this period, to be considered as the Actors on a most conspicuous Theatre, which seems to be designed by Providence for the display of human greatness and felicity.[39]

Although no one had foreseen it at the start, The Cause not only meant independence from the British Empire, it also meant the creation of an American Empire in its stead. In that sense, the war for independence was a continuation of the French and Indian War for control over the eastern third of North America. The Treaty of Paris (1763) had eliminated France from contention. Now the Peace of Paris (1783) eliminated Great Britain.* Almost inadvertently, the Americans had acquired an empire of their own. No prominent founder knew more about the Native American presence in the newly acquired American domain than Washington. But in his Circular Letter he chose to ignore the roughly 100,000 occupants of the trans-Appalachian region, whose forebears had been living there for several centuries. The ingredients for an American tragedy were obviously in play, and Washington knew it, despite his silence.[40]

Although he had made the point previously in his private correspondence, now Washington publicly proposed that the occupation and settlement of the western domain would define America's domestic agenda for generations to come. (Over a century later, Frederick Jackson Turner made westward expansion the central theme in American history.) Those western horizons fundamentally altered the political chemistry for postwar America by creating a collective interest that all the states shared in common. Managing this extraordinary asset required the provincial representatives in the Confederation Congress to think nationally rather than locally or regionally. The west created a gravitational field that would exert relentless pressure on the states to function together as a permanent union or lose the bounty they had so providentially acquired. "We have indeed so plain a road before us," Washington observed, "that it must be worse than ignorance if we miss it."[41]

Over in Paris, French and British diplomats had just negotiated the definitive treaty, though word did not reach America until late July. During the celebratory dinner, a French delegate proposed a toast to "the growing greatness of America," now poised to become "the great-

---

* The terms "Treaty of Paris" and "Peace of Paris" were used interchangeably to describe the diplomatic agreement ending the war for independence. The former term refers to the provisional treaty between the United States and Great Britain in 1782; the latter to the additional cluster of treaties among Great Britain, France, Spain, and the Netherlands in 1783. That the agreement ending the Seven Years' War in 1763 is also called the Treaty of Paris is an occasionally confusing coincidence.

est empire in the world." The British negotiating team had the good grace to second the toast, but with a smile one diplomat added, "and they will speak English every one of 'em." If there was such a thing as a European consensus, it recognized the enormous potential of the newly arrived American republic but harbored serious reservations about the capacity of the inherently weak American government to manage its enormous assets.[42]

Letters among delegates in the congress suggest that no one was sure how large the western domain was, but most members were eager to resolve the Virginia claim in order to start earning revenue from land sales. "It is said by good judges that the tract acquired comprehends some five hundred thousand square miles," wrote one Massachusetts delegate, "and some men who are acquainted with that country assert that the value of it is sufficient to discharge the public debt." Washington's vision appeared to be coming true alongside Robert Morris's previous prediction: the west and the debt were interacting to create a collective response as "the Union." But the sectarian edges were still showing during the debate over the Virginia cession, and even the common debt was viewed from a state-based perspective. Eventually, in 1861, the sectional split over slavery in the western territories became the immediate cause of the Civil War.[43]

In this pre-Darwinian era, uncertainty and ignorance prevailed as the delegates speculated about what was really "out there," some worrying that future settlements would encounter mastodons and dinosaurs in the unexplored territory. The "plain path" forward that Washington envisioned was already becoming crowded with reluctant travelers and imagined monsters.

THE SUMMER AND FALL of 1783 became an extended epilogue, an overlong ending to an overlong war. The major British player throughout the epilogue was General Guy Carleton, who was ordered down from Quebec to assume command of the British evacuation of New York. Sir Guy was the only senior British officer who could claim that he had won his piece of the war, since he had repelled all American efforts to capture Quebec, thereby assuring that Canada would remain a British colony. His mission was both unprecedented and monumental: the former because Great Britain had never lost a foreign war and did not know how to manage defeat; the latter because the British garrison at New York contained fifteen thousand troops, twenty-nine thousand loyalists, and three thousand former slaves, and transporting a population that large necessitated the largest amphibious operation in British naval history.*

Though fewest in number, the ex-slaves were the biggest problem because of a short paragraph inserted into the provisional Treaty of Paris at the last minute, stipulating that all slaves seized by the British army must be returned to their American owners. The stipulation was the sole contribution of Henry Laurens, who had been released from his cell in the Tower of London just in time to attend the final negotiating session at Versailles. Observers noted that Laurens had become a pale replica of his former self, broken by his imprisonment and, even more so, by the death of his son. One can only guess at what the spirit of John Laurens thought about his father's insistence on recovering all ex-slaves, which defied everything the younger Laurens had fought and died for.[44]

Once apprised of the "Laurens stipulation," the Virginia planter class hired a score of agents to recover more than three hundred former slaves they claimed were now residing in New York. The most prominent Virginian of all wrote to one of the agents requesting assistance: "Some of my own slaves may probably be in New York," explained

---

* Carleton was actually the senior British officer in North America, but Germain loathed him for personal reasons. Carleton had voted to convict Germain of treason for alleged cowardice at the Battle of Minden. Germain also blamed Carleton, not Howe, for failing to rescue Burgoyne at Saratoga.

Washington, "but I am unable to give descriptions. If by chance you should come at the knowledge of any of them, I will be much obliged to you for securing them, so I may obtain them again."[45]

At their first conference Carleton promised to look into Washington's request, but on the larger question he called attention to the language of the provisional treaty, which referred to ex-slaves who had been seized by the British army, whereas the vast majority of Blacks under his protection had fled to the British army voluntarily. He could hardly be expected to violate his code of honor as a British officer by ignoring the promise of freedom offered to these obviously desperate souls. As it turned out, there were four Mount Vernon slaves—Daniel Paine, Maurice Salt, Harry Washington, and Deborah Payne—who had already been evacuated on ships bound for Nova Scotia. If Washington and his fellow Virginia planters could prove in the courts that their former slaves were taken against their will, Carleton was sure the British government would provide compensation. Otherwise, these former slaves were now free men and women.[46]

This was not a conversation that Washington wanted to pursue, for it exposed the delusion prevalent among southern slave owners that their slaves could not possibly have run away to freedom, when the vast majority had done precisely that, and Washington knew it. He advised Benjamin Harrison, the governor of Virginia, to drop the subject, since there was "little expectation that any of these characters will be returned," and he himself had "little enthusiasm for it."[47]

There were deep reasons for Washington's reticence. The war had become a conversion experience for him on the slavery question. At the start, he had been a typical Virginia squire who regarded his slaves as property, like cows and pigs. Since then he had watched African American soldiers under his command suffer and die for The Cause. He had seen his trusted manservant Billy Lee perform his duties for him on a day-to-day basis for eight years. He had listened to his three fondest aides—Lafayette, Laurens, and Hamilton—expound on slavery as a blatant stain that must be removed sooner or later if The Cause was to mean anything, and he had frequently nodded in agreement with their youthful convictions.

He knew the direction that postwar America needed to go, which was some kind of gradual emancipation plan. But he also knew that all the states south of the Potomac would vehemently oppose such a plan. And any effort to impose the long-term solution risked destroying the infant republic before it could get to the long term. The state-based character of the Confederation Congress virtually assured that outcome. For now, then, all wisdom dictated deferral. While waiting, however, Washington did not want this name associated with any scheme to recover lost slaves. The very topic touched a nerve that was too painful to contemplate, for at Mount Vernon he was caught up in the same web of shame that entrapped the entire south, and he did not know how to extricate himself.[48]

British transport ships were departing New York Harbor throughout the fall, and in mid-November Carleton apprised Washington that the final disembarkation was looming. It was imperative that Washington occupy the city on the heels of the British evacuation, since Carleton expected looting and score settling against residents deemed closet loyalists to break out as soon as the last British soldiers departed. Washington concurred by bringing his small residue of eight hundred continental troops down from West Point to Harlem. Joined by a delegation headed by Governor George Clinton, who insisted that New York state, not the Continental Army or Confederation Congress, was liberating the city, the parade marched down Manhattan on November 25.

One historian has described the city as "a kind of civic corpse." The western side of Manhattan remained a charred ruin of burned houses, churches, and warehouses left to rot after the great fire of 1776. Not a tree was standing anywhere on the island, all having been cut down for firewood. The shoreline of the eastern side of Manhattan was strewn with the decayed bodies of dead prisoners of war from the ghost ships in the East River, where more than eleven thousand American prisoners had died of disease and malnutrition, their bodies thrown into the river.

At the Battery on the southern end of the island, departing British troops had greased the flagpole, so they would not have to see the Stars and Stripes floating in the breeze as they sailed out of the harbor. But a small group of savvy American sailors fashioned nails and cleats to the flagpole and raised the flag to cheers and a thirteen-gun cannon salute, all in time to frustrate the British culprits rowing out to their ships.

Washington had always thought the war would end in New York, but in a final battle that redeemed his earlier debacle on Long Island. Instead, New York was only the scene of a symbolic triumph. And Carleton saw to it that there would be no surrender ceremony. After all, the British army had never lost New York, indeed had not really lost the war. It was deciding to vacate the premises and cut its losses in a war that was no longer worth its cost, leaving the Americans to fend for themselves. And the British were leaving the Americans with a gruesome reminder of how much the war had cost them. After a seven-year British occupation, New York was a deliberately devastated city, haunted by the ghosts of more dead defenders of The Cause than anywhere else on the continent.

The feared outbreak of hostilities against closet loyalists never occurred. Instead there were three days of festivities, capped off by a fireworks display put on by Knox's artillerymen, which ended with a final volley of a hundred red, white, and blue rockets streaming into the night sky. Washington was eager to head south, ultimately to retirement at Mount Vernon. Before departing, he invited all the officers in the army who were available to attend a farewell ceremony at Fraunces Tavern on December 5 for a final gathering of "the few."

It was really "the fewest of the few." During the previous spring, before the army at Newburgh was disbanded, Washington had attempted to schedule a farewell dinner for all officers. The dinner was canceled when a majority of the junior officers declined to attend, their refusal accompanied by the statement that "the present period is more adapted to sorrow than mirth." The prevailing presumption was that Washington had failed them, although the congress and state legislatures were the obvious culprits in refusing to provide back pay and pensions. Washington, somehow, should have found a way to overcome such disgraceful behavior. Despite his emotional speech at Newburgh, a majority of the officers' corps, while not willing to mutiny, were not able to embrace Washington's moral injunction to let virtue be their only reward.

Only forty officers showed up at Fraunces Tavern, Steuben, Knox, and McDougall the only senior generals present. Greene and Lafayette were away, Laurens farthest away in the hereafter. But Hamilton, who was in the city, was conspicuously absent. Those attending were the small but hard residue of officers whose loyalty to Washington was synonymous with their semi-sacred commitment to The Cause. As a result, the emotional intensity in the room merits comparison with any postwar gathering of surviving veterans in American history. It is also the only recorded occasion when Washington cried in public. Alonzo Chappel painted a justifiably famous depiction of the scene, and Colonel Benjamin Tallmadge, the head of Washington's spy network, left a detailed account in his memoirs, published seventy-five years later.[49]

As Tallmadge remembered it, when Washington entered the room, the officers stood in silence, seeing that their customarily composed commander in chief was on the verge of tears. No one spoke until Washington asked them to fill their wineglasses and proposed a toast: "With a heart full of love and gratitude," he trembled, "I now take leave of you. I most devotedly wish that your latter days may be as prosperous and happy as the former ones have been glorious and honorable." When everyone had downed their glasses of wine, he finished his toast: "I cannot come to each of you, but shall feel obliged if each of you will come and take me by the hand." Henry Knox was nearest to Washington, who extended his hand, then both men embraced, sobbing together, the scene Chappel captured.[50]

"In the same affectionate manner," Tallmadge recalled, "every officer in the room marched up to, kissed, and parted with the General-in-Chief." Men who had retained their composure amid scenes of unspeakable horror broke down for an extended moment of mutual affection as the "band of brothers" gathered around their chief for the last time. "It was indeed too affecting to be of long continuance," Tallmadge remembered, "for tears of deep sensibility filled every eye—and the heart seemed too full, that it was ready to burst from its wanted abode." The officers followed Washington out of the tavern, "in mournful silence," down to the wharf, then watched as twenty-two oarsmen rowed him toward New Jersey, returning the gesture when Washington stood up in the boat and waved his hat, "bidding us a silent adieu."

Washington was an aficionado of exits, but this one was special, for it marked the end of his nearly eight years of service alongside men who shared his understanding of an experience that defied description in words. (Characteristically, he made no mention of the scene in his diary or correspondence.) Like the deepest meaning of The Cause itself, if you had not lived it, no one could explain it to you.[51]

On the way south toward Annapolis, where the Confederation Congress had just established its roving residence, Washington stopped for three days in Philadelphia. He stayed at the baronial estate of Robert Morris just outside the city, called the Hills, where the two old friends commiserated about the problematic fate of the postwar government and the shameful treatment of the army. The chief piece of official business was the calculation of pay due Washington for his expenses incurred during the war. He had vowed to serve without salary, but had kept a meticulous record of his expenses, which totaled £8422, a tidy sum, but less than half of what a British commanding general would have earned over the same span of time.[52]

Accompanied by two aides, Washington reached Annapolis, the unlikely new capital of the United States, on December 19. For two days he attended ceremonial dinners and dances, where witnesses reported long lines of elegantly coiffed women "eager to get a touch" of him. The dinners featured toasts in his honor. (The obligatory thirteen toasts meant that inebriation became a patriotic act.) Washington's final toast contained a political statement that some guests found inappropriate and offensive, though the etiquette of the occasion forbade criticism: "Competent powers to Congress for general purposes." Many guests presumably raised their glasses and nudged one another in disapproval while sustaining a forced smile.[53]

The political context was also awkward. Only twenty delegates were present at Annapolis, insufficient to constitute a quorum. By refusing to call a quorum, the president of the congress avoided embarrassment by skirting the legalities. And the president was none other than Thomas Mifflin, the mastermind of the misnamed Conway Cabal, whom Washington had forced to resign from the army after Mifflin was accused of profiteering as quartermaster general. Also present in the audience was Horatio Gates, Washington's self-appointed heir apparent and the covert leader of the failed mutiny at Newburgh. Washington chose to float above the emotional wreckage, making a point to shake hands with both former antagonists. This, after all, was his moment, and they were the ones who would have to swallow their pride.

Mifflin avoided frequent interaction with Washington by appointing the newest delegate from Virginia, Thomas Jefferson, to manage the arrangements of the ceremony. Jefferson also drafted Mifflin's final speech closing the session, and might also have made stylistic suggestions that found their way into Washington's speech.

"Mr. President," Washington began, his hands visibly trembling, "the great events on which my resignation depended having at length taken place, I now have the honor of offering my sincere congratula-

tions to Congress and of presenting myself before them to surrender
into their hands the trust committed to me, and to claim the indul-
gence of retiring from the service of my country." Witnesses recalled
that his voice faltered at this point; he temporarily lost his composure,
"and the whole house felt his agitation." Then he recovered: "Happy
in the confirmation of our independence and sovereignty, and pleased
with the opportunity afforded the United States of becoming a respectable nation, I resign with satisfaction the appointment I accepted with
diffidence." He said "nation," not "confederation," choosing not to conceal his more expansive hopes for The Cause.

Next Washington expressed his hope that congress would acknowledge the "distinguished merits" of the officers' corps, pointing to his
two aides, both of whom wore the insignia of the Society of the Cincinnati. He was channeling the painful emotions released at Fraunces
Tavern, here to a congress dominated by delegates—Jefferson obviously
excepted—poised to cast the Continental Army into the outer darkness. He was rubbing their faces in their own shame.

He ended succinctly, but melodramatically, with words that had
Jeffersonian overtones: "Having now finished the work assigned me,
I retire from the great theatre of action, and bidding farewell to the
august body under whom I have long acted, I offer here my commission
and take leave of all the employments of public life." He then walked
straight to the door behind his aides while the applause was still ring-
ing, mounted Nelson, and rode toward Mount Vernon with Billy Lee
at his side. It was the greatest exit, and perhaps the most consequential
moment, in American history.[54]

Jefferson understood what he had just witnessed. "The moderation
and character of a single man," he wrote a friend, "has probably prevented the revolution from being closed, as most other have been, by
a subversion of the liberty it was intended to establish." Jefferson was
thinking of Caesar and Cromwell. If he had access to a crystal ball, he

could have mentioned Napoleon, Lenin, Stalin, Mao, Castro, and a host of African dictators.[55]

Washington's resignation was reported with awe and amazement in European newspapers from London to Vienna. When word reached George III, he expressed disbelief. "If he does that," he declared, "he will become the greatest man in the world." He did, and at least for the moment, he was.[56]

PROFILE

JOSEPH PLUMB MARTIN

If Billy Lee was the invisible man, Joseph Plumb Martin was the Zelig of the American Revolution. He keeps popping up in almost every dramatic scene, from the debacle on Long Island in 1776 to the trenches at Yorktown in 1781, where he comes face-to-face with Washington crawling through the mud.

His memoir, published fifty years after the fact in 1830, entitled *Private Yankee Doodle,* has struck some historians as too good to be true, meaning that his story has so many memorable details of so many crucial moments that no single person could have experienced them all. He must have had several published histories at the elbow as he wrote, so the critics say, and inserted himself as an eyewitness.

On the other hand, his account has all the earmarks of a true war story. He never exaggerates his own significance, never glorifies battle, and pokes fun at his own youthful foibles. In his own unassuming way, Martin provides a Tolstoyan view of war, a recovery of the authentic emotional experience of the ordinary soldier at the ground level.

Martin's memoir, then, is a meditation on the importance of the ordinary, which focuses on the day-by-day struggle for survival. For Martin, that struggle took the form of foraging for food, which becomes a running joke throughout his story. The major theme is not bravery, but resilience, both his own and the Continental Army's, to

endure despite hardships that subsequent generations could not possibly comprehend, and apparently
preferred to forget.

By the time he wrote, the
enforced amnesia about the essential role of the Continental Army
had become received wisdom. What
Martin called "the myth of the militia" dominated the folklore, making
Minutemen rather than regulars like
Martin the heroes of the story. As one
of the few surviving continentals, he
felt a special obligation to challenge
that slanted version of history:

Joseph Plumb Martin and his wife,
Lucy Clewley Martin, date unknown.

> It has been said by some that the Revolutionary Army was need-
> less; that the Militia was competent for all that the crisis required.
> But I still insist that they would not have answered the end as well
> as regular soldiers, who were there, and there obliged to be, and
> could not go away when we pleased.

After the war, Martin settled in what is now Stockton Springs, Maine,
married, raised a family, worked a small farm, and apparently became
a local character known for his dry wit. Late in the game, in the 1820s,
he began receiving an annual pension of $96. He still had his hair and a
bemused smile in the only visual rendering, done shortly before he died
at eighty-nine in 1850.

EPILOGUE

Legacies

The American narrative is morally unresolvable because
the society that saved humanity in the great conflicts of
the twentieth century was also a society built on enormous
crimes—slavery and the extinction of the native inhabitants.
—Robert D. Kaplan, *Earning the Rockies* (2017)

ʃ

Great Britain found it difficult to process defeat. Benjamin West's
portrait of the preliminary peace negotiations at Paris in 1782 left
the right side of the portrait blank because the British diplomatic team
refused to sit for a painting. The blank space served as an eloquent illus-
tration of British inability to acknowledge America's lopsided triumph.
No British statesman wanted to become the enduring face of imperial
humiliation. And no postwar commission was appointed to probe the
deeper reasons this awkward and awful moment had arrived. In the
wake of the war, neither the British government nor the British press
were disposed to ask "How did this happen?" The operative question
was "Who lost America?" It was a season for scapegoats.

The most available targets were the generals, chiefly Howe, Burgoyne, and Clinton. Despite the stigma of Yorktown, Cornwallis did
not make the list, in part because his designated status as the second
coming of Hannibal made demonization difficult, in part because the

unloved and chronically obnoxious Clinton was easier to blame for the Yorktown debacle. Both Howe and Burgoyne had used their seats in Parliament to mount a compelling defense of their conduct while the war was still ongoing. Clinton began writing his memoirs in 1782, echoing many of the same arguments, while blaming Howe for failing to destroy the Continental Army on Long Island, which might have won the war before it became a protracted struggle. But Clinton's memories had no direct impact on the postwar debate, since they were not published until the twentieth century.[1]

Though it did not appear until 1794, an American-born British officer, Charles Stedman, wrote a two-volume history of the war that synthesized the arguments of Howe, Burgoyne, and Clinton's defenders in the officers' clubs throughout London. Stedman's lengthy argument for the defense sought to absolve the British army, which in his account performed at worst capably, at best brilliantly, but had been given a mission that was inherently impossible, because it underestimated the depth of the American resistance and overestimated loyalist support. His major argument was that the search for scapegoats needed to look beyond the battlefield. All signs on the blame trail pointed toward Whitehall, specifically to George Germain.[2]

As the chief architect of British strategy during the war, Germain was an eminently plausible target. It helped that he carried the baggage of being "the coward of Minden," a stigma that senior British officers had always held against him, and that could now be trotted out again to verify his scapegoat status. There had also been whisperings of his questionable relationship with Richard Cumberland, a Germain protégé, and those whispers could now become spoken, albeit elliptically, as clinching evidence of his moral depravity. From the day he was dismissed as American Secretary in 1782 to the day he died at his Sussex country home in 1785, Cumberland at his side, Germain carried the label as "the man who lost America."[3]

In retrospect, Germain was actually the ideal stand-in for George III, who had ignited the imperial engine in 1774, then kept it running at full throttle in spite of mounting evidence that he had led his beloved British Empire into a war without end. But His Majesty could not serve as a scapegoat, since he was the symbolic embodiment of the British nation itself, and therefore could not become the face of the catastrophe without prompting a wholesale reassessment of the entire imperial agenda.[*]

Apparently, George III glimpsed privately what could not be acknowledged publicly. In a somewhat meandering memorandum to himself, he admitted that "the late conflict" had proven "an expense of blood and treasure worth more at this instant than all we have ever received from America." He even questioned what he called "the entire Colonial Scheme," meaning the elemental assumption that all aspiring empires, by definition, must acquire foreign colonies in order to qualify as imperial powers.[4]

He was clearly influenced by *Four Letters on Important National Subjects,* a series of essays published in 1783 by Josiah Tucker, an Anglican minister and aspiring economist. Tucker posed the most probing question of all: Why did the British Empire need colonies? "America was ever a Millstone hanging about the Neck of this Country," he claimed, "and as we ourselves had not the wisdom to cut the Rope, and let the Burthen fall off, the Americans have kindly done it for us."[5]

Whereas Tucker was arguing that all colonies per se were liabilities because they were not cost effective, George III was predisposed to draw a distinction between different kinds of colonies, obviously based on the painful American experience. "A people spread over an immense tract of fertile land, industrious because free, and rich because industrious," in other words the former British colonies in North America, "could never be conquered at a cost that justified the effort, most especially

---

[*] The war cost Great Britain an estimated £115,654,914—in modern terms nearly $150 billion. Casualty estimates vary, based on whether to count Hessians and loyalists, and how to interpret often unreliable after-action reports from the battlefield. The most educated guess is that roughly fifty thousand British soldiers and sailors died in the war, the majority from disease.

when one realizes that such former colonies will inevitably become a Market for the Manufactures and Commerce of the Mother Country."[6]

It was a distinction that proved prophetic. Over the course of the next century and beyond, Great Britain would pour vast resources into occupying India, the Middle East, and huge swaths of ground in Africa, all regions populated by nonwhite inhabitants with decidedly non-Western visions of civilization. In Canada, Australia, and New Zealand, however, British policy was designed to avoid the American mistake by imposing a more calculated kind of imperial power, eventually allowing these former colonies to go in peace. It helped that they all spoke English.

Finally, one more specific legacy of the British defeat was a drastic reduction in the annual budget provided to George III for purchasing the loyalty of peers and commoners in Parliament. His distribution of royal patronage, it was now clear, had shifted the balance of power within the King-in-Parliament arrangement by making a near majority of Parliament agents of His Majesty. As a result, George III's avowed defense of Parliament's sovereignty was effectively a defense of his own imperial agenda masquerading as a principled embrace of the Whig tradition. British kings and queens after George III in the nineteenth century were more than symbolic figures, but no British monarch ever again exercised the political power that George III enjoyed from 1773 to 1783.

GREAT BRITAIN RECOVERED from the humiliation suffered at the hands of their upstart American cousins. Indeed, the British Empire went on to enjoy a level of success under Queen Victoria not seen since the headiest days of Rome. But there was no second act for the Native American population. For the roughly 100,000 Native Americans living between the Appalachians and the Mississippi, the American victory in 1783 proved an unmitigated calamity from which history would provide no rescue. American acquisition of the eastern third of the continent triggered a tidal wave of western migration that required no guidance from government. Indeed, any effort to block or restrain the westward flow of settlers would have proven just as futile in 1783 as the British effort to do so with the Proclamation of 1763. As a result, the indigenous population east of the Mississippi was fighting a holding action against the odds—ultimately, it was a matter of sheer numbers—that rendered them the biggest losers in the war for American independence.[7]

The clairvoyance of hindsight actually obscures the choices perceived by the Native tribes caught in the moment. It never occurred to most tribal chiefs that the scratch of a pen in Paris had dispossessed them of lands they had lived on for centuries. (The assumption that land was property that could be owned by mere mortals was also incomprehensible.) From the Native American perspective, the British intruders had been replaced by the American intruders, but there seemed no reason to believe that this change would make the future dramatically different from the past. The exception was the Iroquois Confederacy, whose alliance with Great Britain had cost them dearly (i.e., Sullivan's scorched-earth campaign in 1778), a devastating experience that allowed them to glimpse the inexorable power building to the east.[*8]

For the more western tribes, in that vast expanse stretching south from the Ohio Valley through what is now Tennessee, Alabama, and Mississippi, the war between the whites had remained a distant event of little consequence for their daily lives. Until the front edge of the looming American invasion reached their tribal borders, most Native leaders presumed, as one Shawnee chief put it, that "our island" was both safe and impregnable. Nothing in their previous experience equipped them to regard themselves as tragic victims. The mixed-blood Creek chief

---

* The exception to the exception was the Oneida tribe, which had sided with the Americans. Their tribal lands were purportedly off-limits to white settlements. Their chief, Grasshopper, was Washington's invited guest to observe the British surrender at Yorktown.

Alexander McGillivray let it be known that he could field an army of five thousand Creek warriors fully capable of repelling any and all white invaders.[9]

Between 1783 and 1785 the Confederation Congress appointed commissioners to negotiate treaties with the Six Nations, the Ohio tribes, and the Cherokees. Actually "negotiate" is a misleading term. The Treaty of Paris had defined the Native American population in the entire trans-Appalachian region as "a conquered people" who should be grateful to be consulted at all. "You are mistaken in supposing that you can make what terms you please," one American commissioner explained. "It is not so. You are a subdued people." The Native tribes were effectively ordered to surrender a portion of their tribal land or face war with the United States.[10]

From the very start, this explicit expression of American power struck some observers as too conspicuously coercive. Not only did the conquest theory make the United States appear to be just another imperial power in the European mode, its undisguised rejection of Native American rights was sure to provoke a series of Indian wars on the frontier that would prove expensive in blood and treasure. And the Ohio tribes were soon to demonstrate that they were a much more formidable enemy than anyone had initially imagined; indeed, the conquest theory could not possibly apply to them, since they had never been conquered.

An alternative approach that sidestepped these problems was proposed by Philip Schuyler even before the war ended. A former general in the Continental Army who also happened to be Hamilton's father-in-law, Schuyler had extensive experience as a negotiator with the Six Nations that informed his more gradual and indirect version of removal. In the Schuyler scheme, the United States could afford to recognize Native rights and negotiate generous terms for the indigenous population because all treaties would prove temporary arrangements that would become null and void once the demographic wave of white settlements reached Indian Country.

"As our settlements approach their lands," Schuyler explained, "they must, from scarcity of game, retire further back, and dispose of their lands, until they dwindle comparatively to nothing, as all savages have done when compelled to live in the vicinity of civilized people." Until the first wave of white settlers arrived, some semblance of mutual consent could guide official American policy, making it more compatible with the anti-imperial principles of The Cause. And not so inadvertently, costly wars could be avoided because demography would eventually do the work of armies.[11]

In truth, what Schuyler described as a cultural collision that would cause Native American tribes to disintegrate upon contact with white civilizations was more biological than cultural. Settlers of European ancestry carried diseases, chiefly smallpox and measles, that most Native Americans had never encountered. The Native Americans were therefore vulnerable to epidemics capable of generating mortality rates of 90 percent. The weapons of mass destruction in the eighteenth century were viruses; and the reason the Native population collapsed upon contact with the front edge of white settlements was that they were defenseless against such biological weapons. What Schuyler described as the march of civilization was in fact annihilation in slow motion led by a barrage of microbes that cleared the way.[12]

Within the Confederation Congress there was little dissent about the proper direction of policy—staged removal—but considerable confusion about who should manage it. In August 1786 congress enacted an ordinance claiming "the sole and exclusive right of regulating the trade and managing the affairs with the Indians, not members of any states." This seemed clear enough and appeared to sustain Washington's belief that integrating the western domain into the union would become the great project that virtually forced the embryonic confederation to function as a nation-state. But in the same ordinance the Confederation Congress qualified its claim to jurisdiction, declaring that federal authority only obtained "provided that the legislative right of any state within its own limits be not infringed or violated." This huge loophole seemed to sanction separate treaties that New York, North Carolina, and Georgia negotiated with indigenous tribes within their borders, creating constitutional confusion about who was really in charge.[13]

Another kind of mixed message was sent in the Northwest Ordinance (1787). On one hand, the ordinance defined the terms for establishing territories and soon-to-be states in the region stretching from the north side of the Ohio River to the Mississippi. The clear implication was that any Native American presence in the northwest was presumed to be temporary, despite treaties with the Ohio tribes that said otherwise. On the other hand, the ordinance contained a reassuring promise that American policy toward the indigenous population would always be conducted in accord with the consensual principles of a republic rather than the coercive principles of an empire:

> The utmost faith shall always be observed towards the Indians; Their lands and property shall never be taken from them without their consent; and in their property, rights, and liberty, they shall never be invaded or disturbed, unless by just and lawful wars authorized by Congress; but laws founded on humanity and justice shall, from time to time, be made for preventing wrongs being done to them.[14]

Whether this rhetorical promise was designed to deceive the multiple tribes or soothe the conscience of delegates in congress is difficult to know. Given the relentless reality of removal, it is hard to believe it achieved either purpose. At least from the Native Americans' perspective, the United States was a much more dangerous imperial power than Britain, France, or anything they could have possibly imagined. From the perspective of the infant American republic, it was born betraying the principles it claimed to be founded on. Although the culmination of Indian removal did not occur for fifty years—during the presidency of

Andrew Jackson—it was embedded in the American founding from the start; and as Washington observed during his own presidency, nothing short of a "Chinese wall" could have altered the outcome.[15]

THE LOYALISTS ALSO have a compelling claim as losers, and in their case the losses did not require decades to arrive. For over a century it was fashionable to dismiss the loyalists as faceless traitors. Eventually, historians began to recover the loyalist experience more empathetically. Bernard Bailyn's biography of Thomas Hutchinson in 1974 set a new standard for dispassionate insight and an appreciation of Hutchinson's truly tragic fate.[16]

The scholarly pendulum has swung even further when it comes to the roughly 60,000 loyalists who became exiles, chiefly to Canada and England, with smaller numbers to the Bahamas, east Florida, Jamaica, and eventually to Sierra Leone. When recovered, these stories are almost always poignant—most especially, those of the nearly 10,000 escaped slaves, about half of whom died of smallpox.[17]

Less noticed, indeed almost invisible, are the vast majority of loyalists, approximately 400,000 souls, who chose to remain in the United States. We know that some of them moved to different communities, and some joined the westward migration "over the mountains." But most remained where they were, endured persecution, house arrest, or incarceration during the war, then were gradually treated like penitent sinners welcomed back into the congregation as memories of the war faded. Gradual reassimilation was the dominant trend, and although how it occurred varied from place to place, it merits more attention than it has received.

While there is no question that loyalists were ostracized, threatened, and routinely denied their rights, except for the terror campaigns by both sides in the southern theater they were rarely killed. Unlike the French or Russian revolutions, there were no mass executions at the guillotine or firing squad wall. The loyalist diaspora was so large compared with later revolutions because banishment, not death, was the ultimate punishment. The loyalists, to be sure, were victims but, compared with the losing side in subsequent revolutions, they were extremely fortunate victims. And before they became victims, loyalist troops were generally regarded as the most savage and vengeful soldiers in the British army. If roles had been reversed, and the British had somehow won the war, these loyalists would have been cheering as their neighbors were marched to the gallows.

MUCH LIKE "Indian removal," perhaps more so, slavery defied the core principles of The Cause. It was impossible for advocates of independence to ignore the contradiction, since the British press kept hurling their hypocrisy at them, starting with Samuel Johnson's sarcastic question: "How is it we hear the loudest yelps for liberty among the drivers of Negroes?" Most members of the American resistance regarded Johnson as an implacable Tory, but he was making a powerful point, and they knew it.

In 1775, a year before she wrote her "Remember the Ladies" letter to her husband, Abigail Adams called attention to the awkward fact that slavery, like patriarchy, contradicted everything John claimed to be fighting for: "I wish there was not a single slave in the province," she wrote, "for it always appeared to me a most ingenuous scheme to fight for freedom while we are daily robbing and plundering those who have as good a right to freedom as we have."[18]

In 1781, while drafting his *Notes on the State of Virginia* (1785), Thomas Jefferson described slavery in words that anticipated the language of abolitionist leader William Lloyd Garrison in the 1830s: "Slavery is a perpetual exercise of the most boisterous passions, and the most unremitting despotism on the one part, and degrading submission on the other. I tremble for my country when I reflect that God is just, and that his justice cannot sleep forever." No prominent member of the revolutionary generation, to include slave owners south of the Potomac, ever attempted to argue that slavery was morally compatible with the values of the Declaration of Independence. The only question was how to end it.[19]

Jefferson's answer to that question was beguilingly simple: wait, and allow slavery to die a natural death. In the rarefied region where Jefferson's mind did its best work, slavery was an anachronism, a vestige of the medieval world of witches, miracles, and feudal laws, appropriately described as the "dark ages." Slavery was a doomed institution in the modern world as Jefferson saw it, especially in the kind of enlightened republic the United States aspired to become. As a result, emancipation was both inevitable and self-enacting. The end of slavery was baked into America's future.[20]

During the latter years of the war and its immediate aftermath, the Jeffersonian vision enjoyed considerable credibility, as an antislavery movement swept across the northern states. Vermont (1777) and New Hampshire (1779) made slavery illegal in their state constitutions. The Massachusetts courts followed suit (1783). Pennsylvania (1780) and Rhode Island (1784) passed laws ending slavery within their borders. Connecticut (1784) adopted a gradual emancipation plan. New York and New Jersey, which contained the largest slave populations north of the Chesapeake, proved more resistant, deferring plans for gradual emancipation into the next century. But defenders of slavery in all the northern states were clearly fighting a losing battle. Abolition was more a question of when than whether.[21]

Nor was that all. Historians have been late to recognize the emergence of what became the first wave of the abolition movement in the 1780s. (The standard histories described the antislavery movement starting with Garrison's appearance in the 1820s.) Prominent veterans of the war years threw their energies into the crusade against slavery, viewing the commitment as a continuation of their campaign on behalf of The Cause. Upon returning from Paris, Franklin joined and soon became president of the Pennsylvania Abolition Society, declaring that he intended to make emancipation his final campaign. Alexander Hamilton and John Jay joined forces to create the New York Society for the Manumission of Slaves (1785). In Virginia, Jefferson led the successful fight that permitted slave owners to free their slaves at their own discretion, and proposed a plan whereby all slaves in Virginia born after 1800 would eventually be freed. While serving in the Confederation Congress, he also drafted the Ordinance of 1784, which included a provision that prohibited slavery in all the western territories; it lost by a single vote. But the provision was enacted in the Northwest Ordinance, which forbade slavery in all territory north of the Ohio River.[22]

Under the still-glowing embers of The Cause, slavery appeared to be on the road to extinction: the slave trade was generally regarded as a criminal act; slavery was dead or dying throughout the northern states; the expansion of slavery into the western territories looked at best uncertain; plans for gradual emancipation were proliferating in Virginia, where Lafayette urged Washington to take the lead by establishing a haven for freed slaves in what is now West Virginia; slavery was in the process of being isolated in the states of the Deep South; Virginia, which had the largest slave population of all the states, also contained the largest number of freed slaves; it looked like the beachhead for the final surge of an antislavery movement—indeed, the first such movement in the modern world—destined to sweep across the Carolinas and Georgia and deliver the full promise of The Cause by eliminating its most glaring contradiction.[23]

Hindsight, clairvoyant as always, allows us to notice wartime decisions that should have complicated Jefferson's moral categories and the unspoken presumption that emancipation had the wind of history at its back. Yes, Jefferson did attempt to place a somewhat garbled paragraph blaming both the slave trade and slavery itself on George III in America's founding document. But the delegates in congress deleted the paragraph, preferring to leave such an explosive issue off the revolutionary agenda. It was merely the first occasion—many would follow—when any direct attack on this peculiar institution was deemed too threatening to risk a collapse of the fragile union.

Yes, John Laurens merits admiration for his insistence that emancipation was a moral imperative that flowed naturally from the full meaning of The Cause. But Laurens charged ahead in his frontal attack on slavery with the same youthful ardor he charged into a hail of British bullets and his premature death. The South Carolina legislature rejected his proposal for recruiting a black regiment as a preposterous pipe dream. In a state where 60 percent of the population was black, virtually all of them slaves, the Laurens dream of gradual emancipation was generally regarded as a nightmare.

Yes, more than five thousand African Americans fought for The Cause during the war, and the predominantly Black Rhode Island regiment earned the reputation as the elite combat unit in the Continental Army. But roughly eight to ten thousand African American slaves fled to the British army over the course of the war, obviously choosing to grasp immediate freedom under British protection rather than trust any vague promise of future freedom once independence was won.

Moreover, no one celebrating the American triumph in 1783 could possibly know what the first census of 1790 would reveal about the size of the slave population—namely, that it was approaching 700,000, up from 500,000 in 1776. Despite the steady march of abolition in the northern states, the slave population south of the Potomac was growing explosively, doubling every twenty to twenty-five years. Antislavery advocates who believed the future was on their side had been deluding themselves. The window for ending slavery was closing, not opening. Another unforeseeable development, the emergence of the Cotton Kingdom in the early years of the nineteenth century, effectively sealed the window shut.

Despite initiating the first wave of the antislavery movement in the western world, the revolutionary generation failed to end slavery when it was still vulnerable to gradual removal short of war because they misread the time that was running on the political clock. In a sense they made the same kind of mistake as the British, who underestimated the depth of the American resistance. But the American mistake flowed directly from the different meanings of The Cause itself.

As Jefferson, Hamilton, Lafayette, and Laurens could all testify, The Cause had egalitarian implications that were incompatible with slavery, and it was that self-evident truth which energized the antislavery movement in the postwar years. But one of the chief strengths of The Cause, which allowed what we might call the American Evolution to succeed by avoiding the self-destructive path of the French Revolution, was its latency, its capacity to delay the full promise into the future. (Washington kept up a running joke with Rochambeau after the war about hot soup. The French gulped it down and burned their throats, while the Americans blew on their soup until it cooled down.) This deferral dimension of The Cause produced prudent revolutionaries, who worried about attempting to implement reforms too quickly. John Adams was the most eloquent advocate for the deferral strategy.[24]

But slavery needed to become the exception to that rule. It needed to be ended before the numbers—both the size of the slave population and the cost of compensating owners—became impossible, before the memories of the revolutionary agenda faded, before the cancer spread to the southwestern territories. None of the prominent founders realized that they were racing against time. All were apprehensive of generating a sectional split when the infant republic was too fragile to survive such a trauma. And their apprehensions were not unfounded; indeed, they were realistic assessments of the political threat that any explicit abolitionist agenda posed to the union.

Washington was typical of first-wave abolitionists in the postwar years, who knew that emancipation eventually needed to be placed on the political agenda, but who also lacked any sense of urgency in reaching that goal. As he explained to an old army friend, John Mercer, "I mean never to possess another slave by purchase, it being among my first wishes to see some plan adopted by the legislature by which slavery in this Country may be abolished by slow, sure, and imperceptible degrees."[25]

He reiterated his insistence on going slow to Robert Morris: "I can only say that there is not a man living who wishes more sincerely than I do to see a plan adopted for the abolition of it," then adding, "but there is only one proper and effected mode by which it can be accomplished, and that is by legislative authority; and this, as far as my own suffrage will go, shall never be wanting."[26]

In 1785 Washington received a letter from Robert Pleasants, a Quaker who had freed his own slaves in 1782, urging Washington to follow his example or risk staining his reputation: "For notwithstanding thou art now receiving the tribute of praise from a grateful people, the time is coming when all actions will be weighed in an equal balance, and undergo an impartial explanation." How would it sound to posterity, Pleasants asked rhetorically, "if the great hero of the war, the destroyer of tyranny and oppression, persists in keeping a number of People in absolute slavery, who were by nature equally entitled to freedom as himself?"[27]

Washington did not respond, telling friends that he seldom listened to advice from Quakers, whom he could never quite forgive for sitting out the war. But Lafayette, whom he regarded as an adopted son, offered the same advice, albeit in a more positive format. "Such an Example as Yours," Lafayette wrote, "Might Render It a General Practice." When rumors reached William Gordon in Boston, who was writing the first history of the war, that Washington was contemplating freeing his slaves, Gordon became ecstatic. "I should rejoice beyond measure should your just counsels [with Lafayette] produce it, and thereby give the finishing stroke and last polish to your political character."[28]

But Washington continued to struggle with the decision. Whether his example would have made a difference in the crucial state of Virginia is an unanswerable question. He kept deferring until 1799, when he drafted his will, freeing all the slaves he owned at Mount Vernon upon the death of his wife. On the most consequential issue facing the revolutionary generation, its greatest leader could not lead.*[29]

NEITHER AN American nation nor a viable national government existed at the end of the war. All the political energy belonged to "pluribus," not "unum." Historians who talk about the looming emergence of a proverbial nation-state in postwar America are reading later developments into a revolutionary legacy that, in truth, regarded the creation of an American nation as a betrayal of The Cause. Those poised on the cusp of the moment envisioned a North American version of Europe, thirteen separate countries, always vying for dominance, loosely linked in a domestic League of Nations. It would become a political model for the Confederate States of America.[30]

Josiah Tucker, the same Anglican divine who had described Great Britain's loss of its North American empire as more a blessing than a curse, joined the lists again to assure his countrymen that the term "United States" was a comical contradiction, indeed "one of the most idealistic and most visionary Notions that ever was conceived by the writers of romance." Try as one might, Tucker argued, it was impossible to imagine that those rowdy Americans "could ever be united under any auspices of Government whatsoever. Their fate seems to be a Disunited People till the End of Time."[31]

Prominent American voices echoed the same message, albeit less

---

* Washington owned about half the 317 slaves at Mount Vernon when he died in December 1799. Martha owned the remainder, which she had inherited upon her first husband's death. There is strong evidence that Martha did not share Washington's antislavery convictions, but she did honor the terms of his will. When the slaves at Mount Vernon learned that their emancipation was contingent on Martha's death, rumors circulated that they planned to poison her. She promptly freed them in 1801.

enthusiastically. Writing from London, Abigail Adams lamented that her husband faced the awkward task of representing an American government that did not exist. (Appointing John Adams to serve as the first minister to the Court of St. James's was a brilliant stroke, like appointing Martin Luther as ambassador to the Vatican.) Abigail described the current delegation in the Confederation Congress as "beardless boys," who thought that "foreign affairs" referred to infidelity abroad. She compared them to one member of Parliament who kept referring to "the island of Virginia." Given the current state-based structure, she and John were a diplomatic team resigned to playing the role of clowns in a farce.[32]

Recently arrived in the Virginia legislature, Thomas Jefferson concurred with Abigail's assessment of his new colleagues: "The members of Congress are no longer, generally speaking, men of worth or distinction. For Congress is not, as formerly, held in respect. There is dread of its power, though it has none." Benjamin Harrison, the governor of Virginia, went further, worrying that the very survival of the Confederation Congress "seems to be problematic." Like Jefferson, he looked back to better days, "when the eyes of the world were upon us, and we were the wonder and envy of all." But now, Harrison concluded, "we are sinking faster in esteem than we rose," and the European powers were "gathering like buzzards to feast on the spoils of our demise." The center could not hold because it did not exist.[33]

Then there was the experience of John Jay. In 1784 he was appointed superintendent of foreign affairs. (Jay carried all the prestige of his recent triumph in Paris, and used it as leverage to negotiate a move of the federal capital from Annapolis to New York, where his wife and family resided.) As his first act, Jay sent a letter to all the state governors, requesting them to forward all correspondence relating to foreign policy to his office. Few governors responded, none complied. The states presumed they could each make their own foreign policy.

The same thing happened when Jay ordered several southern states

to observe Article IV of the Treaty of Paris, which required them to pay
the £4 million in prewar debts they owed to English bankers, over half
of it owed by Virginia planters. Not a single southern state responded,
even when Jay apprised them that all treaties carried the force of "laws
of the land," an anticipation of what became the supremacy clause in
the U.S. Constitution. The Virginia delegates expressed their outrage
that Jay believed he could lecture them on the law. They obviously presumed their debts could be finessed. As Jay explained in frustration to
Richard Henry Lee, currently serving as president of the Confederation
Congress: "I have some Reason, Sir, to apprehend that I have come into
the Office of Foreign Affairs with ideas of my Duties and Rights somewhat different from those of the Congress." He had presumed that the
American government needed to speak with a single voice in foreign
policy, and he was hired to provide that voice. He was wrong. There
were thirteen separate voices.[34]

We need to understand why Jay was wrong. Those historians who
look back at postwar America through the lens of the looming Constitutional Convention unknowingly bend the evidence to fit what will
soon happen. The political legacy of the revolutionary war thus becomes
"pre-national." If instead we view the same extended moment through
the lens of the war itself—that is, the previous decade (which is how it
was actually experienced)—the more accurate way to describe the political legacy is "antinational." One might press the evidence more firmly
and propose "antigovernment."

By 1783–84 the vast majority had come to regard the creation of an
American nation-state as a preposterous distortion of The Cause. The
structural weakness and periodic dysfunction of the state-based confederation framework was actually reassuring, just as the marginal status
of the Continental Army throughout the war had been a source of comfort rather than concern. Anyone proposing political reform expanding
the meaning of The Cause in a national direction faced a barrage of
invective from self-appointed True Whigs loaded with all the quasi-

paranoid conspiratorial accusations previously leveled at Parliament and the British ministry. Outspoken nationalists like Jay, Hamilton, and Washington were outliers on the far fringe.

The same top-bottom coalition that had worked so well to generate and then mobilize the resistance against efforts at imperial reform performed the same task after the war to stymie any national agenda. From above, any proposed increase of government power at the federal level was demonized as a domestic incarnation of British tyranny. From below, the same women and men who had gone house to house enforcing allegiances to The Cause were unwilling to surrender control over their lives to representatives in faraway places whom they did not know personally. Nothing in their lives prepared them to "think continentally," as Hamilton had urged. Any government beyond local or state borders was a foreign government, "them" rather than "us."

There were, then, two enduring political legacies firmly embedded in the American founding at the very start: first, any robust expression of government power, most especially at the federal level, was placed on the permanent defensive; second, conspiracy theories that might otherwise have been dismissed as preposterous shouts from the lunatic fringe enjoyed a supportive environment because of their hallowed association with The Cause. Both legacies gave American political thought a decidedly oppositional edge, much surer about what it was against than what it was for, prepared to block any hostile takeover from above by any aspiring dictator or domestic version of British tyranny, but incapable of decisive action at the national level to face or resolve the two embedded tragedies of slavery and Native American genocide in slow motion.

Acknowledgments

A special salute to the small army of editors whose work over many decades has provided historians and biographers with scholarly editions of the papers and correspondence generated by the most prominent founders. The net result is the fullest account of a political elite ever assembled in recorded history.

While researching and writing this book I frequently listened to advice from voices in the past stored in my memory. These are former teachers and mentors who have left us but never left me: Edmund S. Morgan, Eric McKitrick, Elting Morison, C. Vann Woodward, and William McFeely.

Four historians read the entire manuscript, catching multiple gaffes and providing advice I could not afford to ignore: Chet Atkinson, whose knowledge of the military story is unsurpassed; Richard Brown, who brought the same level of hard-earned wisdom to the political and ideological issues at stake; Paul Staiti, whose perspective as an art historian added a visual dimension no one else could have offered; and Susan Dunn, who has a preternatural knack for knowing when the reader needs more, and when less is more.

Clay Jenkinson allowed me to try out certain still-forming thoughts on his radio program, *The Jefferson Hour*; Stacy Schiff, who is working on a biography of Samuel Adams, listened to me hold forth in multiple conversations and shared thoughts in her inimitable voice. The subtitle was Stacy's suggestion. Steve Smith, the most veteran Ellis editor of all, made me think harder about Valley Forge and proved himself the reigning champion in that space where substance meets style.

My longtime assistant, Linda Fernandes, continued to disguise my digital incompetence, read my handwritten drafts as no one else on the planet can now do, greeted me every day with "What have we got?" and signed off with "What else do you need?" She was joined for this book by Louise Harlow, a former actress and current archivist, who kept sending me old, out-of-print books that I could have never found otherwise and who gave the whole project a vibrant sense of her adventurous spirit.

My agent, Bob Barnett, negotiated the contract with his customary poker-faced style. Bob also kept me in the loop as we coped with the enforced isolation caused by the Covid crisis.

At Norton, Bob Weil lived up to his reputation as one of the few editors who still line-edits. Someday, Bob needs to publish his marginalia, though I have urged him to consider scaling back his use of the word "evoke." His able assistant, Haley Bracken, deftly handled finicky questions about maps and illustrations, and made Norton feel more like family than a corporation. Lauren Abbate quietly oversaw the production of the printed book.

The Norton team responsible for the cover demonstrated infinite patience with my artistically challenged suggestions. Two friends with more educated eyes, Wendy Watson and Leo Echaniques helped me see what Norton proposed with greater insight..

Two labradoodles, Phoebe and Lucy, napped behind me throughout the writing process. They somehow knew instinctively when to nose me out of my chair and take me for a walk.

Ellen Wilkins Ellis brought me back from the eighteenth century with her commanding, steel-magnolia style, forgave me any lapses when I appeared to be listening but wasn't, and kept the keel of the family balanced during my oblivious moments. Ellen is my Abigail.

Notes

The notes below represent my attempt to provide documentation for all quotations in the text, the vast majority of which came from primary sources, most often from the correspondence of the chief characters in my story. When that story crosses over contested historical terrain, I have cited secondary sources that strike me as seminal in order to pay my respect to historians who preceded me. My accounting on that score, however, is far from exhaustive, because such a standard would burden the book with notes that outweigh the text itself.

I have silently modernized spelling and punctuations, except when the eighteenth-century version is not confusing and adds a distinctive flavor the reader might find revealing.

ABBREVIATIONS

Titles

AmAr   Peter Force, ed., *American Archives,* 9 vols. (Washington, D.C., 1833–1853).

AFC   Lyman Butterfield et al., eds., *Adams Family Correspondence,* 11 vols. to date (Cambridge, Mass., 1963–).

AP   Robert J. Taylor et al., eds., *The Papers of John Adams,* 15 vols. to date (Cambridge, Mass., 1983–).

DA   Lyman H. Butterfield, ed., *The Diary and Autobiography of John Adams,* 4 vols. (Cambridge, Mass., 1966).

DAR   K. B. Davis, ed., *Documents of the American Revolution 1770–1783,* 21 vols. (Shannon, Ireland, 1972–1981).

FP   Barbara Oberg et al., eds., *The Papers of Benjamin Franklin,* 28 vols. to date (New Haven, Conn., 1959–).

GP   Richard K. Showman, ed., *The Papers of Nathanael Greene,* 8 vols. to date (Chapel Hill, N.C., 1976–).

HP   Harold C. Syrett and Jacob E. Cooke, eds., *The Papers of Alexander Hamilton,* 26 vols. (New York, 1961–1979).

JCC   W. C. Ford et al., eds., *Journals of the Continental Congress,* 24 vols. (Washington, D.C., 1904–1937).

JP   Julian Boyd et.al., eds., *The Papers of Thomas Jefferson,* 30 vols. to date (Princeton, N.J., 1950–).

LDC   Paul H. Smith et al., eds., *Letters of Delegates to Congress, 1774–1789*, 29 vols. (Washington, D.C., 1976–2000).

LP   David R. Chestnutt and C. James Taylor, eds., *The Papers of Henry Laurens*, 17 vols. (Columbia, S.C., 1968–2003).

MP   E. James Ferguson et. al., eds., *The Papers of Robert Morris*, 9 vols. (Pittsburgh, 1973–1999).

PAR   Gordon S. Wood, ed., *The Pamphlets of the American Revolution*, 2 vols. Library of America (New York, 2011).

PWCS   W. W. Abbot and Dorothy Twohig, eds., *The Papers of George Washington: Confederation Series*, 6 vols. (Charlottesville, Va., 1992–1997).

PWPS   W. W. Abbot and Dorothy Twohig, eds., *The Papers of George Washington: Presidential Series*, 20 vols. to date (Charlottesville, Va., 1987–).

PWRS   W. W. Abbot, Dorothy Twohig, and Philander D. Chase, eds., *The Papers of George Washington: Revolutionary War Series*, 22 vols. to date (Charlottesville, Va., 1985–).

WAR   Clifford J. Rogers, Ty Seidule, and Samuel J. Watson, eds., *The West Point History of the American Revolution* (New York, 2017).

WMQ   *William and Mary Quarterly*, 3rd series.

WW   James C. Fitzpatrick, ed., *Writings of George Washington*, 39 vols. (Washington, D.C., 1931–1939).

Persons

AA   Abigail Adams
AH   Alexander Hamilton
BF   Benjamin Franklin
GW   George Washington
HL   Henry Laurens
JA   John Adams
JD   John Dickinson
JL   John Laurens
NG   Nathanael Greene
RM   Robert Morris
TJ   Thomas Jefferson

CHAPTER ONE: THE RUBICON

1. *FP* 4:225–35.
2. Three works are seminal: Edmund S. Morgan and Helen M. Morgan, *The Stamp Act Crisis: Prologue to Revolution* (Chapel Hill, N.C., 1953); Bernard Bailyn, *The Ideological Origins of the American Revolution* (Cambridge, Mass., 1967); and Pauline Maier, *From Resistance to Revolution: Colonial Radicals and the Development of American Opposition to Britain, 1765–1776* (New York, 1972).
3. Thomas Pownall, *Administration of the Colonies* (London, 1764); subsequent editions appeared in 1765, 1767, 1774, and 1777.
4. *PAR* 1:1–24.
5. Ibid., 25–40.

6. Ibid., preface by Gordon Wood, which provides a succinct overview of the problems facing Great Britain after 1763. For the demographic flow across the imaginary line, see Kevin Phillips, *1775: A Good Year for Revolution* (New York, 2012), 165–68.

7. Two American historians, Charles McLean Andrews and Lawrence Gibson, each wrote multivolume chronicles of the imperial story as experienced on the American side. For the British side, see Charles R. Ritchie, *British Politics and the American Revolution, 1763–1783* (Norman, Okla., 1954), Bernard Donoughue, *British Politics and the American Revolution, 1773–1775* (London, 1964), and more recently, and helpfully, Andrew Jackson O'Shaughnessy, *The Men Who Lost America: British Leadership, the American Revolution, and the Fate of the Empire* (New Haven, Conn., 2013).

8. William Blackstone, *Commentaries on the Laws of England* (London, 1765), 49–50. See also Gordon Wood, "The Problem of Sovereignty," *WMQ* 68 (October 2011): 592–77.

9. *DA* 3:284.

10. *AP* 1:103–28.

11. Ibid., 127–28.

12. John J. McCusker and Russell R. Menard, *The Economy of British America, 1607–1789* (New York, 1991) remains the best overview. For the administrative problems and costs, see Michael Kammen, *Empire and Interest: The American Colonies and the Politics of Mercantilism* (Ithaca, N.Y., 1970).

13. Lytton Strachey, *Eminent Victorians* (London, 1986), 9.

14. An old but still reliable survey of the various interpretive schools of thought is Esmund Wright, ed., *Causes and Consequences of the American Revolution* (Chicago, 1966).

15. *PAR* 1: 121–330.

16. Ibid., 405–90; Dickinson quoted in Morgan and Morgan, *The Stamp Act Crisis*, 142–43.

17. Richard D. Brown, *Revolutionary Politics in Massachusetts: The Boston Committees of Correspondence and the Towns* (Cambridge, Mass., 1970); Richard Ryerson, *The Revolution Has Now Begun: The Radical Committees of Philadelphia, 1765–1776* (Philadelphia, 1978); T. H. Breen, *American Insurgents, American Patriots: The Revolution of the People* (New York, 2010); Mark Puls, *Samuel Adams: Father of the American Revolution* (New York, 2006); John C. Miller, *Samuel Adams: Pioneer in Propaganda* (Boston, 1936). My keen sense is that Samuel Adams has yet to find a modern biographer capable of telling his story with the political and psychological insight it requires. In that sense he remains the "missing link" between the top-down and bottom-up interpretations of the American Revolution.

18. The standard account remains Benjamin W. Labaree, *The Boston Tea Party* (New York, 1964). See also L. F. S. Upton, "Proceeding of Ye Body Respecting the Tea," *WMQ* 22 (1965): 287–300, which contains the Adams quotations. Brown, *Revolutionary Politics in Massachusetts*, 149–77, includes material on the political context not available elsewhere.

19. BF to Thomas Cushing, 22 March 1774, *FP*.

20. George III's Address to the House of Lords, 7 March 1774, *AmAr* 1:6; George III to Lord North, 11 November 1774, quoted in Donoughue, *British Politics and the American Revolution*, 49.

21. See *New York Gazette, and Weekly Mercury*, 15 April, 1776, for Clarke quotation.

22. See *AmAr* 1:61–66, 104–12, 129–32 for the texts of the major Coercive Acts. Earl of Dartmouth to General Gage, 9 April 1774, ibid., 245–46. In addition to these punitive actions against Massachusetts, Parliament also passed the Quartering Act and the Quebec Act, which are noticed here only in passing.

23. Ibid., 34, 46, 50–51, 74.

24. Ibid., 167. For the term "sleeping sovereignty," see Donoughue, *British Politics and the American Revolution*, 19, 215.

25. Edward Gibbon to Lord Sheffield, 31 January 1774, J. E. Norton, ed., *The Letters of Edward Gibbon*, 3 vols. (London, 1956), 1:217.

26. Edward Gibbon to Lord Sheffield, 15 May 1775, ibid., 296.

27. Edward Gibbon, *The Decline and Fall of the Roman Empire*, ed. Moses Hadas (New York, 1969), 25–41.

28. BF to Jane Macon, 1 November 1773, *FP* 20:458.

29. Ibid., 391–99.

30. See *FP* 21:37–70, for the hostile treatment of Franklin before the Privy Council.

31. *PAR* 2: 588.

32. Samuel Adams to Arthur Lee, 18 May 1774, *AmAr* 1:332; to Arthur Lee, 20 August 1774, ibid., 726. Picking up the motto of the resistance movement as his title, David Ammerman's *In the Common Cause: American Response to the Coercive Acts of 1774* (New York, 1975) remains the authoritative account of the crisis, which I found more reliable than the recent effort by Robert Parkinson, *Thirteen Clocks: How Race United the Colonies* (Chapel Hill, 2021).

33. Thomas Jefferson, *A Summary View of the Rights of British America*, *PAR* 2: 85–108; James Wilson, *Considerations on the Nature and Extent of the Legislative Authority of the British Parliament*, ibid., 109–46; William Henry Drayton, *A Letter from Freeman of South Carolina*, ibid., 147–84.

34. For the role of the Committees of Correspondence, see Brown, *Revolutionary Politics in Massachusetts*, 121–40, and Ammerman, *In the Common Cause*, 19–34. See also the reminiscence of John Adams, JA to Jedidiah Morse, 22 December 1815, *The Works of John Adams, Second President of the United States*, 10 vols., ed. Charles Francis Adams (Boston, 1850–1860), 10:196–97. The quotation is from Richard Henry Lee to Arthur Lee, 28 June 1774, *AmAr* 1:489.

35. Open Letter from Members of the Late House of Burgesses in Virginia, 27 May 1774, *AmAr* 1: 350–51.

36. Earl of Dartmouth to Governor Gage, 3 June 1774, ibid., 380–82. See also John Shy, "The Empire Militant: Thomas Gage and the Coming of War," in *A People Numerous and Armed: Reflections on the Military Struggle for Independence* (New York, 1976), 72–107.

37. *AmAr* 1:764, 768, 782; Brown, *Revolutionary Politics in Massachusetts*, 208.

38. *AmAr* 1:745, 747, 748, 752.

39. Governor Gage to Earl of Dartmouth, 2 September 1774, ibid., 767–69.

40. Gage's correspondence to Dartmouth became more pessimistic in the late fall of 1774, thereby sealing his fate. The quotation comes from an unidentified British officer in London, in Donoughue, *British Politics and the American Revolution*, 210.

41. Ammerman, *In the Common Cause*, 139–49, for a convenient summary of the resolutions during the summer of 1774. *AmAr* 1:380–662, for the fullest documentary record of the resolutions themselves.

42. *AmAr* 1:893–938; Ammerman, *In the Common Cause*, 89–401; Joseph Galloway's Proposed Resolution, 28 September 1774, *LDC* 1: 112–19; Julian Boyd, *Anglo-American Union: Joseph Galloway's Plans to Preserve the British Empire, 1774–1788* (Philadelphia, 1941); GW to Robert Mackenzie, 9 October 1774, *LDC* 1:166–67.

43. The scene is recounted in JA to AA, 16 September 1774, *AFC* 1:156.

44. JA to William Tudor, 29 September 1774, *AP* 2:177.

45. Suffolk County Resolves, 9 September 1774, *AmAr* 1:776–79.

46. *DA* 2:134; JA to AA, 29 September 1774, *AFC* 1:163.

47. Samuel Adams to Joseph Warren, 25 September 1774, *LDC* 1:100.

48. *AmAr* 1:914.

49. South Carolina Delegates, Report to the South Carolina Provincial Congress, 4 January 1775, *LDC* 1:292–95. This report provoked a debate over the reasons rice was excluded from the boycott, but no mention of the slave trade was made.

50. *AmAr* 1:915.

51. David Ammerman was the first historian to notice and document the extraordinary political impact of the Continental Association, in *In the Common Cause*, 103–24. Most recently, T. H. Breen has amplified the analysis of the enforcement mechanism of local committees in *American Insurgents, American Patriots*, 185–206.

52. *AmAr* 1:387–88, 392, 417, 1011, 1141, 1171–72; 2:140–42, 170–71.

53. See *AmAr*. 1:1262, for Daniel Dunbar's painful conversion.

54. The calculated moderation of the American posture from 1774 to 1776 is the main theme of the next chapter.

55. The decision to focus on British policy after 1763 was made after lengthy debates in closed sessions of the Rights and Grievances Committee. It was presented as a resolution to the full congress and approved on October 14. It begins, "We pass over for the present and proceed to state such Acts and measures as have been adopted since the last war, which demonstrate a system formed to enslave America." *AmAr* 1:914.

56. Ibid., 917.

57. Ibid., 918.

58. Ibid., 921.

59. Pitt's remarks were recorded by Arthur Lee during a walk with Pitt on December 25, 1774. Ibid., 1058–59.

60. Jay's reputation as a major figure within the revolutionary generation is currently undergoing restoration. The biography by Walter Stahr, *John Jay* (New York, 2005), is an important contribution to that worthy cause.

61. Much like Jay, Dickinson's prominent role, most especially in the decade before independence was declared, is also being rediscovered. See William Murchison, *The Cost of Liberty: The Life of John Dickinson* (Wilmington, Del., 2013) for a cogent and quite convincing reappraisal.

62. *AmAr* 1:921–28.

63. Ibid., 934–37.

64. This is the moment when Dickinson and John Adams began to part company, and when the distinction between moderates and radicals began to become a relevant description of divisions within the Common Cause. The gap between the two camps was fully exposed in the Second Continental Congress. By then, George III's commitment to the sovereignty principle completely undermined Dickinson's moderate posture. By clinging to it, Dickinson made himself into a reluctant revolutionary and therefore, as Adams saw it, not quite fairly, a pathetic patriot who chose to remain on the far side of the Rubicon.

65. JD to Arthur Lee, 27 October 1774, *LDC* 1:250. Also, JD to Joshua Quincy Jr., 28 October 1774, ibid., 251.

66. JD to William Pitt, 21 December 1765, quoted in Morgan and Morgan, *The Stamp Act Crisis*, 261–62.

67. *PAR* 2: 496.
68. Ibid., 463–96; JA to AA, 17 June 1775, *AFC* 1:216.
69. Pitt's speech in the House of Lords, 20 January 1775, *AmAr* 1:1493–98.
70. George III quoted in Donoughue, *British Politics and the American Revolution*, 272–73.
71. *AmAr* 1:842.
72. Ibid., 1:1268–69.
73. Shy, *A People Numerous and Armed*, 193–224, emphasizes the decisive role played by militia in controlling the American interior throughout the war, a war for hearts and minds effectively won even before independence was declared. Piers Mackesy, *The War for America, 1775–1783* (Lincoln, Neb., 1993) makes the same argument as seen from the British side, which faced intractable strategic problems rooted in the inability to subjugate an entire population already dedicated to resistance. For the most recent and comprehensive account of the early years of the war, see Rick Atkinson, *The British Are Coming: Lexington to Princeton, 1775–1777* (New York, 2019). See also Mary Beth Norton, *1774: The Long Year of Revolution* (New York, 2020).
74. Two recent historians, Kevin Phillips in *1775: A Good Year for Revolution* and T. H. Breen in *American Insurgents, American Patriots*, focus on the impact of the Continental Association, operating at the local level, to galvanize the resistance movement in late 1774 and early 1775. This is where the "bottom-up" perspective on the American Revolution is most persuasive.

CHAPTER TWO: PRUDENCE DICTATES

1. For the original and edited drafts of the Declaration, along with historical interpretations of the text, see Joseph J. Ellis, ed., *What Did the Declaration Declare?* (Boston, 1999).
2. Three books provide different versions of 1775–76: Allen French, *The First Year of the American Revolution* (Boston, 1934); Kevin Phillips, *1775: A Good Year for Revolution* (New York, 2012); and David McCullough, *1776* (New York, 2005).
3. See John Shy, *A People Numerous and Armed: Reflections on the Military Struggle for American Independence* (New York, 1976), for the role of the militia in controlling the countryside; T. H. Breen, *American Insurgents, American Patriots: The Revolution of the People* (New York, 2010), for the role of civilians.
4. Jack N. Rakove, *The Beginnings of National Politics: An Interpretive History of the Continental Congress* (New York, 1979) is the authoritative account of the congress; Charles Royster, *A Revolutionary People at War: The Continental Army and American Character, 1775–1783* (New York, 1979), 25–53, focuses on the crescendo of patriotic passion, called *rage militaire*, in the months before independence was declared.
5. This tribute to the role of mostly invisible American patriots "out there" in the countryside needs to be accompanied by an appreciation of what it felt like if one happened to be a lukewarm patriot or outright loyalist. Breen, *American Insurgents, American Patriots*, makes it quite clear that leaders of the resistance could not afford to respect the rights of their recalcitrant neighbors. In a revolutionary situation, standard rules of civility did not apply.
6. The Burke quotation comes from a speech in the House of Commons in 1768, quoted in Bernard Bailyn, *The Ideological Origins of the American Revolution* (Cambridge, Mass., 1967), 158–59.
7. TJ to John Randolph, 25 August 1775, *LDC* 1:707–8.
8. *AmAr* 2:52–59, 1867–69, for *Petition* and *Declaration*. The latter was initially drafted by

Jefferson, then revised by Dickinson, whose revised version, contrary to Jefferson's latter-day claim, took a firmer stance toward British aggression than Jefferson's had.

9. Dickinson's long-standing reputation, popularized in the play 1776, as the weak-kneed appeaser and "the Man Who Would Not Sign the Declaration of Independence," has been rescued from marginalization by his most recent biographer, William Murchison, in *The Cost of Liberty: The Life of John Dickinson* (Wilmington, Del., 2013). The words "do the right thing, rightly" are Murchison's.

10. *LDC* 1:371–91, for Dickinson's notes for speeches and debates in late spring and early summer of 1776. These often cryptic and rambling ruminations show Dickinson attempting to reconcile his diplomatic agenda with his growing realization that George III had made it abundantly clear that he had no interest in negotiations.

11. Ibid., 378.

12. Ibid., 39–81. Franklin commiserated with Dickinson's dilemma, but based on his experience in London, had concluded that all efforts at diplomacy would fail because the British ministry "has neither Temper nor Wisdom enough to seize the Golden opportunity." BF to Jonathan Shipley, 7 July 1775, ibid., 604–7.

13. JA to Moses Gill, 10 June 1775, *AP* 2:21. See also JA to James Warren, 22 April 1776, *AP.* 4:135.

14. DA 1:256.

15. JA to James Warren, 24 July 1775, *LDC* 1:658–59.

16. Jeremy Black, *George III: America's Last King* (New Haven, Conn., 2006) is a reliable and readable biography. For a succinct and riveting overview of George III's early career, see Andrew Jackson O'Shaughnessy, *The Men Who Lost America: British Leadership, the American Revolution, and the Fate of the Empire* (New Haven, Conn., 2013), 17–46.

17. Shaughnessy, *The Men Who Lost America*, 22–27, for George III's proclamations and speech to Parliament; see also *AmAr* 1:1465, 1542.

18. George III to Lord North, 18 August 1775, John Fortesque, ed., *The Correspondence of George the Third from 1760 to December 1783*, 6 vols. (London, 1927–1928), 3:248.

19. *AmAr* 2:961–62; Shaughnessy, *The Men Who Lost America*, 175–77; see also Gerald S. Brown, *The American Secretary: Lord George Germain, 1775–1778* (Ann Arbor, Mich., 1963).

20. JA to John Trumbull, 13 February 1776, *AP* 4:22.

21. Murchison, *The Cost of Liberty*, 131–50, which describes Dickinson's awkward posture as a measure of his principled integrity.

22. There are three excellent biographies: Eric Foner, *Tom Paine and Revolutionary America* (New York, 1976); John Keane, *Tom Paine: A Political Life* (Boston, 1995); and Harvey J. Kaye, *Thomas Paine and the Promise of America* (New York, 2005).

23. Philip Foner, ed., *The Complete Writings of Thomas Paine*, 2 vols. (New York, 1945) 1:4–5, 28–29, 36–39.

24. Ibid., 30–31, 45.

25. JA to William Tudor, 12 April 1776, *AP* 4:118.

26. Unknown to JA, 9 June 1775, ibid., 3:18–19.

27. "Humanity" to JA, 23 January 1776, ibid., 411.

28. James Sullivan to JA, 12 April 1776, ibid., 4:212–13.

29. JA to James Sullivan, 26 May 1776, ibid., 208–13; JA to John Winthrop, 23 June 1776, ibid., 332–33.

30. AA to JA, 31 March 1776, *AFC* 1:370.

31. AA to Mercy Otis Warren, 27 April 1776, *AP.*, 396–98.

32. AA to JA, 7 May 1776, ibid., 402.

33. JA to James Warren, 22 April 1776, *AP* 4:136–37.

34. JA to Mercy Otis Warren, 16 April 1776, ibid., 124.

35. JA to John Winthrop, 12 May 1776, ibid., 183–84.

36. Editorial note, *Thoughts on Government*, ibid., 65–73; JA to AA, 17 May 1776, *AFC* 1:410.

37. See *AP* 4:86–93, for the text of *Thoughts on Government.*

38. Ibid., 83–84.

39. JA to James Warren, 15 May 1776, ibid., 186.

40. JA to William Cushing, 9 June 1776, ibid., 245.

41. JA to AA, 2 June 1776, *AFC* 2:3.

42. The interaction between the advancing political agenda in Philadelphia and the advancing British military agenda in New York is the main focus of my *Revolutionary Summer: The Birth of Independence* (New York, 2013).

43. See *AmAr* 6:702–4, for Topsfield and western Massachusetts's towns. Pauline Maier, *American Scripture: Making the Declaration of Independence*, (New York, 1997), 47–96, was the first modern history to focus attention on the reports from the countryside as "the other declarations."

44. *AmAr* 6:755, 876–68, 951–67. Several coastal towns, especially on Cape Cod, were more divided, presumably because of apprehension that they would be targeted by the British fleet. See ibid., 705–6, for Barnstable's hesitation.

45. Ibid., 5:1206–8.

46. Ibid., 6:461–62, 1524.

47. Ibid., 5:1047–47.

48. Ibid., 6:1618, 1623–29; editorial note, *FP* 22:551–52.

49. *AmAr* 6:755, for Pennsylvania's instructions to delegates in congress.

50. See Richard A. Ryerson, *The Revolution Is Now Begun: The Radical Committees of Philadelphia* (Philadelphia, 1978), 207–40, for the way artisans and mechanics created committees that effectively seized control of the resistance movement in and around Philadelphia in the wake of the Coercive Acts. Paine was their champion, and removing the property qualification to vote was their highest priority.

51. Ibid., 260–88, and William Hoageland, *Declaration: The Nine Tumultuous Weeks When American Became Independent, May 1–July 4, 1776* (New York, 2010), 105–42, tell the story of how Samuel and John Adams both worked behind the scenes to mobilize support for a new Pennsylvania constitution.

52. *AmAr* 6:957–67; JA to James Warren, 20 May 1776, *LDC* 4:41.

53. AA to JA, 27 November 1775, *AFC* 1:329–30.

54. JCC 1:320–27, for the resolution creating Dickinson's committee. For the context of the Dickinson Draft, see Merrill Jensen, *The Articles of Consideration: An Interpretation* (Madison, Wisc., 1940), 126–39. For a more recent overview, see David Hendrickson, *Peace Pact: The Lost World of the American Founding* (Lawrence, Kans., 2003), 127–38.

55. JA to Joseph Hawley, 25 August 1776, *LDC* 5:60–62.

56. Ellis, ed., *What Did the Declaration Declare?*, provides a sampling of the historical interpretations of the context for the semi-sacred event, plus the original draft and revisions of the Declaration itself. The following paragraphs represent my efforts to digest the scholarship in a succinct and accessible fashion.

57. TJ to James Madison, 30 August 1823, and TJ to Henry Lee, 8 May 1825, both quoted in editorial note, *JP* 1:415. See also ibid., 413–33, for Julian Boyd's long note on the multiple drafts of the document.

58. One can make a plausible, but unprovable, case that Jefferson's original intention was to blame George III for slavery itself, not just the slave trade. Since he was blaming the king for everything else, why not include slavery in the indictment, thereby placing slavery on the list of British transgressions that Americans are morally obliged to put on the road to extinction? I have made that case in *American Dialogue: The Founders and Us* (New York, 2018), 19–21. But even if Jefferson was contemplating making emancipation part of America's founding document, he chose not to do so, knowing full well that the delegates would delete it.

59. Jefferson's language in this deleted paragraph actually replicates the language used in several of the town and county resolutions pouring into the congress in response to the request of May 20 for a referendum on independence. For the sentimental streak in Jefferson, see Andrew Burstein, *The Inner Jefferson: Portrait of a Grieving Optimist* (Charlottesville, Va., 2000).

60. Lincoln quoted in Donald E. Fehrenbacher, ed., *Lincoln's Speeches and Writings* (New York, 1989), 2:19, from a letter to Henry Pierce in 1859. See Richard Brookheiser, *Founders' Son: A Life of Abraham Lincoln* (New York, 2014) for the fullest study of Lincoln's appropriation of Jefferson's message to posterity, although Brookheiser, correctly I believe, thinks Washington was Lincoln's major lodestar.

61. These are the most studied words in American history. My fullest effort at comprehending Jefferson's thought process at the time is in *American Sphinx: The Character of Thomas Jefferson* (New York, 1997), 55–59. The most distinctive phrase is "the pursuit of happiness" in lieu of "property" in the original Lockean trinity of "life, liberty, and property." The change had major antislavery implications. Jefferson borrowed the phrase from George Mason, who coined it in his draft of the Virginia constitution, then under consideration in Williamsburg and reported in the Philadelphia press.

62. Resolutions, 9 July 1776, *Journal of the Provincial Congress of New York* (Albany, N.Y., 1816), 1:518.

CHAPTER THREE: THE ESCAPE

1. David Hackett Fischer, *Washington's Crossing* (New York, 2004). On Leutze's painting, see Ann Hawkes Huton, *Portrait of Patriotism: Washington Crossing the Delaware* (Radnor, Pa., 1959), and Raymond L. Stehl, "Washington Crossing the Delaware," *Pennsylvania History and Biography* 31 (1964): 269–94.

2. For coverage, or lack of coverage, of the Battle of Long Island, see the following newspapers during August, September, and October 1776: the *Connecticut Courant*, the *Independent Chronicle* (Boston), the *New England Chronicle*, the *Newport Mercury*, the *Pennsylvania Packet*, and the *Virginia Gazette.*

3. This conclusion was reached by both British and American historians of the New York campaign. See, especially, William B. Willcox, *Portrait of a General: Sir Henry Clinton and the War of Independence* (New York, 1964), and Piers Mackesy, *The War for America, 1775–1783* (Cambridge, Mass., 1964). The chief threat to the survival of the Continental Army after 1776 came not from the British army, but the unwillingness of state governments to provide the money and men to sustain more than a token force.

4. These questions have been addressed from multiple angles, most accessibly in the following books: Benson Bobrick, *Angel in the Whirlwind: The Triumph of the American Revolution* (New York, 1999); Bruce Blevin, *Under the Guns: New York, 1775–1776* (New York, 1972); Thomas Fleming, *1776: Year of Illusions* (New York, 1972); Ira Gruber, *The Howe Brothers and the American Revolution* (New York, 1972); David McCullough, *1776* (New York, 2005); and Barnet Schecter, *The Battle for New York: The City at the Heart of the American Revolution* (New York, 2002).

5. Paul Lockhart, *The Whites of Their Eyes: Bunker Hill, the First American Army, and the Emergence of George Washington* (New York, 2011). On Howe's experience during the battle, see the essay by Maldwyn Jones in George Billias, ed., *George Washington's Opponents: British Generals and Admirals in the American Revolution* (New York, 1969), 39–72. For the quotation on the impact of Bunker Hill on Howe's subsequent career, see Henry Lee, ed., *Memoirs of the War in the Southern Department*, 2 vols. (Philadelphia, 1812), 1:55.

6. Christian Di Spigna, *Founding Martyr: The Life and Death of Joseph Warren* (New York, 2018).

7. John Shy, *A People Numerous and Armed: Reflections on the Military Struggle for American Independence* (New York, 1976). See also Kevin Phillips, *1775: A Good Year for Revolution* (New York, 2012), 9–17, for the sheer size of the militia in New England. For deeper background, see John Shy, *Toward Lexington: The Role of the British Army in the Coming of the American Revolution* (Princeton, N.J., 1965).

8. GW to Burwell Bassett, 19 June 1775, *PWRS* 1:12–14; *PWCS* 10:367–68, for purchases in early June.

9. GW to Joseph Reed, 10 February 1776, *PWRS* 3:87–92.

10. General Orders, 27 February 1776, ibid., 379–81.

11. GW to John Hancock, 7 January 1776, ibid., 18–21.

12. GW to John Hancock, 20 December 1776, *PWRS*, 7:382.

13. GW to John Hancock, 9 February 1776, *PWRS*, 3:274–75.

14. John Hancock to GW, 17 March 1776, *PWRS*, 4:16–17.

15. The seminal work on the Continental Army is Charles Royster, *A Revolutionary People at War: The Continental Army and the American Character* (Chapel Hill, N.C., 1979).

16. Charles Lee to GW, 16 February 1776, *PWRS* 4:339–41.

17. William Howe to George Germain, 26 April 1776, quoted in Trevor S. Anderson, *The Command of the Howe Brothers During the American Revolution* (New York, 1936), 120.

18. This assessment of the size and scale of the British expeditionary force is a distillation of accounts by Blevin, *Under the Guns*, 327–29, Gruber, *The Howe Brothers*, 72–88, and Schecter, *The Battle for New York*, 95–111.

19. The quotation characterizing Germain is from Mackesy, *The War for America*, 55. An excellent overview of Germain's career is available in Stanley Weintraub, *Iron Tears: America's Battle for Freedom, Britain's Quagmire, 1775–1783* (New York, 2005), 26–44. See also Andrew Jackson O'Shaughnessy, *The Men Who Lost America: British Leadership, the American Revolution, and the Fate of the Empire* (New Haven, Conn., 2013), 165–206. Germain's correspondence on the logistical and political issues at stake can be found in *DAR*, 2:150–58.

20. Gerald S. Brown, *The American Secretary: The Colonial Policy of Lord George Germain, 1775–78* (Ann Arbor, Mich., 1963), 127; Mackesy, *The War for America*, 55.

21. Gruber, *The Howe Brothers*, remains the authoritative work. The pair are also central players in Mackesy, *The War for America*. See also Kevin Phillips, *The Cousin's War: Reli-*

gion, Politics, Civil Warfare, And The Triumph Of Anglo-America (New York, 1999), which emphasizes the American sympathies of the Howes. The papers of both brothers were lost in a fire that consumed the family estate in the nineteenth century, so there are some things we will never know about their personal convictions.

22. *DAR*, 12:54–56.

23. General Orders,14 April 1776, *PWRS* 4:59. Martha arrived on April 16 and set up residence at the mansion of Abraham Mortimer, at what is now the corner of Varick and Charlton Streets.

24. GW to George Augustine Washington, 31 May 1776, *PWRS* 6:413.

25. Editorial note, ibid., 5:569, for efforts to restrict British naval mobility. BF to GW, 22 July 1776, *PWRS*, 421–22, on the claims of David Bushnell about a submarine. Editorial note, ibid., 6:528, on the intriguing efforts of the underwater vessel named *Turtle*.

26. *GP* 1:231–32, which also provides a map of the fortifications on Brooklyn Heights. More detailed maps and descriptions of the Long Island battlefield are provided in *WAR*, 72–78.

27. Terry Golway, *Washington's General: Nathanael Greene and the Triumph of the American Revolution* (New York, 2005) is the best biography, though the more we learn about Greene, the more we want to know. His distinctive voice first enters the story of the American Revolution at this moment.

28. NG to Christopher Greene, 9 June 1774, *GP* 1:232–33.

29. The interaction of political and military agendas is the main theme of my *Revolutionary Summer: The Birth of Independence* (New York, 2013).

30. For Washington's stay in Philadelphia from May 21 to June 12, see *PWRS* 4:363–68. For his conference with delegates of the Continental Congress, see *JCC* 4:389–91.

31. JA to NG, 22 June 1776, *GP* 1:238–40. For Adams's work on the Board of War and Ordnance, see editorial note in *AP* 4:260–78.

32. Pennsylvania Committee of Safety to GW, 11 July 1776, *PWRS* 5:271–73; Thomas Mifflin to GW, 6 August 1776, ibid., 581–82.

33. GW to John Hancock, 10 July 1776, ibid., 260.

34. Council of War, 12 July 1776, ibid., 280.

35. GW to John Hancock, 12 July 1776, ibid., 283–85. Today, the site of Fort Washington lies in the shadows of the majestic George Washington Bridge.

36. Lord Howe to GW, 13 July 1776, ibid., 296–97.

37. John F. Roche, *Joseph Reed: A Moderate in the American Revolution* (New York, 1957), 84–85; GW to John Hancock, 14 July 1776, *PWRS* 5:306.

38. Memorandum of an Interview with Lieutenant Colonel James Patterson, 20 July 1776, ibid., 398–402; GW to Horatio Gates, 19 July 1776, ibid., 402.

39. Lord Howe to GW, 6 August 1776, ibid., 402.

40. NG to GW, 15 August 1776, *GP* 1:287.

41. GW to John Hancock, 26 August 1776, *PWRS* 6:115–16. Putnam, who was barely literate, left few letters and has no modern biographer. See ibid., 6:128, for Reed's remark.

42. Clinton's recollection of the decision is in his *The American Rebellion: Sir Henry Clinton's Narrative of His Campaigns, 1775–1782*, ed. William B. Willcox (Hamden, Conn., 1971), 41–42. See also Schecter, *The Battle for New York*, 132–34.

43. Schecter, *The Battle for New York*, 141–43; E. J. Lowell, *The Hessians and Other German Auxiliaries of Great Britain in the Revolutionary War* (New York, 1884), 65–67.

44. Lord Stirling to GW, 29 August 1776, *PWRS* 6:159–62; See *AmAr* 2:107–8, for Wash-

ington's remark; Paul David Nielson, *William Alexander, Lord Stirling* (Tuscaloosa, Ala., 1989), 44; for the casualties, see editorial note, *PWRS* 6:142–43.

45. Willcox, ed., *The American Rebellion*, 44.

46. Schecter, *The Battle for New York*, 166–67, for Putnam's comment on Howe's decision.

47. Sir William Howe, *The Narrative of Lieutenant General William Howe* (London, 1780), 31–32. In his testimony to Parliament, Howe quoted directly from his letter to Germain of 3 September 1776, available in *DAR*, 12:217–18.

48. George Germain to William Howe, 3 October 1776, quoted in Weintraub, *Iron Tears*, 75.

49. Joseph Reed to Esther Reed, 2 September 1776, The Papers of Joseph Reed, New-York Historical Society. Reed left no written record of this recommendation to Washington.

50. Fleming, *1776: Year of Illusions*, 162–63, provides the fullest account of Mifflin's animus against Washington.

51. Council of War, 29 August 1776, *PWRS* 6:153–55; Benjamin Tallmadge, *The Memoir of Colonel Benjamin Tallmadge* (New York, 1858), 10.

52. The standard work on Glover is George Billias, *General John Glover and His Marblehead Mariners* (New York, 1960). The quotation is from Alexander Graydon, *A Memoir of His Own Time* (Philadelphia, 1846), 176.

53. See Henry P. Johnston, *The Campaign of 1776 Around New York and Brooklyn* (Brooklyn, 1878), 2:85, for the Tilghman quotation; Joseph Plumb Martin, *Narrative of a Revolutionary Soldier* (New York, 2001), 171.

54. Graydon, *Memoir*, 168; George F. Scheer and Hugh Rankin, eds., *Rebels and Redcoats* (New York, 1957), 171.

55. Tallmadge, *Memoir*, 11.

56. Ibid., 12–13.

57. Sir George Collier, "Admiral Sir George Collier's Observations on the Battle of Long Island," *New-York Historical Society Quarterly* (October 1964), 304.

58. Charles K. Bolton, *Letters of Hugh Earl Percy from Boston and New York* (Boston, 1972), 69.

59. *DA* 3:415–31, for John Adams's recollection of the debate over Sullivan's testimony to the Continental Congress.

60. John Witherspoon's Speech in Congress, 5 September 1775, *LDC* 5:108–13; JA to AA, 6 September 1776, ibid., 113–15.

61. *DA* 3:419–20.

62. Ibid., 422.

63. Report to Congress, 13 September 1776, *FP* 2:606–8.

64. Journal of Ambrose Serle, 22 August–15 September, 1776, in Library of America, *The American Revolution: Writings from the War of Independence*, ed. John Rhodehamel (New York, 2001), 215–16.

65. New York Committee of Safety to GW, 31 August 1776, *PWRS* 6:185–86; John Morin Scott to GW, 31 August 1776, ibid., 189–90; Rufus Putnam to GW, 3 September 1776, ibid., 210–11.

66. Joseph Reed to Esther Reed, 2 September 1776, quoted in Roche, *Joseph Reed*, 92.

67. Captain Collins quoted in Schecter, *The Battle for New York*, 175.

68. NG to GW, 5 September 1776, *PWR* 6:222–24.

69. GW to John Hancock, 8 September 1776, ibid., 248–52.

70. Petition from Certain General Officers, 11 September 1776, ibid., 279.

71. Council of War, 12 September 1776, ibid., 285–89; GW to John Hancock, 14 September 1776, ibid., 308–9.

72. Schecter, *The Battle for New York*, 179–82; GW to John Hancock, 15 September 1776, *PWR* 6:313–17, for Washington's after-action report.

73. Editorial note, *PWRS* 6:316–17, for descriptions of Washington's efforts to stop retreating troops at Kip's Bay; editorial note, *GP* 1:301–2, for Greene's comment on Washington's effort at martyrdom.

74. GW to Lund Washington, *PWRS* 6:440–41.

75. Ibid., 442.

76. GW to John Hancock, 18 September 1776, ibid., 331–37, which includes an editorial note and a map of the battlefield.

77. Blevin, *Battle of Manhattan*, 83–106, and McCullough, *1776*, 217–20, provide concise summaries of the battle. Henry P. Johnston, *The Battle of Harlem Heights* (New York, 1897), contains information not found elsewhere. For Knowlton's last words, see Ashbel Woodward, *Memoir of Colonel Thomas Knowlton* (Boston, 1861), 238.

78. General Orders, 17 September 1776, *PWRS* 6:320–21.

79. GW to John Hancock, 25 September 1776, ibid., 393–98.

80. Ibid., 400–401.

81. GW to John Hancock, 11–13 October 1776, ibid., 534–36, for Washington's report on Howe's intentions; Roche, *Joseph Reed*, 86–92, for Reed's whispering campaign.

82. Council of War, 16 October 1776, *PWRS* 6:576–77.

83. Washington later had second thoughts about leaving the garrison at Fort Washington, telling Greene, "I am therefore inclined to think it will not be prudent to hazard the men and Stores at Mount Washington," then adding "but as you are on the spot, leave it to you to give such Orders." See GW to NG, 8 November 1776, *GP* 1:342–43. Greene probably assumed, incorrectly, that the garrison could be evacuated across the Hudson.

84. William Howe to George Germain, 30 September 1776, editorial note, *PWRS* 6:533; see also Gruber, *The Howe Brothers*, 127–34.

85. Martin, *Narrative of a Revolutionary Soldier*, 44–46.

86. Billias, *General John Glover*, 121.

CHAPTER FOUR: THE FEW

1. Wayne Boodle, *The Valley Forge Winter* (University Park, Pa., 2002), and Bob Drury and Tom Clavin, *Valley Forge* (New York, 2018) provide comprehensive overviews. My briefer effort at telling the story is in *American Creation* (New York, 2007), 58–86.

2. Joseph Plumb Martin, *A Narrative of a Revolutionary Soldier* (New York, 2001), 144–45; GW to John Bannister, 21 April 1778, *PWRS* 14:577–78.

3. Albigence Waldo, "Diary of Albigence Waldo," *Pennsylvania Magazine of History and Biography* 21 (1897): 306.

4. Benjamin Rush to NG, 1 February 1778, *GP* 2:267. See also Benjamin Rush to GW, 26 December 1777, *PWRS* 13: 7–8.

5. GW to HL, 23 December 1777, *PWRS* 12:683.

6. Boodle, *Valley Forge Winter*, tends to argue that the special significance of Valley Forge has been exaggerated. Robert K. Wright, *The Continental Army* (Washington, D.C., 1983), also places Valley Forge in the larger context of systemic deprivation throughout the war.

Wayne E. Carp, *To Starve the Army at Pleasure: Continental Army Administration and American Political Culture* (Chapel Hill, N.C., 1993), as its title suggests, makes Valley Forge a dramatic example of a long-standing indifference toward the Continental Army.

7. John Marshall, *The Life of George Washington*, 2 vols. (Philadelphia, 1842), 1:213–43. For a comprehensive analysis of deaths and desertions at Valley Forge, see editorial note, *PWRS* 14:235–38.

8. The correspondence of the delegates in 1777, when the revisions of the Dickinson Draft were being made, can be found in *LDC*, especially vols. 2–4. Washington's first Circular Letter to the States, 29 December 1777, is in *PWRS* 13:36–37.

9. Editorial note, *PWRS* 13:78–79, for a brief summary of the background to the whispering campaigns against Washington.

10. NG to GW, 8 January 1778, ibid., 424–33.

11. Gouverneur Morris to HL, 25 February 1778, *LDC* 13:351.

12. GW to HL, 5 January 1778, *PWRS* 13:147–48; NG to GW, 16 February 1778, ibid., 176–77.

13. William Steward to GW, 12 January 1778, ibid., 276–77.

14. John Lacey to GW, 26 January 1778, ibid., 351; George Gibson to GW, 19 March 1778, *PWRS*, 14:226–28.

15. GW to John Armstrong, 27 March 1778, *PWRS*, 14: 276–77.

16. NG to William Greene, 7 March 1778, *GP* 2:300–4. General Orders, 24 March 1778, *PWRS* 14:285–86, for Greene's official appointment. Once the Camp Committee moved out, Greene made the Moore House his new headquarters, where he was soon joined by Caty, his vivacious wife.

17. *PWRS* 13:40–42, for editorial note on background to the machinations of Mifflin, Rush, and Gates. For Washington's after-the-fact summary of the cabal, see GW to Gouverneur Morris, 18 May 1778, *PWRS*,15:156–57.

18. GW to Rev. William Gordon, 23 January 1778, *PWRS*,13:322–23.

19. Kenneth R. Rossman, *Thomas Mifflin and the Politics of the American Revolution* (Chapel Hill, N.C., 1952), 9–137, for the fullest treatment of the plotting as it was being exposed.

20. Marquis de Lafayette to GW, 30 December 1777, *PWRS* 13:68–70.

21. HL to GW, 2 January 1778, ibid., 120–21, which contains the "Thoughts of a Farmer" accusations.

22. Richard Henry Lee to GW, 2 January 1778, ibid., 121–22, which contains the British forgeries. GW to HL, 31 January 1778, ibid., 392–93.

23. GW to Richard Henry Lee, 28 October 1777, *PWRS*, 12:40–42.

24. Charles Royster, *A Revolutionary People at War: The Continental Army and the American Character* (Chapel Hill, N.C., 1979), 179–89, for Conway's ostracization at Valley Forge.

25. GW to William Livingston, 12 March 1778, *PWRS* 14:163–64.

26. Morgan quoted in Henry Lee, ed., *Memories of the War in the Southern Department* (Philadelphia, 1812), 390–91.

27. GW to Colonel John Fitzgerald, 28 February 1778, *PWRS* 13:694–95.

28. Ira Gruber, *The Howe Brothers and the American Revolution* (New York, 1972), is the authoritative work on the subject. The best brief treatment is in Andrew Jackson O'Shaughnessy, *The Men Who Lost America: British Leadership, the American Revolution, and the Fate of an Empire* (New Haven, Conn., 2013), 83–122.

29. JA to AA, 30 July 1777, *AFC* 2:296–97. See Gruber, *The Howe Brothers* 224–67, for

Howe's strange voyage to the Chesapeake. Max Mintz, *The Generals of Saratoga: John Burgoyne and Horatio Gates* (New Haven, Conn., 1990), features the role of swarming militia at Saratoga.

30. O'Shaughnessy, *The Men Who Lost America*, 96–114; Stanley Weintraub, *Iron Tears: America's Battle for Freedom, Britain's Quagmire, 1775–1783* (New York, 2005), 109–31, for anti-Howe coverage in the British press.

31. Sir William Howe to Lord Germain, 22 October 1777, quoted in Gruber, *The Howe Brothers*, 273.

32. NG to GW, [?] January 1778, *PWRS* 13:424–25.

33. James Verdun to GW, 3 January 1778, ibid., 132–36; Arthur St. Clair to GW, 5 January 1778, ibid., 151–57; Henry Knox to GW, 4 February 1778, ibid., 449–50.

34. GW to Continental Congress Camp Committee, 29 January 1778, ibid., 376–409.

35. Ibid., 377. Washington repeated this message, almost word for word, in GW to John Bannister, 21 April 1778, *PWRS*, 14:574.

36. GW to HL, 10 April 1778, ibid., 459–64; AH to George Clinton, 13 February 1778, *HP* 1:425–28. See also editorial note, *PWRS* 13:220, for a summary of the debate in the Continental Congress on the pension question.

37. For first impressions of Steuben, see William Gordon to GW, 9 January 1778, *PWRS* 13: 187–88; HL to GW, 19 February 1778, ibid., 598. The reigning biography is Paul Lockhart, *The Drillmaster of Valley Forge: The Baron von Steuben and the Making of the American Army* (New York, 2008).

38. For comments on Steuben's drilling procedures, see *PWRS* 12:557; *PWRS*, 13:187–88, 306, 598; *PWRS*, 14:223–25.

39. Quoted in Lockhart, *Drillmaster of Valley Forge*, 104.

40. *PWRS* 13:435–36, for Martha's arrival on February 5.

41. Royster, *A Revolutionary People at War*, 191–254. Royster's landmark study of the Continental Army is an extended tribute to the contributions made by the small core of veteran troops during the war, the "faceless few" who, for too long, have remained shrouded in obscurity.

42. Quoted in ibid., 210. For examples of grousing about rank, see *PWRS* 13:79–81, 314–15, 494–96, 602.

43. NG to GW, 26 November 1777, *PWRS*, 12:409.

44. Royster, *A Revolutionary People at War*, 204.

45. Gregory D. Massey, *John Laurens and the American Revolution* (Columbia, S.C., 2000), is the standard biography. The completed edition of the Laurens Papers affords an excellent opportunity for a joint biography of Henry and John that provides a truly distinctive window into slavery as the proverbial ghost at the banquet in the revolutionary era.

46. Lafayette's remark is quoted in HL to John Gervais, 13 December 1777, *LDC* 12:145.

47. JL to HL, 23 January 1778, *LP* 12:404–5.

48. JL to Francis Kimlock, 12 April 1776, quoted in Massey, *John Laurens and the American Revolution*, 63.

49. JL to HL, 2 February 1778, *LDC* 12:390–93.

50. For this early state of Hamilton's career as a budding abolitionist, see Ron Chernow, *Alexander Hamilton* (New York, 2004), 94–123.

51. Rhode Island Council of War to GW, 19 January 1778, *PWRS* 13:284–85; JL to HL, 14 January 1778, *LP* 12:305–6.

52. GW to HL, 20 April 1778, *PWRS* 14:570–71.

53. GW to Lund Washington, 15 August 1778, *PWRS*, 16:315.

54. Lord North's correspondence with George III in late 1777 and early 1778 provides the best window into his beleaguered mentality. See John Fontescue, ed., *The Correspondence of King George the Third from 1760 to December 1783*, 6 vols. (London, 1927–1928), vol. 4. See also O'Shaughnessy, *The Men Who Lost America*, 47–80.

55. Stacy Schiff, *The Great Improvisation: Franklin, France, and the Birth of America* (New York, 2005) 126–40, recovers this chapter in Franklin's career with the stylistic flair it requires and deserves.

56. GW to HL, 18 April 1778, *PWRS* 14:547.

57. GW to John Bannister, 21 April 1778, ibid., 573–76.

58. GW to HL, 20 April, 1778, ibid., 679–81.

59. HL to GW, 24 April 1778, ibid., 615–17; *JCC* 10:114–15.

60. Lockhart, *Drillmaster of Valley Forge*, 114–16. There is also an excellent description of this grand parade in Edward G. Lengel, *General George Washington: A Military Life* (New York, 2005), 269–70.

61. GW to Alexander McDougall, 5 May 1778, *PWRS* 5:15; JL to HL, 12 May 1778, *LDC* 13:295; HL to Steuben, 10 May 1778, ibid., 288.

62. GW to Gouverneur Morris, 28 May 1778, *PWRS* 15:260–62.

63. This account of the Mischianza draws on three secondary accounts: O'Shaughnessy, *The Men Who Lost America*, 207–11; Gruber, *The Howe Brothers*, 274–300; and Lengel, *General George Washington*, 273–74.

CHAPTER FIVE: THE PROTRACTION

1. See the sumptuous painting *The Death of the Earl of Chatham* (1781), by John Singleton Copley.

2. William Howe, *The Narrative of Lieutenant General William Howe* (London, 1780); also John Burgoyne, *A Letter from Lieutenant General Burgoyne to His Constituents upon His Resignation* (London, 1779); Piers Mackesy, *The War for America, 1775–1783* (Cambridge, Mass., 1964), 252, for the quotation from General Graves.

3. Mackesy, *The War for America*, and Andrew Jackson O'Shaughnessy, *The Men Who Lost America: British Leadership, the American Revolution, and the Fate of an Empire* (New Haven, Conn. 2013) are the best accounts of the war from the British perspective. Mackesy believes that the war was both defensible and winnable. O'Shaughnessy disagrees on both accounts. I tend to side with O'Shaughnessy, most especially after French entry into the war in 1778.

4. *WW* 13:43, editorial note for Germain's orders to Clinton.

5. See Henry Clinton, *The American Rebellion: Sir Henry Clinton's Narrative of His Campaigns, 1775–1782*, ed. William B. Willcox (Hamden, Conn., 1971), 119, for Clinton's account of his wholly defensive mission after 1778. See also O'Shaughnessy's chapter on Clinton in *The Men Who Lost America*, 207–246, which is entitled "The Scapegoat."

6. See Herbert Butterfield, *George III, Lord North and the People 1779–80* (New York, 1968), 116–40, for North's growing reluctance about the war. See also Mackesy, *The War for America*, 153–55, 183–84.

7. George III to Lord North, 17 March 1778, John Fortescue, ed., *The Correspondence of King George the Third from 1760 to December 1783*, 6 vols. (London, 1927–1928) 4:65. See also Charles K. Ritcheson, *British Politics and the American Revolution* (Norman, Okla., 1954), 247–48, and Ian Christie, *The End of the North Ministry, 1780–1782* (London, 1958), 140–49.

8. John Brewer, *The Sinews of Power: War, Money, and the English State, 1688–1783* (New York, 1989).

9. Louis Namier, *The Structure of Politics at the Accession of George III* (London, 1929).

10. Alan Valentine, *Lord George Germain* (Oxford, 1962), 39–42; O'Shaughnessy, *The Men Who Lost America*, 187–95.

11. Samuel Shaw to John Lamb, 12 July 1780, *The Memoir of the Life and Times of General John Lamb* (New York, 1857), 243.

12. Council of War, 24 June 1778, *PWRS* 15:530–21.

13. AH to GW, 20 June 1779, ibid., 536.

14. NG to GW, 18 June 1778, ibid., 441–42.

15. Joseph Plumb Martin, *Narrative of a Revolutionary Soldier* (New York, 2001), 10–11, for his recollection of Washington's anger upon encountering Lee in retreat.

16. Editorial note, *PWRS* 15:576.

17. GW to Thomas Nelson, 20 August 1778, *WW* 12:343.

18. For critical assessments of Lee, see JL to HL, 30 June 1778, *LP* 14:30; GW to Charles Lee, 30 June 1778, *WW* 12:132–33. The fullest defense of Lee is in Theodore Thayer, *The Making of a Scapegoat: Washington and Lee at Monmouth* (Port Washington, N.Y., 1976).

19. Editorial note, *PWCS* 1:401, for Lee's duel with Laurens.

20. GW to Count d'Estaing, 29 September 1778, *WW* 12:516–18.

21. Robert J. O'Connell, *Revolutionary: George Washington at War* (New York, 2019), which coined the term "Redcoat Central" for New York.

22. Jonathan R. Dull, *The French Navy and American Independence: A Study of Arms and Diplomacy* (Princeton, N.J., 1975), 65–73.

23. For Washington's frequent lamentations about lack of support for the Continental Army, see *WW* 13:178–80, 346–47; 19:104–5, 174–76, 235, 391–94, 481–83. This is the central theme of Wayne E. Carp, *To Starve the Army at Pleasure: Continental Army Administration and American Political Culture* (Chapel Hill, N.C., 1993).

24. GW to President of Congress, 22 July 1780, *WW* 19:235.

25. GW to Benjamin Harrison, 18 December 1778, *WW* 13:466–68; see also GW to Joseph Reed, 12 December 1778, ibid., 382–85; GW to Gouverneur Morris, 4 October 1778, ibid., 231–32; GW to John Augustine Washington, 12 May 1779, *WW*, 15:57–60.

26. GW to Fielding Lewis, 6 July 1780, *WW*, 13:175–80.

27. GW to NG, 31 March 1778, *PWRS* 14:367–68.

28. O'Connell, *Revolutionary*, 213–48, which describes this contested region as "Dangerland."

29. John Graves Simcoe, *Simcoe's Military Journal: A History of the Queen's Rangers* (New York, 1844).

30. GW to Anthony Wayne, 27 November 1780, *WW* 20:407; see also General Orders, 2 January 1780, *WW*, 17:362.

31. GW to HL, 14 November 1778, *WW*, 13:256–57.

32. GW to Horatio Gates, 6 March 1779, *WW*, 14:199–201; GW to John Sullivan, 31 May 1778, *WW*, 15:189–93.

33. Edwin G. Burrows, *Forgotten Patriots: The Untold Story of American Prisoners During the Revolutionary War* (New York, 2008), estimates that 30,000 Americans were captured and 18,000 died in captivity. Robert P. Watson, *The Ghost Ships of Brooklyn: An Untold Story of the American Revolution* (New York, 2017), estimates that 11,000 American prisoners died on board one notorious prison ship, the *Jersey*, in Brooklyn Harbor.

34. GW to President of Congress, 15 December 1779, *WW* 17:272–73.

35. GW to Joseph Jones, 3 May 1780, *WW*, 18:453. For the same theme, see *WW*, 17:425–28; 18:207–11; 21:213–16.

36. Circular Letter from Congress to the States, 13 September 1779, quoted in David Hendrickson, *Peace Pact: The Lost World of the American Founding* (Lawrence, Kans., 2003), 71–72; Charles Thomson to RM, 29 June 1781, *LDC* 11:362, for the budget figures.

37. William W. Crosskey and William Jeffrey, eds., *Politics and the Constitution in the History of the United States*, 3 vols. (Chicago, 1953–1980), 3:136, for the Boston Conventions. Carp, *To Starve the Army at Pleasure*, 202–3, for the Hartford convention.

38. Article II, Articles of Confederation, available as appendix in my *The Quartet: Orchestrating the Second American Revolution* (New York, 2015), 221.

39. GW to John Armstrong, 10 January 1783, *WW* 26:26–27; Andrew R. McLaughlin, *The Confederation and the Constitution* (New York [1905], 1962), 45–46.

40. *HP* 2:649–56.

41. Ibid., 650–51.

42. Ibid., 655–56.

43. For the land claims, see *JCC* 19:99–100, 208–13, 233–64; 20: 502–11; 524–26; 21:281–84. For the Butler quotation, see *LDC* 18:462–63.

44. See Stanley Elkins and Eric McKitrick, "The Founding Fathers: Young Men of the Revolution," *Political Science Quarterly* 76 (June 1961): 181–216, for an early argument about the connection between veteran officers of the Continental Army and nationalists at the Constitutional Convention.

45. GW to HL, 15 March 1779, *WW* 14:241–45.

46. Mackesy, *The War for America*, 153–59, 183–85, provides a splendid summary of deliberations in the British ministry and its shift in focus toward the Caribbean. Lord Sandwich, Lord of the Admiralty, was the strongest advocate for regarding the southern coastal cities as mere platforms for the major mission in the Caribbean.

47. *WAR*, 146–49, for Campbell's successful campaign in Georgia and his remark about the "Rebel flag."

48. GW to President of Congress, 15 March 1779, *WW* 14:241–45; see also GW to Benjamin Lincoln, 30 July 1779, ibid., 16: 16–19.

49. JC to HL, 2 February 1778, *LP* 12:390–93; Gregory D. Massey, *John Laurens and the American Revolution* (Columbia, S.C., 2000), 134–35.

50. *WAR*, 152–59, provides the Rutledge terms of surrender and excellent maps of the region. Among the many accounts of the British siege, I found John S. Pancake's version in *The Destructive War: The British Campaign in the Carolinas, 1780–1782* (Tuscaloosa, Ala., 1985), 56–72, most cogent.

51. Pancake, *Destructive War*, 73–80.

52. Frank and Mary Wickwire, *Cornwallis and the War of Independence* (London, 1971),

remains the best biography. The profile in O'Shaughnessy, *The Men Who Lost America*, 247–88, is extremely insightful about Cornwallis's mentality on the eve of the southern campaign.

53. For the Battle of Camden, see *WAR*, 155–63; Pancake, *The Destructive War*, 91–107; and Michael Stephenson, *Patriot Battles: How the War of Independence Was Fought* (New York, 2007), 311–20.

54. Francis Rawdon to Alexander Leslie, 24 October 1780, *DAR* 18:189–90; Charles O'Hara to Duke of Grafton, 1 November 1780, "Letters to the Duke of Grafton," *The South Carolina Historical Magazine* 65 (July 1964): 159–60; Charles Cornwallis to Henry Clinton, 16 October, 1781, *The Cornwallis Papers: The Campaigns of 1780 and 1781 in the Southern Theatre*, 6 vols., ed. Ian Saberton (Uckfield, Ireland, 2010), 2:41–42, and 4 December 1781, ibid., 3:17–19.

55. Pancake, *The Destructive War*, 108–21.

56. Stephenson, *Patriot Battles*, 321–29; *WAR*, 164–65; Charles Cornwallis to Henry Clinton, 4 December 1781, *The Cornwallis Papers*, 3:27–28.

57. GW to NG, 14 July 1780, *WW* 19:169; GW to Committee of Cooperation, 17 August 1780, ibid., 391–94; GW to Samuel Ward, 31 August 1780, ibid., 481–83.

58. Nathaniel Philbrick, *In the Hurricane's Eye: The Genius of George Washington and the Victory at Yorktown* (New York, 2018), 8–10, also provides a much fuller explanation of the technical and tactical problems of moving a naval force in the age of sail.

59. GW to NG, 25 September 1780, *WW* 20:84–85; GW to George Clinton, 26 September, ibid., 43.

60. General Orders, 26 September 1780, ibid., 95.

61. GW to The Commission for Redressing the Grievances in the New Jersey Line, 27 January 1781, *WW*, 21:147–48; General Orders, 30 January 1781, ibid., 158–66.

62. GW to Benjamin Lincoln, 30 July 1779, *WW*, 16:16–19; Council of War, 1 April 1780, *WW*, 18:195; GW to JL, 26 April 1780, ibid., 300.

63. GW to Benjamin Lincoln, 30 July 1779, *WW*, 16:16–19; Council of War, 1 April 1780, *WW*, 18:195; GW to John Laurens, 26 April 1780, ibid., 300.

64. GW to NG, 27 February 1781, *WW*, 21:304.

65. NG to GW, 31 October 1780, *WW*, 20:321.

66. Don Higginbotham, *Daniel Morgan, Revolutionary Rifleman* (Chapel Hill, N.C., 1961), 122–46; Stephenson, *Patriotic Battles*, 321–29.

67. Higginbotham, *Daniel Morgan*, 135–55; *WAR*, 166–69; Pancake, *The Destructive War*, 122–40; Stephenson, *Patriotic Battles*, 321–29.

68. Charles O'Hara to the Duke of Grafton, 20 April 1781, "Letters to the Duke of Grafton," 174. There have been various reasons offered to explain Cornwallis's decision to hurl his dwindling army into the southern equivalent of no-man's-land. My sense is that Greene's army gave him a specific target to practice his professional calling, namely to fight and win on a conventional battlefield. Once inland, he was also beyond the reach of Clinton's interference. A defensive posture also ran against the grain of his personality, which became more fatalistic after the death of his wife.

69. *WAR*, 170–75; Pancake, *This Destructive War*, 172–86; Stephenson, *Patriotic Battles*, 330–38; most fully, Laurence Babits and Joshua Howard, *Long, Obstinate, and Bloody: The Battle of Guilford Court House* (Chapel Hill, N.C., 2009).

70. NG to TJ, 18 March 1781, *JP* 5:156; NG to Anne-César, Chevalier de Luzerne, 28 April 1781, *GP* 8:167–68.
71. GW to JL, 9 April 1781, *WW* 21:439.

CHAPTER SIX: THE CHESAPEAKE

1. Wiley Poag, *Chesapeake Invader: Discovering America's Great Meteorite Crater* (Princeton, N.J., 1999), 3–26.
2. See William B. Willcox, *Portrait of a General: Sir Henry Clinton and the War of Independence* (New York, 1964), 370–71, for Clinton's view of Arnold's Virginia campaign.
3. GW to Marquis de Lafayette, 13 July 1781, *WW* 22:367–69.
4. Lord Germain to Henry Clinton, 2 May 1781, quoted in John S. Pancake, *The Destructive War: The British Campaign in the Carolinas, 1780–1782* (Tuscaloosa, Ala., 1985), 151.
5. Charles Cornwallis to Henry Clinton, 12 April 1781, *The Cornwallis Papers: The Campaigns of 1780 and 1781 in the Southern Theatre*, 6 vols., ed. Ian Saberton (Uckfield, Ireland, 2010), 4:317–18.
6. Charles Cornwallis to Henry Clinton, 15 April 1781, ibid., 321–25.
7. Conference with Count Rochambeau, 23 May 1781, *WW* 22:105–7; see Donald Jackson and Dorothy Twohigs, eds., *The Diaries of George Washington*, 6 vols. (Charlottesville, Va., 1976–1979), 3:369–70, for Washington's diary entries concerning the meeting with Rochambeau.
8. GW to TJ, 8 June 1781, *WW* 22:178–79.
9. Jackson and Twohig, eds., *Diaries of George Washington*, 3:403; GW to RM, 2 August 1781, *WW* 22:424.
10. Charles Cornwallis to Henry Clinton, 10 July 1781, *The Cornwallis Papers* 4:411–12.
11. Johann von Ewald, *Diary of the American War*, trans. and ed. by Joseph P. Tustin (New Haven, Conn., 1979), 305.
12. Count Rochambeau to Count de Grasse, 11 June 1781, quoted in Charles L. Lewis, *Admiral de Grasse and American Independence* (Annapolis, Md., 1945), 123–25.
13. RM to GW, 13 August 1781, *MP* 2:50–55.
14. RM to Governors, 16 July 1781, ibid., 1:305.
15. See Henry Clinton to Lord Germain, 9 June 1781, *WW* 22:132, where Clinton apprises Germain that spies had intercepted letters revealing Washington's intention to attack New York.
16. GW to Marquis de Lafayette, 2 September 1781, *WW* 23:75.
17. Franklin and Mary Wickwire, in their authoritative biography of Cornwallis, blame his hesitation on the confusing orders he received from Clinton. See *Cornwallis: The American Revolution* (Boston, 1970), 349–55. Clinton spent the lion's share of his memoir defending his behavior and trying to shift blame to Cornwallis. Unfortunately for Clinton, his memoirs were not published until the twentieth century. The British press at the time made him the scapegoat and Cornwallis the victim.
18. Nathaniel Philbrick, *In the Hurricane's Eye: The Genius of George Washington and the Victory at Yorktown* (New York, 2018), 179–203, provides the most comprehensive account of the naval side of the Yorktown campaign, to include the Battle of the Chesapeake.
19. GW to Robert Howe, 24 September 1781, *WW* 23:132.
20. Joseph Plumb Martin, *Narrative of a Revolutionary Soldier* (New York, 2001), 198–99.

General Orders, 5 October 1781, Regulations for the Service of the Siege, *WW* 23:179–85, provided fifty-five points of guidance to assist the French engineers.

21. GW to President of Congress, 16 October 1781, *WW* 23:227–29, provides the official report on the attack led by Hamilton and Laurens.

22. Conditions within British lines were truly horrific, with body parts strewn everywhere. Because freed slaves were enlisted to repair trenches and barricades under fire, they suffered almost twice the casualty rate of British regulars. For the fullest description of the battle on the ground, see Richard Ketchum, *Victory at Yorktown* (New York, 2004).

23. GW to Charles Cornwallis, 18 October 1781, *WW* 23:237–38. The British fleet sent to rescue Cornwallis sailed from New York on October 13, arriving with five thousand troops on October 28. Speculation at the time, and later, that Cornwallis would have been rescued if he had held out for ten days is highly dubious. Admiral Graves would have most probably suffered the same fate with his smaller British fleet as he did in the Battle of the Chesapeake a month earlier.

24. The most detailed description of the surrender scene, almost a cinematic rendering, is in Thomas J. Fleming, *The Perils of Peace: America's Struggle for Survival After Yorktown* (New York, 2007), 1–2, 8–12.

25. Martin, *Narrative of a Revolutionary Soldier*, 152; Ludwig von Closen, *Revolutionary Journal 1780–83*, trans. by Evelyn M. Acorub (Chapel Hill, N.C., 1958), 138–42.

26. GW to NG, 6 February 1783, *WW* 26:104.

27. Ian Christie, *The End of North's Ministry, 1780–1782*, 340–42.

28. Ibid., 275–76, for Pitt's speech in Commons. See also Andrew Jackson O'Shaughnessy, *The Men Who Lost America: British Leadership, the American Revolution, and the Fate of the Empire* (New Haven, Conn., 2013), 200–202, for the collapse of North's majority and the emergence of Charles James Fox and William Pitt the Younger as strident critics of Germain in the wake of Yorktown.

29. See Stanley Weintraub, *Iron Tears: America's Battle for Freedom, Britain's Quagmire* (New York, 2005), 311, for the Cornwallis quotation upon returning to England as a paroled prisoner of war.

30. See O'Shaughnessy, *The Men Who Lost America*, 201, for Germain's spirited remark to North when apprised of his removal.

31. See Fleming, *The Perils of Peace*, 150–52, for a succinct summary of the multiple machinations in the British government after North's departure, rendered even more melodramatic by George III's personal hatred of Rockingham.

32. See O'Shaughnessy, *The Men Who Lost America*, 320–52, for the best brief biography of Sandwich, an undeserving casualty of Yorktown.

33. For the Battle of Les Saintes, see Philbrick, *In the Hurricane's Eye*, 240–42.

34. GW to NG, 16 November 1781, *WW* 23:347; GW to Thomas Nelson, 27 October 1781, ibid., 271–72.

35. GW to John Armstrong, 1 January 1783, *WW*, 26:26–27; GW, Circular Letter to the States, 22 January 1782, *WW*, 23:458–61; *MP* 4:506, for Morris's estimate of the amount needed and amount actually collected from the states.

36. GW to NG, 18 December 1782, *WW* 25:448.

37. GW to James McHenry, 12 March 1782, *WW*, 24:63: Washington mentions the warning from Adams in GW to NG, 17 October 1782, *WW*, 25:265; the remark by Franklin is in GW to NG, 23 September 1782, ibid., 195.

38. GW to William Gordon, 23 October 1782, ibid., 287, where Washington responds to the charge that he is prolonging the war and sustaining the size of the Continental Army in order to stage a military coup.

39. GW to AH, 2 May 1780, *WW*, 18:320; GW to Lewis Nicola, 22 May 1782, *WW*, 24: 272–73, which also reproduces sections of Nicola's letter to Washington.

40. Charles Rappleye, *Robert Morris: Financier of the American Revolution* (New York, 2010), now the standard biography.

41. See James Grant, *Money of the Mind* (New York, 1992), for the concept of credit in a capitalistic economy. See also Thomas K. McCraw, *The Founders and Finance: How Hamilton, Gallatin, and Other Immigrants Forged a New Economy* (Cambridge, Mass., 2012), 56–73.

42. RM to Gouverneur Morris, 3 April 1782, *MP* 4:510.

43. BF to RM, 26 July 1781, *MP.*, 1:5.

44. RM, Circular Letter to the Governors, 27 July 1781, ibid., 396.

45. Charles Thomson's Notes on Debate of 2 August 1782, *LDC* 19: 21–22, provides the fullest account of the response to Morris's report of July 29.

46. RM to AH, 28 August 1782, *HP* 3:154.

47. GW to AH, 4 March 1783, ibid., 279.

48. Resolution of the New York Legislature, 20 July 1782, ibid., 110–13; RM to Matthew Ridley, 9 September 1782, *MP* 6:552.

49. AH to GW, 24 March 1783, *HP* 3:304–5.

50. David Howell to William Greene, 30 July 1782, and David Howell to RM, 31 July–2 August 1782, *LDC* 6:678, 691–92.

51. The term "True Whig" did not designate a formal school of thought but was what an ardent faction, claiming to speak for the original and purest meaning of The Cause, called themselves. The faction emerged in the summer of 1782 in response to Morris's fiscal program. Its antigovernment posture, and predisposition for conspiracy theories made it the most attractive legacy of the founding era for the Confederate States of America in 1861.

52. Arthur Lee to Samuel Adams, 6 August 1782, *LDC* 19:25–26; for Madison's critique of Lee, see *MP* 5:388. For the fullest exposure of Lee during his quasi-paranoid vendettas against Franklin in France, see Stacy Schiff, *The Great Improvisation: Franklin, France, and the Birth of America* (New York, 2005), 220–27.

53. Bernard Bailyn, *The Ideological Origins of the American Revolution* (Cambridge, Mass., 1967), was the first historian to pay close attention to the conspiratorial dimension of revolutionary ideology; Wayne E. Carp, *To Starve the Army at Pleasure: Continental Army Administration and American Political Culture* (Chapel Hill, N.C., 1963), made it a major source of the widespread suspicion of the Continental Army throughout the war.

54. See *MP* 7:685–89, for selections from the *Freeman's Journal*. See also ibid., 502–6, 559–95.

55. RM to Horatio Gates, 28 January 1783, ibid., 378; RM to GW, 27 February 1783, ibid., 475.

CHAPTER SEVEN: THE EXIT

1. Ian Christie, *The End of the North Ministry, 1780–1782* (London, 1958), 284–86.

2. Walpole quoted in Stanley Weintraub, *Iron Tears: America's Battle for Freedom, Britain's Quagmire, 1775–1783* (New York, 2005), 119.

3. GW to NG, 6 August 1782, *WW* 24:471; GW to James McHenry, 18 July 1783, ibid.,

388; Thomas J. Fleming, *The Perils of Peace: America's Struggle for Survival After Yorktown* (New York, 2007), 163–71.

4. Stacy Schiff, *The Great Improvisation: Franklin, France, and the Birth of America* (New York, 2005), 338–49.

5. Aranda Notes, *The Selected Papers of John Jay*, 5 vols., ed. Elizabeth M. Nuxoll (Charlottesville, Va., 2010), 2:270–72; Richard Morris, *The Peacemakers: The Great Powers in the Search for American Independence* (New York, 1965), 309–10.

6. *DA* 3:37–38; the moment was recalled later in JA to James Lloyd, 6 February 1815, *The Works of John Adams, Second President of the United States*, 10 vols., ed. Charles Francis Adams (Boston, 1850–1860), 10:115.

7. Christie, *The End of the North Ministry*, 310–12; Weintraub, *Iron Tears*, 324–28; Samuel Flagg Bemis, *The Diplomacy of the American Revolution* (Bloomington, Ind., 1957), 212–13.

8. For debates over control of western land, see *LDC* 17:283–85, 319–21, and 18:72–79; *JCC* 19:99–100, 208–13, 253–64.

9. Charles Thomson's Notes of Debates of 27 August 1782, *LDC* 19:96–99.

10. AH to JL, 14 August 1782, *HP* 3:144–45.

11. Gregory D. Massey, *John Laurens and the American Revolution* (Columbia, S.C., 2000), 225–28.

12. General Orders, 12 August 1782, *WW* 25:8–9.

13. GW to Joseph Jones, 14 December 1782, ibid., 430–31.

14. See *JCC* 24:291–92; *LDC* 19:579–81, for James Madison's notes on the meeting with McDougall and other officers.

15. AH to GW, 13 February 1783, *HP* 3:253–55; GW to AH, 4 March 1783, *WW* 26: 185–88. The authoritative work on the Newburgh conspiracy is Richard H. Kohn, *Eagle and Sword: The Beginnings of the Military Establishment in America* (New York, 1975), 17–39. See also the scholarly article by Kohn, "The Inside History of the Newburg Conspiracy: America and the Coup d'état," *WMQ* 27 (1970): 187–220.

16. Remarks on the Situation of the Army, 20 February 1783, *HP* 3:264.

17. GW to AH, 11 March 1783, ibid., 286–87; GW to President of Congress, *WW* 26:229–32; GW to Joseph Jones, 12 March 1783, ibid., 213–16.

18. GW to AH, 31 March 1783, *HP* 3:310; GW to AH, 4 April 1783, ibid., 315–16.

19. AH to GW, 8 April 1783, ibid., 317–21.

20. Note on conversation between Hamilton and Madison on Washington's recent loss of popularity, *WW* 26:188; see Charles Rappleye, *Robert Morris: Financier of the American Revolution* (New York, 2010), 343–44, for a splendid synthesis of the behind-the-scenes plotting about Washington's role.

21. GW to the Officers of the Army, 15 March 1783, *WW* 26:222.

22. Ibid., 223.

23. Ibid., 224.

24. AH to GW, 17 March 1783, *HP* 3:292.

25. AH to John Jay, 25 July 1783, ibid., 416–17.

26. GW to George Bland, 4 April 1783, *WW* 26:285.

27. See Rappleye, *Robert Morris*, 355–57, for Morris's last days in office signing checks.

28. Joseph Plumb Martin, *Narrative of a Revolutionary Soldier* (New York, 2001), 279–81. Almost fifty years later, in 1828, the Congress voted pensions for the handful of surviving

veterans; Martin was one of them. See Charles Royster, *A Revolutionary People at War: The Continental Army and the American Character* (Chapel Hill, N.C., 1979), 321, for "vultures" quotation.

29. Minor Meyers, *Liberty Without Anarchy: A History of the Society of the Cincinnati* (Charlottesville, Va., 1983), 4–9.

30. Henry Knox to GW, 21 February 1784, *PWCS* 1:142–44, provides a summary of the hostile response to the society, amplified in the editorial notes. See also William Evan Davies, "The Society of the Cinninnati in New England, 1783–1800," *WMQ* 5 (1948): 3–25.

31. TJ to GW, 16 April 1784, *LDC* 21:521–24; BF to GW, 14 November 1786, *PWCS* 4:364–65.

32. NG to GW, 29 August 1784, *PWCS* 2:59–61.

33. See *LDC* 21:472, for the Lee quotation. The deliberate weakness of the Articles of Confederation is most fully exposed in David Hendrickson, *Peace Pact: The Lost World of the American Founding* (Lawrence, Kans., 2003).

34. Fleming, *The Perils of Peace*, 290–91; Kenneth Bowling, "New Light on the Philadelphia Mutiny of 1783," *Pennsylvania Magazine of History and Biography* 99 (1977): 419.

35. AH to Major William Jackson, 19 June 1783, *HP* 3:397–98; Report on Conference with Supreme Council of Pennsylvania on the Mutiny, 20 June 1783, ibid., 399–400; AH to JD, 29 June 1783, ibid., 408–9.

36. Resolutions on Measures to Be Taken in Consequence of the Pennsylvania Mutiny, 21 June 1783, ibid., 401–2; AH to JD, 25 September 1783, ibid., 438–58.

37. GW to Benjamin Harrison, 18 January 1784, *PWCS* 1:56.

38. Ibid., 57.

39. GW, Circular Letter to the States, 8 June 1783, *WW* 26:483–96.

40. This theme is developed more fully in my *American Quartet: Orchestrating the Second American Revolution* (New York, 2015), 26–41. The role of the west in Washington's thinking was most clearly articulated by W. W. Abbot in "George Washington, the West and the Union," in *George Washington Reconsidered*, ed. Don Higginbotham (Charlottesville, Va., 2001), pages 198–211. Abbot also demonstrates that Washington doubled his holdings in western land to a total of sixty thousand acres in the decade after the war.

41. GW to Edward Newenham, 10 June 1784, *PWCS* 1:440.

42. See Walter Stahr, *John Jay* (New York, 2006), 170–71, for the exchange between French and British negotiators. See O'Shaughnessy, *The Men Who Lost America*, 43, for George III's belief that the Americans would regret their departure from the British Empire.

43. Virginia Delegates to Benjamin Harrison, 3 September 1782, *LDC* 19:125; William Ellery to Francis Dana, 3 December 1783, *LDC*, 21:177; David Howell to William Greene, 5 February 1784, ibid., 341; Deed of Virginia Cession, 1 March 1784, ibid., 412–14.

44. See *LP*, 16:78–80, for Laurens's last-minute role at Versailles.

45. GW to Daniel Parker, 28 April 1783, *WW* 26:364.

46. Substance of a Conference Between General Washington and Sir Guy Carleton, 6 May 1783, ibid., 402–3; Commissioners of Embarkation at New York to GW, 18 January 1784, *PWCS* 1:50–56.

47. GW to Benjamin Harrison, 30 April 1783, *WW* 26:370.

48. See Dorothy Twohig, "'That Species of Property': Washington's Role in the Controversy

over Slavery," in Higginbotham, ed., *George Washington Reconsidered*, 114–38; Henry Wienick, *An Imperfect God: George Washington, His Slaves, and the Creation of America* (New York, 2003); and most recently, Mary V. Thompson, *"The Only Avoidable Subject of Regret": George Washington, Slavery and the Enslaved Community at Mount Vernon* (Charlottesville, Va., 2019).

49. Fleming, *The Perils of Peace*, 312–13; Robert Watson, *The Ghost Ships of Brooklyn: An Untold Story of the American Revolution* (New York, 2017).

50. Benjamin Tallmadge, *Memoir of Colonel Benjamin Tallmadge* (New York, 1858), 275–76.

51. Ibid., 287–88.

52. *MP* 8:09–10 provides Morris's commentary on the fact that the war had almost bankrupted him, and that he was therefore afraid that his check to Washington would bounce.

53. Fleming, *The Perils of Peace*, 319–20. The Virginia delegation, Jefferson excepted, later recorded their discomfort at Washington's conspicuous nationalism.

54. GW, Address to the Congress on Resigning His Commission, 23 December 1783, *WW* 26:284–86.

55. TJ to Joseph Jones, 16 April 1784, *JP* 7:106–7.

56. Robert C. Alberts, *Benjamin West* (New York, 1978), 123. Alberts cites as his source Elkanah Watson, *Memoir, Men, and Times of the Revolution* (New York, 1856), 227.

EPILOGUE: LEGACIES

1. William Howe, *Narrative of Lieutenant General William Howe in a Committee of the House of Commons* (London, 1780); *A Letter from Lieutenant General John Burgoyne to His Constituents upon His Resignation* (London, 1779); Henry Clinton, *The American Rebellion: Sir Henry Clinton's Narrative of His Campaigns, 1775–1782*, ed. William B. Willcox (Hamden, Conn., 1971),.

2. Charles Stedman, *The History of the Origin, Progress, and Termination of the American War*, 2 vols. (Dublin, 1794).

3. Piers Mackesy, *The Coward of Minden: The Affair of Lord George Sackville* (London, 1979); Andrew Jackson O'Shaughnessy, *The Men Who Lost America: British Leadership, the American Revolution, and the Fate of the Empire* (New Haven, Conn., 2013), 201–3.

4. Draft memorandum, no date, Royal Archives, quoted in Stanley Weintraub, *Iron Tears: America's Battle for Freedom, Britain's Quagmire, 1775–1783* (New York, 2005), 326–27.

5. Josiah Tucker, *Four Letters on Important National Subjects* (London, 1783).

6. Weintraub, *Iron Tears*, 327.

7. Frederick E. Hoxie, Ronald Hoffman, and Peter J. Albert, eds., *Native Americans and the Early Republic* (Charlottesville, Va., 1999) is an excellent collection of scholarly essays on the Native American predicament during and after the war.

8. Daniel K. Richter, *Facing East from Indian Country: A Native History of Early America* (Cambridge, Mass., 2001).

9. John W. Caughey, *McGillivray of the Creeks* (Norman, Okla., 1931), 90–91.

10. For the treaties, see Wilcomb E. Washburn, ed., *The American Indian and the United States: A Documentary History*, 4 vols. (New York, 1973), 4:2267–77.

11. Philip Schuyler to President of Congress, 29 July 1783, *JCC* 3: 601–7. Washington endorsed the Schuyler strategy: see GW to James Duane, *WW* 27:133–40.

12. Elizabeth A. Fenn, *Pox Americana: The Great Smallpox Epidemic of 1775–82* (New York, 2001). For the pre-epidemic cultural context of Native American tribes, see Daniel K. Richter, *Before the Revolution: America's Ancient Pasts* (Cambridge, Mass., 2011).

13. Washburn, ed., *The American Indian and the United States*, 2:2140–43; Reginald Horseman, *Expansion and American Indian Policy, 1783–1812* (Lansing, Mich., 1967), 36–39.

14. Washburn, ed., *The American Indians and the United States*, 2:2144–50.

15. GW to Secretary of State, 1 July 1796, *WW* 35:112.

16. Bernard Bailyn, *The Ordeal of Thomas Hutchinson* (Cambridge, Mass., 1974). For earlier and sympathetic treatments of the loyalists, see William H. Nelson, *The American Tory* (Westport, Conn., 1961); Wallace Brown, *The King's Friends: The Composition and Motives of the American Loyalists* (Providence, R.I., 1966); and Robert M. Calhoun, *The Loyalists in Revolutionary America, 1760–1781* (New York, 1973).

17. For the overall loyalist diaspora, see Maya Jasanoff, *Liberty's Exile: American Loyalists in the Revolutionary World* (New York, 2011). For the ex-slaves, see Cassandra Pybus, *Epic Journey's of Freedom: Runaway Slaves of the American Revolution and Their Global Quest for Liberty* (Boston, 2006).

18. AA to JA, 12 November 1775, *AFC* 1:324.

19. Merrill D. Peterson, ed., *The Portable Thomas Jefferson* (New York, 1975), 214–15, is the most accessible source for Jefferson's remarks on slavery in his *Notes on the State of Virginia*.

20. For a fuller assessment of Jefferson's version of the slavery dilemma, see my *American Dialogue: The Founders and Us* (New York, 2018), 13–48.

21. Paul J. Polgar, *Standard Bearers of Equity: America's First Abolition Movement* (Chapel Hill, N.C., 2019); see also Arthur Zilversmit, *The First Emancipation: The Abolition of Slavery in the North* (Chicago, 1967), 109–38, and Gary B. Nash, *Race and Revolution* (Madison, Wisc., 1990), 3–24.

22. For this antislavery phrase of Jefferson's career, see my more expansive treatment in *American Dialogue*, 17–27.

23. Robert McColley, *Slavery in Jefferson's Virginia* (Urbana, Ill., 1964).

24. William W. Freehling, "The Founding Fathers, Conditional Antislavery, and the Non-radicalism of the American Revolution," in his *The Reinterpretation of American History: Slavery and the Civil War* (New York, 1994), 76–84. For the running joke about hot soup, see Count Rochambeau to GW, 11 April 1790, *PWPS* 5:326; GW to Count Rochambeau, 10 August 1790, *PWPS*, 6:231–32.

25. GW to John Francis Mercer, 9 September 1786, *PWCS* 3:243.

26. GW to Robert Morris, 12 April 1786, *PWCS*, 4:15–16.

27. Robert Pleasants to GW, 11 December 1785, *PWCS*, 3:449–51.

28. Marquis de Lafayette to GW, 14 July 1785, ibid., 121; William Gordon to GW, 30 August 1784, *PWCS*, 2:63–64. Mary V. Thompson, *"The Only Unavoidable Subject of Regret": George Washington, Slavery and the Enslaved Community at Mount Vernon* (Charlottesville, Va., 2019), 293–330.

29. See, for example, Jack Rakove, *The Beginnings of National Policies: An Interpretive History of the Continental Congress* (Baltimore, 1979), and Merrill Jensen, *The New Nation: A History of the United States During the Confederation* (New York, 1940). For the essential corrective, long overdue, see David C. Hendrickson, *Peace Pact: The Lost World of the American Founding* (Lawrence, Kans., 2003).

30. Jensen, *The New Nation*, is the classic statement of the long-standing interpretation.
31. Josiah Tucker, *Cui Bono?* (London, 1782), 10–11.
32. AA to Charles Storer, 23 March 1786, *AFC* 7:113–14.
33. Editorial note, *LDC* 21:494, for the Jefferson quotation; Benjamin Harrison to GW, 8 January 1784, *PWCS* 1:22–23.
34. John Jay to Richard Henry Lee, *The Selected Papers of John Jay*, 5 vols., ed. Elizabeth M. Nuxoll (Charlottesville, Va., 2010), 4:128.

Index